Black Citymakers

Black Citymakers

*How The Philadelphia
Negro Changed
Urban America*

MARCUS ANTHONY HUNTER

OXFORD
UNIVERSITY PRESS

OXFORD
UNIVERSITY PRESS

Oxford University Press is a department of the University of Oxford.
It furthers the University's objective of excellence in research, scholarship,
and education by publishing worldwide.

Oxford   New York
Auckland   Cape Town   Dar es Salaam   Hong Kong   Karachi
Kuala Lumpur   Madrid   Melbourne   Mexico City   Nairobi
New Delhi   Shanghai   Taipei   Toronto

With offices in
Argentina   Austria   Brazil   Chile   Czech Republic   France   Greece
Guatemala   Hungary   Italy   Japan   Poland   Portugal   Singapore
South Korea   Switzerland   Thailand   Turkey   Ukraine   Vietnam

Oxford is a registered trade mark of Oxford University Press
in the UK and certain other countries.

Published in the United States of America by
Oxford University Press
198 Madison Avenue, New York, NY 10016

© Oxford University Press 2013

First issued as an Oxford University Press paperback, 2015.

Library of Congress Cataloging-in-Publication Data
Hunter, Marcus Anthony.
Black citymakers : how the Philadelphia Negro changed urban America / Marcus Anthony Hunter.
p.   cm.
Includes bibliographical references and index.
ISBN 978-0-19-994813-0 (hardcover): 978-0-19-024967-0 (paperback)
1. African Americans—Pennsylvania—Philadelphia—History.
2. African Americans—Pennsylvania—Philadelphia—Politics and government.
3. African Americans—Pennsylvania—Philadelphia—Social conditions.
4. Urban policy—Pennsylvania—Philadelphia—History.
5. Urban policy—United States—History—Case studies.   6. Philadelphia (Pa.)—History.
7. Philadelphia (Pa.)—Race relations.   8. Philadelphia (Pa.)—Social conditions.   I. Title.
F158.9.N4H86 2013
305.896'073074811—dc23   2012027021

For my parents, Marcus and Shelley Hunter

Contents

List of Tables, Illustrations, Figures, and Graphs

Acknowledgments

It is only right that I begin my acknowledgements with W. E. B. DuBois. While I have always admired DuBois's work, it was not until I started my revisit of his field site, the Black Seventh Ward in Philadelphia, that I began to fully comprehend the magnitude and breadth of ideas and rigor encompassed in *The Philadelphia Negro*. With little money and support, DuBois provided a blueprint for the study of urban America and race relations, completing the research and write-up within a two-year window. His example has been a constant source of inspiration, without which this book could and would not be. In addition to DuBois's example and research, I have been greatly helped by the insights and encouragement of many.

As many before me have noted, a completed book is a reflection of not only the author but also of a larger community and network of support. Without the collective encouragement, critical feedback, and belief of many, this book would have never been able to be completed. My apologies up front for any names I am remiss in not mentioning, with hopes that I will be able to extend a private note of thanks in our next communication.

From the beginning of my graduate studies my mentor, Mary Pattillo, has been a constant force of support, always pushing me to think harder, write better, and to never be afraid to ask new questions. Her work motivated me to pursue sociology; her example and guidance taught me how to be a sociologist. I am grateful to Gary Alan Fine for his insights, encouragement, and general belief in me from the outset of my graduate studies; his penetrating commentary and innovative suggestions have been profoundly impactful. I am deeply grateful to Aldon Morris for his investment in the project from its inception. His comments pushed me; his advice encouraged me; and his example as a scholar inspires me. I thank Charles (Chas) Camic for his feedback, insights, and encouragement. His combination of enthusiasm, kindness, and brilliance provided an invaluable resource for me and he is an example of the sort of sociologist I aspire to be some day.

I am also very grateful to the friends who have provided a foundation of support, many of whom have read this manuscript multiple times: Jean Beaman, Courtney J. Patterson, Mikaela Rabinowitz, Zandria Robinson, and Rashida Z. Shaw. The support and feedback I received from these brilliant women cannot be overstated or repaid. I would also like to thank the organizations that have so generously provided the financial support and resources that allowed me to conduct my dissertation research that led to this book: the American Sociological Association's Minority Fellowship Program, the National Science Foundation (Grant ID #0902399), the Social Science Research Council, the Woodrow Wilson National Fellowship Foundation, Northwestern University, and the Mellon Mays Minority Fellowship Program. I am especially grateful to David Brady, whose support of my work led me to James Cook and Oxford. Despite growing up in a socioeconomically disadvantaged context, as a kid I dreamed of writing a book someday; many thanks to both of these men for helping to make that dream a reality. I am also especially grateful to Cathy J. Cohen, Mignon R. Moore, and Celeste Watkins-Hayes for their unending support and mentorship.

Much of the revision of the book happened as I transitioned to my position as an assistant professor of sociology at Yale University, wherein the sociology faculty, staff, and students have been very supportive. In addition to the sociology department, the encouragement from Yale's African American Studies, Women, Gender, and Sexuality Studies, and LGBT Studies departments has been invaluable. An array of colleagues at Yale have truly enhanced my thinking and writing for this book: Julia Adams, Elizabeth Alexander, Elijah Anderson, Scott Boorman, Gerald Jaynes, and Christopher Wildeman. I am especially grateful to Chris Wildeman and GerShun Avilez for being tremendous compatriots, whose friendship and intellect have been inspiring and invaluable.

I have also been fortunate to benefit from a community of support: Rene Almeling, Dana Asbury, Sandra Barnes, Juan Battle, Debbie Becher, Martha Biondi, Coron Brinson, Japonica Brown-Saracino, Matthew Desmond, Lee Douthitt, Marlese Durr, John Eason, Tahai Exum, Myra Marx Ferree, Dave Ferguson, Wendy Griswold, David Johns, Chris Johnson, Medina Johnson, Nina Johnson, Lauren Miller, Alondra Nelson, Masozi Nyrienda, Franky Hale, Arah Lewis, Lisa Magged, Tobias Mathis, Tracy Meares, Shanee Mitchell, Andrew Papachristos, Robert Peterson, Rashawn Ray, Camika Royal, Beryl Watson-Shaw, Shakuwra Shaw, Anatolli Smith, Tyree Spaid, Nicole Martorano Van Cleve, Marietta Vivian Wells and Frederick Wherry. I am also grateful to the countless fellow alums of Teach For America and

Girard College for their encouragement. Presentations at and discussions with members of the sociology departments at Berkeley, Columbia/Barnard, and Duke have also been especially helpful. My research was greatly helped by the staff at a variety of archives and libraries, namely the Free Library of Philadelphia, African American Museum in Philadelphia, Temple University's Urban Archives, Temple University's Charles Blockson Collection, the City Archives of Philadelphia, the Historical Society of Pennsylvania, Northwestern University Library, and the University of Pennsylvania Libraries.

Upon completing this book, I discovered that my great-great-grand-mother, Jessie Cannon, was one of the many Black Seventh Warders DuBois likely observed. This discovery has led to an even deeper appreciation for *The Philadelphia Negro*, the many black Philadelphians captured in this book, and in particular my family. I am grateful to my parents, Marcus and Shelley, for nurturing my curiosity and providing the love that only a father and mother can. I am grateful to my siblings, Maurice, Maya, Malakiah, and Marqueeah, for their encouragement, humor, and love. I am thankful for the love, example, and trailblazing of my grandparents: George, Mary, Louise, Rose, and Frank. I am also grateful to my aunts, uncles, cousins, nieces, and nephews (from Newark and East Orange, NJ, all the way to Philly!) that together comprise the Hunter, Jones, Sanders, Saunders, Gaines, Bradberry, Brooks, Mitchell, Fairnot, Wells, Carroll, and Taylor clans. And to Dant'e Taylor, my love and gratitude for you is endless. You have listened to every idea, every change, and every dilemma with grace, love and a keen critical eye. I know this book is better because you are in my life providing unyielding love, support, and honesty.

Abbreviations

ADA	Americans for Democratic Action
AME	African Methodist Episcopal
AMEZ	African Methodist Episcopal Zion
BPF	Black Political Forum
CAC	Community Action Council
CCCP	Citizen's Council on City Planning
CCOCE	Citywide Coalition to Oppose the Crosstown Expressway
CCPDCC	Citizens Committee to Preserve and Develop the Crosstown Community
CDCP	Colored Democratic Club of Philadelphia
CORE	Congress of Racial Equality
CRC	Citizens Republican Club
DCC	Democratic City Committee
GPM	Greater Philadelphia Movement
HADV	Housing Association of Delaware Valley
HCC	Hawthorne Community Council
HUD	Department of Housing and Urban Development
NAACP	National Association for the Advancement of Colored People
NNC	National Negro Congress
OEO	Office of Economic Opportunity
OIC	Opportunities Industrialization Centers
OPDC	Old Philadelphia Development Corporation
PAAC	Philadelphia Antipoverty Action Committee
PHA	Philadelphia Housing Authority
PWA	Public Works Administration
RA	Redevelopment Authority
SEPTA	Southeastern Pennsylvania Transportation Authority
SNCC	Students Non-violent Coordinating Committee
USHA	United States Housing Administration

Black Citymakers

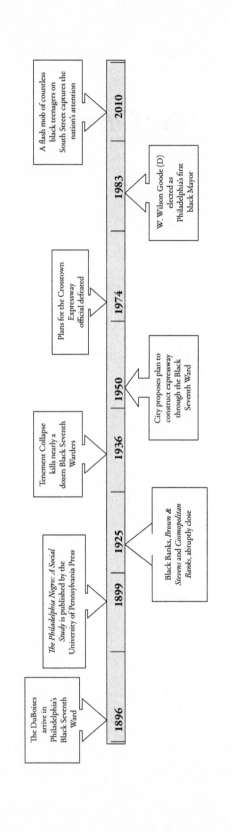

The DuBoises arrive in Philadelphia's Black Seventh Ward

1896

The Philadelphia Negro: A Social Study is published by the University of Pennsylvania Press

1899

Black Banks, *Brown & Stevens* and *Cosmopolitan Banks*, abruptly close

1925

Tenement Collapse kills nearly a dozen Black Seventh Warders

1936

City proposes plan to construct expressway through the Black Seventh Ward

1950

Plans for the Crosstown Expressway official defeated

1974

W. Wilson Goode (D) elected as Philadelphia's first black Mayor

1983

A flash mob of countless black teenagers on South Street captures the nation's attention

2010

I

If These Row Homes Could Talk

THE SMELL OF cooking food, the noise of dishes dropping, pots clanging, and the idle chatter of the hungry were the likely sounds that followed a young man and his wife as they sought refuge in their quaint quarters located at 700 Lombard Street in the heart of Philadelphia's Black Seventh Ward in the fall of 1896 (see Figure 1.1–1.2). The young man, a burgeoning black scholar named William Edward Burghardt (W. E. B.) DuBois, and his new wife, Nina, dropped their belongings to the floor just above the local cafeteria, likely looking around to take their first deep breath in their new home. It had been a bit of journey for the DuBoises, having traveled to Philadelphia from Wilberforce, Ohio, and their hopes were high for the potential prosperity the move from rural Ohio to urban Pennsylvania represented.

Much like many black Americans in the late nineteenth century, the DuBoises' arrival in Philadelphia was no accident. The DuBoises, like scores of black Americans in the wake of Emancipation and Reconstruction, sought new opportunities that urban Northern cities such as Philadelphia, New York, and Boston seemed to hold in store for them. While DuBois differed from the average black migrant during this period, having received his PhD from Harvard University just a few years prior, he was not unlike them in that Philadelphia for him represented an opening of the "door of opportunity...just a crack, to be sure, but a distinct opening."[1] The opportunity that had called him from rural Ohio was from Samuel McCune Lindsay, a white sociologist and professor at the University of Pennsylvania, requesting that DuBois come out and take up a year-long study of the "Philadelphia Negro" and the myriad problems believed to be engendered by this segment of Philadelphia's population.

Often dressed in a sharp, well-fitted suit, DuBois was dapper and took his job seriously. He knocked on the doors of the various row homes along Lombard and South Streets inhabited by Black Seventh Warders, conducted interviews, and wrote in a daily journal to keep track of everyday life in the neighborhood. The Black Seventh Ward, while anchored by the hopes, dreams, and aspirations of black families such as the DuBoises, was no easy place to live. DuBois described the environment surrounding his small room at 700 Lombard as a dangerous one, with "an atmosphere of dirt, drunkenness, poverty, and crime," adding: "Murder sat at our doorsteps, police were our government, and philanthropy dropped with periodic advice."[2] It would, however, provide him with a social scientific laboratory rife with the social ills, disputes, conflicts and possibilities that he would channel a year later into a book aptly titled *The Philadelphia Negro: A Social Study* (*TPN*) published in 1899 by the University of Pennsylvania Press.

In the book, DuBois charged that the problems of the Philadelphia Negro were mere symptoms of the years (centuries for that matter) of prejudice, enslavement, and discrimination under which black Americans had lived for so long. He charged both black and white Philadelphians specifically, and Americans more generally, with the combined duty to enact a series of changes that would help provide access and resources (social, economic, and political) to the Philadelphia Negro. However important and powerful such a proclamation was it would largely fall on deaf ears, and when the post at the University of Pennsylvania did not manifest into something more permanent the DuBoises packed up and left Philadelphia. No longer a "Philadelphia Negro," DuBois would later follow up his ideas and observations in *TPN* from his new intellectual hub at Atlanta University in Georgia.

Today, the neighborhood is neither black nor referred to locally or administratively as the Seventh Ward. Most all the black churches, stores, and social clubs that once lined blocks of Lombard and South Streets are also gone. How and why did this racial shift occur over the course of the twentieth century? Where did the institutions go? Where did the people go? What happened to the "Philadelphia Negroes" of the Seventh Ward? What were the critical historical events that facilitated or frustrated shifts in the racial geography of the Black Seventh Ward? What insights might we glean from DuBois's analysis and observations? These questions are not just specific to the Black Seventh Ward; they are instead indicative of the mysteries embedded in urban change and reflect the rise and decline of urban black neighborhoods across the United States over time. As the Seventh Ward is not only one of the oldest urban black neighborhoods, but also the first to be documented and analyzed in urban research, examining it offers an opportunity to follow cultural and political changes in an urban black neighborhood over what might be imagined as the "life course" of a black enclave—from the creation of a black neighborhood comprising an emergent free black contingent to the enclaves now constituting contemporary black Philadelphia.

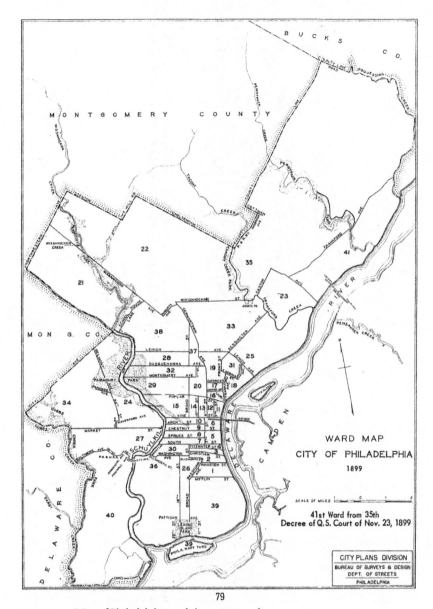

79

FIGURE I.I Map of Philadelphia and the major wards.

Source: http://www.library.upenn.edu/datasets/images/census/1899a.jpg.

FIGURE 1.2 Photographic reproduction of Philadelphia Seventh Ward map. (Published in: W. E. B. DuBois, *The Philadelphia Negro: A Social Study* [Philadelphia: University of Pennsylvania Press, 1899], facing page xx: "Distribution of Negro Inhabitants Throughout the Ward, and their Social Condition."

While DuBois's time as a Philadelphia Negro was perhaps short lived, those who were unable and/or unwilling to leave the city embarked on a journey that would forever change Philadelphia. From many of the row homes wherein DuBois observed and interviewed, black residents forged paths of change, progress, decline, and dispersion that are, at their core, essential contours of contemporary Philadelphia. For example, in 1916, nearly two decades following the publication of *TPN* and the departure of the DuBoises, black Philadelphians staged a boycott of local white-owned businesses in the Seventh Ward located on South Streets just a few yards from the doorstep of 700 Lombard Street, where the DuBoises once lived. Angered by the alleged price-gouging practices of white businessmen and the general unfair treatment of black customers, black Philadelphians embarked on a boycott of several months against the South Street Businessmen's Association, refusing to patronize the various white-owned business along South Street. Seeking to exert their influence on the finances of the white businesses comprising the South Street Businessmen's Association, Black Seventh Warders pooled food and other resources in an effort to bring attention to the injustices they faced during their daily round.

Although the boycott would end with moderate success at best, it would give rise to a mantra of economic self-sufficiency. Such a mantra would spur on a period of revitalization in the Black Seventh Ward, resulting in the development of many black-owned and operated businesses along South and Lombard Streets, including theaters, banks, and social clubs. It was, indeed, an unprecedented experiment in the creation of indigenous institutions relying almost exclusively on black patronage.

Less than a decade later, however, the Black Seventh Ward would again become the site of contention. This time, though, black anger would be directed at other black Philadelphians, namely black banking duo Edward C. Brown and Andrew Stevens. Waiting in long lines, and bearing a terribly cold rainstorm in mid-February of 1925, black depositors withdrew their savings *en masse* from the two black banks Brown and Stevens owned and managed. This banking collapse greatly impacted the financial livelihoods of many black Philadelphians, and the hardships it induced were compounded by the stock market crash just four years later in 1929, when the nation began its downward spiral into the Great Depression.

As was the case for citizens across the United States, the decades following the Great Depression were trying ones for black Philadelphians. The Black Seventh Ward was a shadow of its former self, and by the time the Civil Rights Act of 1964 was signed by President Lyndon B. Johnson much of its population dispersed across newly emergent black neighborhoods in North, West, and South Philadelphia. The death of black residents in a tenement collapse in the Black Seventh Ward just before Christmas in 1936, and more than twenty years of urban renewal (from 1950 to 1974), had rocked the neighborhood, leaving little trace of the vibrant black area in which DuBois once lived and researched. By 1990, the area that had once been the center of Black Philadelphia had become a faint memory, kept alive mostly through Odunde (pronounced Oh-Dune-Day), an African-American Festival held annually along South Street, and the revitalization efforts of a working-class black activist Alice Lipscomb.

Fast-forward to early evening on March 20, 2010, just a few yards from where 700 Lombard had stood, young black teenagers are running east and west, north and south in an effort to disperse following a violent flash mob. No longer standing, 700 Lombard Street would provide only a thruway for Philadelphians seeking refuge from the heavy police presence out in full force to respond to the mobs of black teenagers who broke out into seemingly spontaneous acts of collective violence against local store-owners and shop-pers along South Street. Though the flash mobs give the impression that there is a strong black presence in the area, the neighborhood today is split between commercial businesses and upper-middle-class white residences; all that remains of the Black Seventh Ward are murals and placards indicating a black world that once thrived along Lombard and South Streets.

In this book, I argue that the sociopolitical history of the Black Seventh Ward demonstrates that urban black residents were not mere victims of the structural changes impacting American cities like Philadelphia throughout the twentieth century; nor were they mere passive bystanders watching the city change from the windows of their row homes. Rather, as I will show throughout the book, black Philadelphians were agents of urban change, or *citymakers*, albeit sometimes purposeful and inadvertent, but facilitating and frustrating patterns of urban change nonetheless. The importance of this point cannot be overstated, as without an understanding of how a largely migrant black population, such as the Philadelphia Negro, moved from a "problem" populace when DuBois began his study in 1896 to perhaps the most powerful voting bloc in Philadelphia is critical to contextualizing the causes and consequences of structural changes in urban America including public housing policy, deindustrialization, urban renewal, and the rise of the black mayor.

Reiterating and elaborating upon this argument in subsequent chapters, I hone in on the historical moments foreshadowed in this opening. Four, in particular, serve as the empirical foundation of the book: (1) the collapse of two black banks, Brown & Stevens and Cosmopolitan Bank, in 1925; (2) the tenement collapse which killed nearly a dozen black residents in the Seventh Ward in 1936; (3) the nearly twenty-five-year-long black-led protest against urban renewal, namely the proposed construction of the Crosstown Expressway through the Seventh Ward (1950 through the early 1970s); and (4) the election of W. Wilson Goode as Philadelphia's first black mayor in 1983. To a lesser extent I make use of a fifth historical moment, the flash mob on South Street in March 2010, as a lens through which to summarize and examine the implications of this study of the Black Seventh Ward and draw some final conclusions.

Instead of focusing exclusively on the debates black Philadelphians had over economic self-sufficiency, housing reform, urban renewal, or political representation, I also connect the effects of the historical moments encompassing these debates to the shifts in Philadelphia's politics and racial geography over time. Although each historical period I examine in this book is significant in its own right, my goal here is to bring these periods together in one place to fully evaluate their relationship and uncover their combined effects. Revisiting the cultural, economic, and political history of the Black Seventh Ward affords us a richer and fuller understanding of the origins and conditions of urban black residents and neighborhoods today. To make clear and deepen the central claim of the book, I rely not just on the descriptive power of the historical moments I examine, but DuBois's observations in *The Philadelphia Negro* and an analysis of the *political agency* of black Philadelphians as well.

The Black Seventh Ward

Philadelphia, like other cities across the United States, became a key destination for black migrants following Emancipation and through the Great Migration. Along with Chicago's Bronzeville, Pittsburgh's Hill District, Los Angeles's Watts, Washington DC's U-Street/Shaw neighborhood, and New York City's Harlem—hubs for migrant blacks as they moved out of the Jim Crow South—Philadelphia's Seventh Ward emerged as a neighborhood with one of the largest concentrations of blacks during the Great Migration. As DuBois explains in *The Philadelphia Negro*, the Black Seventh Ward was born out of the race riots of the mid-1800s, beginning as a safe haven for blacks as whites instigated a series of race riots that lasted days at a time over several years. As a result, many indigenous black institutions (e.g., churches, markets, and social clubs) were centered in the Seventh Ward. By 1896, when DuBois began his study, "[T]his long and narrow ward, extending from South Seventh street to the Schuylkill river and from Spruce to South street" contained "a fifth of all Negroes" in Philadelphia.[3]

At its peak, the Seventh Ward contained close to 15,000 black residents and was the predominant site of many of the goods, services, and cultural institutions for black Philadelphians. Although the Seventh Ward was both a black and white neighborhood, the area bounded between South and Lombard Streets from 7th to 25th Streets was a distinctive black enclave unto itself (see Figure 1.2).[4] Much like the Black Belt of Chicago, famously examined by sociologists St. Clair Drake and Horace Cayton in *Black Metropolis*, the black South/Lombard Street area of the Seventh Ward was in many ways *a city within a city*.[5]

While the Black Seventh Ward never contained more than twenty percent of the total black population, given the density of the indigenous institutions in the neighborhood and its function as the major port of entry for southern black migrants into Philadelphia, an examination of this neighborhood provides an important sociological, political and historical window into patterns of change in the larger city and Black Philadelphia.

Much like DuBois, I also discovered that the Black Seventh Ward offered important sociological insights into the factors impacting urban change, and provided a way to uncover the historical actors and events that animate contemporary understandings and debates about the economic and political advancement of urban minorities, public and affordable housing, and the consequences of urban renewal and gentrification. Like DuBois's *The Philadelphia Negro*, this book draws its analysis from a combination of archival resources. In particular I make great use of archival data, large-scale data sources (e.g., US Census Reports), oral histories, photographs, and daily news sources to generate a historical narrative and detailed picture of the neighborhood and its residents.[6]

My analysis is structured around several "critical junctures" or crucial historical moments that emphasize the decisions made by a range of black actors at specific choice analytic points that in my view determined the path of particular policies, changes, and reforms.[7] To be clear, the critical junctures I base my analysis upon are not meant to be exhaustive. Rather, such historical moments provide a means to uncover and analyze the variety of black actions and attitudes impacting on and interacting with structural changes throughout the twentieth century. Given the hundred-year period I cover, a discussion of the social history of the Black Seventh Ward vis-à-vis these four critical junctures provides a cohesive and succinct way to discuss the empirical and theoretical importance of changes in the neighborhood and Philadelphia over time and how the agency of urban black residents impacted such changes.

For analytical purposes I have attempted to distill each historical period covered in order to uncover and attend to some of the major lessons, stake-holders, and outcomes of that time. However, this is not at all to suggest that these historical periods represent an exhaustive or complete view of Philadelphia twentieth-century history (or of Black Philadelphia for that matter). As sociologist Eric Klinenberg demonstrates, in his analysis of Chicago's deadly heatwave in the summer of 1995, a focus on moments of crisis and conflict helps to specify the relative importance of human agency, while also making visible the structural conditions and power relations that foster the inequalities embedded in American cities.[8]

The Four Faces of Political Agency

If the tool for understanding and examining urban change in this book is political agency, then what does such agency look like? How do citizens, in this case, black Philadelphians, express this agency and to what end? Who are the key players using such agency and what outcomes are produced because of this behavior? In this book, I focus on the concept of *political agency*[9] to encapsulate what I see as the key attitudes and actions that impact and thus contextualize a variety of key structural changes occurring in Philadelphia and the Black Seventh Ward during the twentieth century. Throughout the book I will focus on what I see as the *four faces* or expressions of political agency—*framing*, *voting*, *mobilization*, and *migration*. To be clear, my con-ception of political agency is also rooted in some important assumptions about urban America. Such assumptions are interwoven throughout my elab-oration of political agency so as to demonstrate the connections. In what follows, I will briefly discuss these faces while also foreshadowing some of the dynamics that are more fully discussed in each of the subsequent chapters of the book.

The first face of political agency can also be thought of as what sociolo-gist David Snow and his colleagues refer to as *framing*—the concise and punchy articulation of a social issue or reality into political terms that are used by citizens to forge alliances and seek social change on a variety of fronts. This first face is where we find culture expressly involved, often in the form of rhetoric or discourse. Indeed, as Frances Fox Piven and Richard A.

Cloward remind us in their classic book *Poor People's Movements*, framing can be an essential tool for "people whose only possible recourse in struggle is to defy the beliefs and rituals laid down by their rulers."[10] The ability of citizens to construct narratives, symbols, and phrases to identify themselves, as well as stakeholders, power, oppression, resources, and inequality, is perhaps the bedrock of political agency.

Richard Iton's *In Search of the Black Fantastic*, for example, demonstrates that black rhetoric and discourse vis-à-vis literature, music, and performance have been powerful tools to articulate black politics and elicit support to address a variety of inequities experienced by black Americans. We also find the importance of discourse as a common and significant expression of political agency in the work of historians such as Robin D. G. Kelley on the actions and attitudes or "infrapolitics" of Southern working-class and poor blacks during the Jim Crow era, and the analysis of social revolutions in countries like Russia by sociologist Theda Skocpol.[11] As I will show in this book, black Philadelphians created powerful rhetoric to generate collective and individual action to address a number of issues of both local and national significance. For example, when urban renewal plans targeted the Black Seventh Ward for expressway construction, black Philadelphians created a powerful discourse that thwarted the expressway plans by positing the roadway as exemplifying "Philadelphia's Mason-Dixon Line," and emphasized that such construction would physically separate blacks and whites, while also producing deadly air pollution.

Voting and *mobilization*, the second and third faces of political agency, spring from framing. Drawing on Albert O. Hirschman's classic typology of "voice" and "exit," both voting and mobilization reflect primary responses of individual agents to structural conditions.[12] When citizens want political change in a representative democracy, such as that in the United States, voting is the formal path to enacting or achieving such change. To be sure, black voting has a complicated history, rife with stories of threats, and of unfair poll taxes levied almost exclusively on black voters, systematically weakening the impact of the black voter (perhaps finally eliminated by the Voting Rights Act of 1965). Myriad scholars have revealed that voting and the process through which voters make decisions regarding the casting of their ballot are fundamental components of civil society generally and modern democracies more specifically.

Discussions of black politics in the post–civil rights era are perhaps the most instructive. Recent research in this area has focused on the role of the black vote and the marked shift from a largely Republican voting base to a

Democratic one among the black electorate. Inquiry in this area has focused on the political attitudes of blacks in the period of "new black politics," an era of postsegregation and increased black electoral representation.[13] In this research scholars have focused particularly on the prominence of what political scientist Michael Dawson refers to as the "linked fate perspective," a political framework that presumes that black people share a common fate. The linked-fate perspective has been shown to influence voting behaviors, particularly the strong support of the Democratic Party among black Americans, while also impacting mobilization efforts and the creation and maintenance of a black political community.[14]

As scholars have shown, however, the pervasiveness of such a perspective does not mean that black attitudes are homogeneous, as the operationalization of the perspective varies among black people dramatically.[15] Acknowledging that the mobilization of indigenous resources often occurs under the guise of a linked-fate perspective, scholars have uncovered the intraracial processes involved in mobilizing a black political constituency.[16] Political scientist Cathy J. Cohen, for example, complicates the notion of linked fate by demonstrating that within black political agendas segments of the population are further marginalized for the sake of a supposed consensus, constituting what she refers to as "secondary marginalization."[17] As we will see in the story of the Black Seventh Ward, black political attitudes are tied to the mobilization of resources, particularly indigenous resources such as the black press, churches, schools, and social clubs, influencing voting practices and outcomes.

Applying Dawson's and Cohen's insights to the local context, black neighborhoods, such as the Black Seventh Ward, are perhaps best understood as linked to one another. Therefore, the decline of one urban black neighborhood influences the rise and politicization of another. Events and debates shaping one urban black neighborhood reverberate throughout the city, particularly in other black neighborhoods. As we will find in the story of the Black Seventh Ward, the decline of that neighborhood influenced the rise of other black neighborhoods in Philadelphia indicating a pattern of interdependency among urban black enclaves.[18]

As social-movement scholars such as sociologists Doug McAdam, Aldon Morris, Charles Tilly and Francesca Polletta, and historians Thomas Sugrue, Martha Biondi, and Rhonda Y. Williams have shown, the third face of political agency, *mobilization*, is often manifested in marches, rallies, private meetings, riots, and/or the creation and establishment of indigenous institutions. For example, when the deaths of nearly a dozen Black Seventh Ward residents occurred due to the collapse of a poorly managed tenement, black activists' mobilization on the issue of housing reform facilitated a lasting policy of race-specific housing policy and construction, wherein working families across race outside of the Seventh Ward would benefit the most. Mobilization is not always the result of a concerted plan. Indeed, violence—like the race riots Sugrue describes and those that sociologist Darnell Hunt examines in South Central Los Angeles in the wake of the Rodney King verdict in April of 1992—demonstrates that mobilization is not always premeditated and can have unexpected consequences such as riots.[19]

Although riots are not the topic of examination in this book, the unplanned mobilization of black Philadelphians is. For example, when city officials began to condemn areas of the neighborhood in the wake of the devastating tenement collapse, outraged residents' individual protests combined into a larger campaign against the city's actions. These conceptions of voting and mobilization as they pertain to black Philadelphians are based on my assumption that urban black neighborhoods represent substantial points within the larger nexus constituting the "black community," containing important indigenous resources that are mobilized or demobilized for political ends. As political scientist Adolph Reed reminds us:

> The group as a coherent entity with an identifiable standpoint, in this case the generic "black community" (or any given black community, for that matter), is a reification that at most expresses the success of some interest networks in articulating their interpretations and programs and asserting them in the name of the group.

In other words, the so-called "black community" at its core is constitutive of a diverse group of interest networks, most often (but not always) based at the neighborhood level, whose combined impact gives rise to the boundaries and politics of the larger black population.[20]

Migration is the fourth face of political agency. As the old adage goes: "People vote with their feet." In other words, the movement from one place to another is often a political act reflecting the needs or desires of those who move. Further, as sociologists John Logan and Harvey Molotch have noted, migration can be an expression of the class status of a citizenry. As they show, those who are poorer migrate more often. However, the existing notion of migration is quite broad.

In my view, there are two broad types of migration, *primary* and *secondary*. *Primary migration*, like that described by historians' (and most recently in Isabel Wilkerson's) discussion of the Great Migration, involves the movement from one city/town/state to another city/town/state some distances apart. *Secondary migration*, on the other hand, involves within-city movement. That is, residents move from one neighborhood within the city to another in the same city. While both are critical expressions of the larger sense of migration as a face of political agency, the focus of this book will largely be on secondary migration. Indeed, as Hirschman reminds us, "withdrawal or exit" is a "'direct' way of expressing one's unfavorable views" of the state and institutions.[21] That is, leaving a place is constitutive of agency.

Often disempowered from the political process in Philadelphia, black Philadelphians responded to structural changes in public housing and urban growth and decline by leaving the Black Seventh Ward and taking up residence in emergent black sections in North, West, and South Philadelphia drawing new boundaries in the racial geography of Philadelphia, thus reshaping the political districts of Philadelphia over time. Here, the major assumption is that neighborhoods often are a major tangible cultural, socioeconomic, and political resource. A neighborhood is a reflection of its residents, shaped by the relationship between its residents and the city. If its residents lack access to mainstream resources and are politically and socially marginalized, then so too is the neighborhood in which they live. This assumption, then, emphasizes the importance of marginalization and racial domination. That is, a neighborhood is a container for local and indigenous resources as well as a place of residence. However, like all resources neighborhoods are limited. Neighborhoods are socially and politically constituted physical areas of the built environment, and as such can contain only portions of the total resources of a city and a given population; neighborhoods are commodities, and are often the tool used by federal, state, and local agencies to designate resources, especially those tied to social welfare programs.

In this way, my concern with political agency seeks, in the words of political scientist James C. Scott, to make the state and structure "legible." As Scott reminds us: "[F]ormal schemes of order are untenable without some elements of the practical knowledge that they tend to dismiss."[22] Indeed, structure can be hard to see analytically and empirically. In my view, agency represents the practical knowledge of which Scott speaks; and political agency provides a fruitful way to gauge the interface between individual agents and state-sanctioned actions, procedures, and policies. Here, then, agency is not situated as more important than or superior to structure. Rather, agency is situated as an empirical and analytic lens to gauge the range of attitudes and actions of black residents as they came up against structural changes over time.

Overview of the Book

The story that follows begins where DuBois's *The Philadelphia Negro* ended. Each chapter begins by bringing us to the scene of a crucial historical moment that in my view both defines the period of change in the Black Seventh Ward while also contextualizing the socioeconomic and/or political structural conditions at the time. I then work backwards from the scene to piece together, through historical narrative, the world of the Black Seventh Ward, and to identify the major players, institutions, and debates that provide a sense of the stakes and political terrain. I focus in particular on the relationship between the structural conditions of the time and the actions and attitudes of black Philadelphians in response to or in anticipation of such conditions.

As we will discover in the story that follows, over the course of the twentieth century black Philadelphians experienced periods of structural opportunity while also navigating the continued lack of access due in large part to discrimination. In this book, I attempt to reconstruct the historical period through the lens of four historical moments to amplify the impact of the political agency of black Philadelphians over time. As a result, I am able to identify and analyze each of the four faces of the political agency of black Philadelphians over time as they related to questions of urban change under the themes of economic self-sufficiency, public housing policy, urban renewal, gentrification, and the post–civil rights context.

Chapter 2 begins this historical journey back into the Black Seventh Ward, focusing in particular on the rise and fall of black banks during the late nineteenth and early twentieth centuries. How have black efforts to combat economic disenfranchisement impacted the urban landscape? In this chapter, I detail how the collapse of indigenous black banks impacted the financial livelihood of black Philadelphians. Developed largely in response to the lack of access blacks had to mainstream banks and credit, black entrepreneurs Edward C. Brown and Andrew Stevens established and managed two banks that relied heavily on black capital. The collapse of these financial systems and subsequent loss of access to economic resources resulted in a multiclass migration of blacks from the neighborhood and an economic depression preceding and magnified by the Great Depression. Subsequently, the Black Seventh Ward transitioned into an overcrowded neighborhood with a high concentration of poverty due to the influx of southern black migrants who replaced long-time black residents but failed to find comparable employment opportunities. Essentially, this chapter investigates and analyzes the mobilizing efforts and rhetoric that were key expressions of black political agency impacting socioeconomic structural conditions.

In chapter 3 I take up a discussion of an issue that has long been key to examinations of urban black residents—public housing. Did urban black residents impact public housing policy and housing reform in Philadelphia, and, if so, in what ways? In this chapter I discuss how the particularly poor housing conditions of the Black Seventh Ward gave rise to the mass development of race-based public housing policy and construction in Philadelphia. In this discussion, I reveal the inadvertent ways that black residents in their quest for housing reform generally, and affordable housing specifically, were complicit in the demise of the Black Seventh Ward and the shifting institutional geography of Black Philadelphia and the racial geography of the city. This chapter, then, focuses in particular on framing, mobilization, and migration as key expressions of political agency impacting housing reform and public housing policy.

Much like public housing, urban renewal has also been key to understanding and examining urban black life and urban change. Did urban black residents in Philadelphia challenge urban renewal plans, and, if so, how did such opposition impact patterns of urban development and change? How did black activism against urban renewal impact urban transportation plans developed under the guise of urban renewal? In chapter 4, I consider the conflict emergent in the Black Seventh Ward as city leaders pursued highway construction plans created from the urban renewal goals for the area. Specifically, I detail how urban renewal efforts in the Black Seventh Ward gave rise to a powerful interneighborhood and interracial alliance established and led by black residents that left an indelible mark on Philadelphia's transportation system, specifically highway construction and public transportation.

Ultimately, I situate urban renewal vis-à-vis the Crosstown Expressway as a critical juncture that amplifies the interdependent relationship among black neighborhoods and the impact of the agency of black residents on urban landscapes. I argue that although urban renewal plans for the Black Seventh Ward virtually destroyed its historic black community, the decline of that area helped to reinforce and extend the prominence of emergent black neighborhoods in North, South, and West Philadelphia. Further, I contend that black-led activism against the Crosstown Expressway demonstrates the important ways in which black residents impact patterns of urban development, particularly urban transportation. Examining the social history of urban renewal in the Black Seventh Ward through the lens of the debate over the Crosstown Expressway, I emphasize the important and lasting impact black residents, entrepreneurs, and leaders have on larger patterns of neighborhood change and the racial geography of the city. In essence, in this chapter I focus on the relationship between structure as expressed through urban renewal, and political agency, namely mobilization and migration.

How have black political victories in post–civil rights Philadelphia impacted patterns of urban black development specifically and urban growth more generally? In chapter 5, I trace the contemporary racial geography of Philadelphia and the Black Seventh Ward, in the wake of W. Wilson Goode's historic election as Philadelphia's first black mayor, focusing specifically on the last two decades of the twentieth century. I reveal that in the post–civil rights context the combined political efforts of various neighborhood councils and leaders facilitated efforts to preserve the cultural legacy of the Black Seventh Ward, especially around the South Street area. The political enfranchisement of black Philadelphians, as indicated by Goode's historic victory, demonstrates how contemporary and historic black neighborhoods changed as the relationship urban blacks had with the local power structure shifted in the post–civil rights era. Whereas chapter 4 focuses on mobilization, namely activism against urban renewal, this chapter focuses on black political rhetoric and mobilization in post–civil rights Philadelphia.

Using the South Street flash mob of March 2010 as a springboard, chapter 6 considers the lessons we might draw from the storied Black Seventh Ward, political agency, and urban change in Philadelphia over time. Further, this chapter recaps the dynamics captured in the substantive chapters to elaborate on the patterns of urban and neighborhood change discussed throughout the book. I reflect on the major lessons that the socioeconomic, cultural, and political history of the Black Seventh Ward and Black Philadelphia teach us about urban and neighborhood change and the role of the political agency of black residents, leaders, and activists in such change.

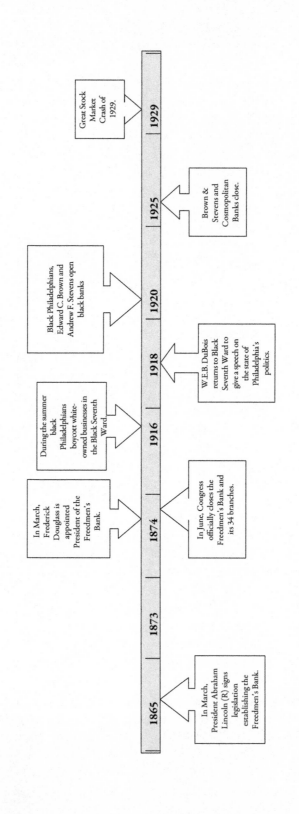

1865 — In March, President Abraham Lincoln (R) signs legislation establishing the Freedmen's Bank.

1873

1874 — In March, Frederick Douglass is appointed President of the Freedmen's Bank.

In June, Congress officially closes the Freedmen's Bank and its 34 branches.

1916 — During the summer black Philadelphians boycott white-owned businesses in the Black Seventh Ward.

1918 — W.E.B. DuBois returns to Black Seventh Ward to give a speech on the state of Philadelphia's politics.

1920 — Black Philadelphians, Edward C. Brown and Andrew F. Stevens open black banks

1925 — Brown & Stevens and Cosmopolitan Banks close.

1929 — Great Stock Market Crash of 1929.

2

A Tale of Two Banks

IN FEBRUARY OF 1925, the Black Seventh Ward again became a site of contention. Unlike previous conflicts, however, this time black Philadelphians were embroiled in an *intraracial* clash—a financial battle with black banking entrepreneurs in the Black Seventh Ward. After a series of massive withdrawals by depositors, or "runs," two black banks, Brown & Stevens and Cosmopolitan, closed suddenly, leaving many to wonder when and if they would ever see their savings returned. While some relied on the goodwill of those in charge of managing the two banks, others sought legal means to recoup their savings.

On February 18, 1925, Teresa A. Williams, Norma B. Winslow, and Clarence L. Smith filed an involuntary bankruptcy suit against the Brown & Stevens and Cosmopolitan Banks. Seeking the repayment of their savings totaling $1,932 ($24,000 in 2010), Williams, Winslow, and Smith were among the nearly 13,000 depositors whose savings were in limbo due to the failure of the two banks.[1] As Table 2.1 indicates, much like these three depositors, many black Philadelphians had placed their savings in the two banks in hopes of establishing financial security for themselves and their families.

The claims of Williams, Winslow, and Smith reflect an important interaction black Americans had during the late nineteenth and early twentieth centuries with banks. Following President Lincoln's signing of the Emancipation Proclamation in January 1863, banks became one of the first experiments to address the social inequality created under slavery. After Emancipation, black Americans had the chance to accumulate wealth. But to protect that wealth, they needed banks. Yet the banks were also "separate but equal," leading to racially disparate risks of being bankrupted by the bank.

Much like that of early American leaders such as James Madison, Alexander Hamilton, and John Jay, and British economist Adam Smith, the logic underlying the establishment of the Freedmen's Bank (and later the Brown & Stevens and Cosmopolitan Banks) determined that banks functioned as institutions that leveraged new economic possibilities. In this view, banks were also a major socializing component in capitalistic economic systems.[2]

Table 2.1 Statement of the financial condition of the Brown & Stevens Bank on February 11, 1925

(Main office and West Philadelphia Branch)

Resources:	$ in 1925	$ in 2010
Loans and Discounts	496,601.10	6,180,000
Overdrafts	12, 582.57	157,000
Stocks and bonds	317,982.22	3,960,000
Mortgages	151,704.89	1,890,000
Real estate	137,842.66	1,710,000
Furniture and fixtures	20,591.80	256,000
Cash on hand	4,627.27	57,600
Due from banks and bankers	24,291.62	302,000
Certificates of deposit	24,500.00	305,000
Expense	42,781.64	532,000
Reserve fund	100,000.00	1,240,000
Shortage	319.22	3,970
Other resources	858.11	10,700
Interest on deposits and interest in active accounts	2,201.37	27,400
Total	1,336,884.47	16,600,000

Liabilities:		
Capital	100,000.00	1,240,000
Surplus	15,000.00	187,000
Undivided profits	2,060.80	25,600
Deposits (individual)	851,355.35	10,600,000
Savings deposits	26,998.28	336,000
Christmas savings deposits	4,382.25	54,500
Due to banks	9,160.34	114,000
Cashier's checks	28,005.26	348,000
Certified checks	4,237.80	52,700
Demand certificates of deposit	80,600.00	1,000,000
Bills rediscounted	175,215.92	2,180,000
Interest and exchange	2,566.80	31,900
Collections	945.06	11,800
Due on real estate	36,330.00	452,000
Excess	26.61	331
Total	1,336,884.47	16,600,000

Source: Walter L. Fleming, *The Freedmen's Savings Bank: A Chapter in the Economic History of the Negro Race* (Westport, CT: Negro Universities Press, 1970) 50; U.S. Senate, 46th Cong., 2nd sess., 1880, Rep. 440; U.S. Senate, *The Freedman's Bank Bill*, 46th Cong., 3rd sess., 1881; U.S. Senate, 62nd Cong., 2nd Session, 1912, Rep. 759, 4.

However, the climate of racial exclusion characterizing the United States generally (and Philadelphia more specifically) rendered race-specific banks the only viable avenue. Indeed, race was a mediating influence in the construction of America's financial sector in the post-Emancipation context, leading to significant social boundaries in the operation and function of banks. As Michèle Lamont and Virág Molnár remind us: "Social boundaries are objectified forms of social differences manifested in unequal access to and unequal distribution of resources (material and nonmaterial) and social opportunities."[3]

Additionally, the incomes, savings, and wealth of black Americans were constructed in ways that can best characterized as what sociologist Viviana Zelizer calls *special monies*—the assignment of "different meanings and designat[ion] of separate uses for particular kinds of money." Indeed, as Zelizer asserts: "Not all dollars are equal."[4] In the case of black Americans post-Emancipation, black assets, especially money, were designated as different, and thus were collected and held by black-specific banking institutions like the Freedmen's and Brown & Stevens Banks. At the same time, the "separate but equal" mantra of the time also meant that black-specific banking institutions were the only financial institutions designed and authorized to handle the savings and incomes of black depositors. Such differentiation regarding "black" money had important implications for the economic livelihoods of black Americans, especially as such separation meant that when these banks collapsed black depositors were left with little recourse to recoup their savings.

While the Brown & Stevens and Cosmopolitan Banks were not the first black-owned banks to fail, the embeddedness of these two banks in the financial livelihood of black Philadelphia was unprecedented and largely unknown to depositors. The impact of the collapse of these two financial institutions was devastating, leading to foreclosures for black business-owners and dire economic straits for poor and working-class black Philadelphians. The collapse of Brown & Stevens and Cosmopolitan Banks ushered in a period of economic decline preceding the larger national economic depression that followed the Great Stock Market Crash of 1929. Without question, the rise and fall of the Brown & Stevens and Cosmopolitan Banks in Philadelphia significantly altered the racial geography of the city and the financial condition of black Philadelphians in the years that followed.

In this chapter, I examine the Black Seventh Ward prior to and following the banking collapse. I begin by detailing the growth and development of the

Black Seventh Ward at the beginning of the twentieth century. In this discussion I show that the economic marginalization of black Philadelphians provided the impetus for the development of a network of indigenous black institutions and services; such growth incentivized redevelopment of the Black Seventh Ward, financially tied black institutions to one another, and facilitated wealth accumulation among black Philadelphians. In particular, I focus on the political agency of black Philadelphians as they grappled with and framed their economic marginalization and on how the lack of access to mainstream banking institutions generated new structural opportunities to pursue economic self-sufficiency. Following this discussion, I consider the banking collapse, its causes, and the larger impact of the failure of the two banks.

In what follows, I demonstrate that the sociopolitical history of black banks is inflected with serious distrust on the part of black depositors because of the acute patterns of financial loss for black depositors. As evidenced in W. E. B. DuBois's analysis in *The Philadelphia Negro*, banking institutions, economic self-sufficiency, and distrust among blacks have a long and important history. Indeed, DuBois identified similar sentiments for banks by Black Seventh Warders, writing: "The Negroes have an inherited distrust of banks and companies."[5]

Complementing DuBois's observations, this chapter charts the origins of such distrust alongside the genealogy of the Brown & Stevens and Cosmopolitan Banks, to demonstrate how structural discrimination facilitated the rise and fall of black banks and the interdependent relations among black residents and wealth. I focus on the black banks in Philadelphia as a reaction to the loss of capital and confidence following the collapse of the Freedmen's Bank, and I provide an analytic lens to understand and examine the structural conditions defining this period of black economic development and urban history.

In this way, indigenous institutions such as black banks provide an important and underexplored method of analyzing and understanding larger patterns of neighborhood change and interdependency. I argue that these banks functioned as the linchpin that sustained the economic livelihood and financial wherewithal of the Black Seventh Ward and Black Philadelphia. Examining the social history of black banks through the lens of the Brown & Stevens and Cosmopolitan Banks, I underscore the important role and lasting impact the political agency of black residents, leaders, and entrepreneurs have on larger patterns of neighborhood change through framing and mobilization.

The Freedmen's Bank

The emergence of black banks in Philadelphia was already shrouded in a sentiment of distrust due to early failures of black banks following Emancipation, particularly the collapse of the Freedmen's Savings and Trust Company (the Freedmen's Bank). As DuBois notes in *The Philadelphia Negro*: "Negroes distrust all saving institutions since the fatal collapse of the Freedmen's Bank." Therefore, an understanding of the sociopolitical history of black banks in Philadelphia (or anywhere in the United States) is distinctly tied to the rise and fall of the Freedmen's Bank.[6]

The economic environment of black Americans prior to, during, and following Emancipation was a precarious and contentious one, as "until the strict drawing of race lines... arising out of Reconstruction there was a noticeable tendency among the emancipated to separate into economic and social classes." This was in part due to the dynamics of slavery prior to Emancipation, wherein "most of those who were free before the war were mulattoes and many of them had property; in Louisiana they formed an important part of the colored population, holding property valued in 1860 at $13,000,000" ($352,000,000 in 2010). Although there are some accounts of black Americans holding considerable savings in white banks prior to the Civil War, following Emancipation many white business leaders and politicians believed it important to develop an institution or corporation that would specifically target the economic improvement of freed blacks.[7]

Several issues converged facilitating the rise of the Freedmen's Bank: the emancipation of black Americans, increased pay of black soldiers, and increased secondary and primary migration of black Americans throughout the North and South. Cases of black soldiers being swindled, for instance, were quite common and underscored the need to establish a formal and central banking institution for newly freed black Americans. As historian of the Freedmen's Bank Walter L. Fleming notes: "swindlers of every kind were always ready for pay day in a Negro regiment, and had little difficulty in getting most of the soldiers' cash."[8] In this way, black consumers were treated much like sociologist Frederick Wherry's description of the "market fool"— individual consumers seen as "idiot[s] unable to manage money."[9]

Upon the conclusion of the Civil War, Northern (and to some extent Southern) white leaders began to lobby the United States Congress to authorize and create a bank for freed blacks that would be loosely affiliated with the Freedmen's Bureau—the federal institution charged with overseeing and facilitating the process of black emancipation following the war's conclusion.

Following a meeting of key political and business leaders on January 27, 1865, plans proposing the Freedmen's Bank were sent to the United States Congress. Congress, in turn, swiftly approved the incorporation of the banking institution, outlining its responsibilities:

> The general business and object of the corporation hereby called shall be to receive on deposit such sums of money as may from time to time be offered, therefore by or on behalf of persons heretofore held in slavery in the United States or their descendants and to invest the same in stocks, bonds, treasury notes and other securities of the United States.[10]

On March 3, 1865, President Abraham Lincoln signed the legislation, entitled the Freedmen's Bank Act, thus authorizing the organization of the bank. As Lincoln signed the legislation, he lauded it a significant step in the realization of black freedom: "This bank is just what the freedmen need."[11]

With the support of prominent white businessmen and politicians, along with reports that the United States Government protected the savings of the bank, the Freedmen's Bank was quickly organized and received tremendous black support. Most important for black confidence in the banking institution was the outreach efforts by the bank's corresponding secretary (and inspector and superintendent of schools for the Freedmen's Bureau), a white northerner named John W. Alvord. Alvord, a minister and an attaché to General William Tecumseh Sherman during the Civil War, was a key proponent of the Freedmen's Bank. As its initial president, Alvord traveled throughout the Black South to encourage black Americans to deposit their money at the bank.

His most successful strategy involved convincing potential depositors that the bank "was part of the Freedmen's Bureau system." Alvord traveled through the South with supposed endorsements from General O. O. Howard (the commissioner of the Freedmen's Bureau): "as an order from Howard...Negro soldiers should deposit their bounty money with him."[12] Alvord also carried a handwritten letter from General Howard to assure skeptics. In the letter, Howard's words were emphatic: "I consider the Freedman's [sic] Savings and Trust Company to be greatly needed by the colored people, and have welcomed it as an auxiliary to the Freedmen's Bureau."[13]

Additionally, the bank provided promotions in their materials such as passbooks. One version of the passbook featured the following statement, in English, German, and French: "The Government of the United States has made this bank perfectly safe." Another edition of the passbook, for example, featured photographs of President Lincoln, General Ulysses S. Grant, and the United States flag, with a poem believed to have been penned by General Howard encouraging black Americans to be frugal and deposit their money with the Freedmen's Bank:

> 'Tis little by little the bee fills her cell;
> And little by little a man sinks a well;
> 'Tis little by little a bird builds her nest;
> By littles a forest in verdure is drest;
> 'Tis little by little great volumes are made;
> By littles a mountain or levels are made;
> 'Tis little by little an ocean is filled;
> And little by little a city we build;
> 'Tis little by little an ant gets her store;
> Every little we add to a little makes more;
> Step by step we walk miles, and we sew stitch by stitch;
> Word by word we read books, cent by cent we grow rich.[14]

Here, then, banks and frugality were pushed heavily as important economic ideals that would address and advance the needs of black Americans in the post-Emancipation period. Such ephemera from the bank also illustrate that the proponents of the bank, as an institution and as a metaphor for an ideology regarding black economic practices and progress, envisioned the Freedmen's Bank as a tool to socialize freed blacks, attempting to teach them the ways to think about their money and the relationship it shares with citizenship—*the more you save the more you're free*. This mantra of frugality, however, was conditioned by the relegation of black incomes and savings to a separate and "special" banking institution structure mostly concerned with collecting savings and not with providing loans.

Due to such recruiting efforts, the bank's list of black depositors grew quickly, and soon thirty-four branches were established in locations across the country including Philadelphia. Observing the popularity of the bank, a reporter in Charleston, South Carolina, observed in 1870: "Go in any forenoon and the office is found full of negroes depositing little sums of money, drawing little sums, or remitting to a distant part of the country where they have relatives to support or debts to discharge."[15] As Tables 2.2 and 2.3 indicate, by January 1874, less than ten years after the establishment of the Freedmen's Bank, deposits at the thirty-four branches totaled $3,299,201

Table 2.2 Listing of deposits held at all branches of the Freedmen's Bank
(c. March 1874)

Branch	Deposits, 1874 ($)	Estimated equivalent, 2010 ($)
Alexandria, VA	21,584	426,000
Atlanta, GA	28,404	561,000
Augusta, GA	96,882	1,190,000
Baltimore, MD	303,947	6,000,000
Beaufort, SC	55,592	1,100,000
Charleston, SC	255,345	5,040,000
Columbus, MS	18,857	372,000
Columbia, TN	19,823	392,000
Huntsville, AL	35,963	710,000
Jacksonville, FL	22,022	435,000
Lexington, KY	34,193	675,000
Little Rock, AK	17,728	350,000
Louisville, KY	137,094	2,710,000
Lynchburg, VA	19,967	394,000
Macon, GA	54,342	1,070,000
Memphis, TN	56,755	1,120,000
Mobile, AL	96,144	1,900,000
Montgomery, AL	29,743	587,000
Natchez, MS	22,195	438,000
Nashville, TN	78,525	1,550,000
New Bern, NC	40,621	802,000
New Orleans, LA	240,006	4,740,000
New York, NY	344,071	6,800,000
Norfolk, VA	126,337	2,500,000
Philadelphia, PA	84,657	1,670,000
Raleigh, NC	26,703	527,000
Richmond, VA	166,000	3,280,000
Savannah, GA	153,425	3,030,000
Shreveport, LA	30,312	599,000
St. Louis, MO	58,397	1,150,000
Tallahassee, FL	40,207	794,000
Vicksburg, MS	104,348	2,060,000
Washington, D.C.	384,789	7,600,000
Wilmington, NC	45,223	893,000

Source: Walter L. Fleming, *The Freedmen's Savings Bank: A Chapter in the Economic History of the Negro Race* (Westport: Negro Universities Press, 1970) 50; U.S. Senate, 46th Cong., 2nd sess., 1880, Rep. 440; U.S. Senate, *The Freedmen's Bank Bill*, 46th Cong., 3rd sess., 1881; U.S. Senate, 62nd Cong., 2nd Session, 1912, Rep. 759, 4.

($65,200,000 in 2010). As the only two northern affiliates of the Freedmen's Bank, New York and Philadelphia branches held total deposits of $344, 071 and $84,657 ($6,810,000 and $1,670,000 in 2010) respectively.[16]

The Freedmen's Bank's success led to a shift from a savings institution to one that also provided loans and credit. This shift was accomplished when Congress amended the bank's charter in 1870. "Before the charter was amended in 1870, no loans could be made by the principal bank or by the branches, for, by the law of 1865, two thirds of all deposits" were to be "invested in United States securities and the remainder held as an available fund."

After 1870, however, Congress authorized the bank to provide mortgages and business loans. Such mortgages and loans were usually given to whites, representing an important contradiction—a black bank using the savings and income of black depositors to advance the economic fortunes of whites who had at their disposal mainstream banks that excluded blacks. This contradiction would soon show itself, as the liabilities created because of lending began to disrupt the viability of various branches. In this way, black depositors were set up to shoulder all the risks, with whites benefiting from their frugality.[17]

Soon after Congress authorized the Freedmen's Bank to provide loans and credit, reports of corruption by the bank's white management diminished black confidence in the bank. For example, in 1872 a rumor that deposits held in North Carolina were being used to support and elect white politicians, including Ulysses S. Grant's successful presidential bid, caused a heavy run on the branches throughout the South. Shortly thereafter, rumors tying the deposits at the Freedmen's Bank with political campaigns spread throughout the North and South, and led to a loss of a half-million dollars of the Freedmen's Bank's total holdings.

Rumors aside, there were also very real accounting issues and serious deficits. Of the thirty-four branches established, half were unprofitably operated, often with white officials taking the money of black depositors to create personal profits for themselves. Bad loans had also been authorized to the detriment of the bank.

In response, the Freedmen's Bank's white management was replaced with a variety of black people, many of whom were inexperienced in the area of banking; thus the organization of the Freedmen's Bank spiraled into chaos and depositors arrived at branches across the country seeking the return of their savings in full. In an effort to win back the confidence of black depositors, in March, 1874 Frederick Douglass was appointed to head the Freedmen's Bank. However, with little experience in the area of banking, Douglass was unable to stop the runs at the bank's branches.[18]

Table 2.3 Total history of deposits held by the Freedmen's Bank
(c.March 1874)

Year	Total deposits, 1874 ($)	Estimated equivalent, 2010 ($)	Annual deposits, 1874 ($)	Estimated equivalent, 2010 ($)	Balance due depositors, 1874 ($)	Estimated equivalent, 2010 ($)	Annual gain, 1874 ($)	Estimated equivalent, 2010 ($)
1866	305,167	6,030,000	305,167	6,030,000	199,283.42	3,940,000	199,283.42	3,940,000
1867	1,624,853.33	32,100,000	1,319,686.33	26,100,000	366,338.33	7,240,000	167,054.91	3,300,000
1868	3,582,378.36	70,800,000	1,957,535.03	38,700,000	638,338.33	12,600,000	271,960.67	5,370,000
1869	7,257,798.63	143,000,000	3,675,420.27	7,260,000	1,073,465.31	21,200,000	435,166.31	8,600,000
1870	12,605,781.95	249,000,000	5,347,983.32	106,000,000	1,657,006.75	32,700,000	583,541.44	11,500,000
1871	19,592,947.36	387,000,000	7,347,165.41	145,000,000	2,455,836.11	48,500,000	798,827.67	15,800,000
1872	31,260,499.97	617,000,000	11,281,313.06	223,000,000	3,684,739.97	72,800,000	1,227,927.67	24,300,000
1873	—	—	—	—	4,200,000	83,000,000	—	—
1874	57,000,000.00	1,130,000,000	—	—	3,299,201	65,200,000	—	—

Source: Walter L. Fleming, *The Freedmen's Savings Bank: A Chapter in the Economic History of the Negro Race* (Westport: Negro Universities Press, 1970) 50; U.S. Senate, 46th Cong., 2nd sess., 1880, Rep. 440; U.S. Senate, *The Freedmen's Bank Bill*, 46th Cong., 3rd sess., 1881; U.S. Senate, 62nd Cong., 2nd Session, 1912, Rep. 759, 4.

Indeed, we need only look to Douglass's "fair and unvarnished narration of [his] connection with" the Freedmen's Savings Bank to ascertain the inner workings of the bank under his leadership.[19] Though he had been urged by others to take the reins of the bank, Douglass later characterized the arrangement as being unknowingly "married to a corpse."[20] His account provides tremendous insights regarding the last days of the Freedmen's Bank in his autobiography, *The Life and Times of Frederick Douglass*:

> I had read of this Bank when I lived in Rochester, and had indeed been solicited to become one of its trustees, and had reluctantly consented to do so....After four months before this splendid institution was compelled to close its doors in the starved and deluded faces of its depositors, and while I was assured by its President [John Alvord] and by its Actuary of its sound condition, I was solicited by some of its trustees to allow them to use my name in the board as a candidate for its Presidency. So I waked [*sic*] up one morning...to hear myself addressed as President of the Freedmen's Bank....On paper, and from the representations of its management, its assets amounted to three million dollars, and its liabilities were about equal to its assets. With such a showing I was encouraged in the belief that by curtailing expenses...we could be carried safely through the financial distress then upon the country....The more I observed and learned the more my confidence diminished....Some of them, while strongly assuring me of its soundness, had withdrawn their money and opened accounts elsewhere. Gradually I discovered that the Bank had sustained heavy losses at [sic] the South through dishonest agents, that there was a discrepancy on the books of forty thousand dollars, for which no account could be given, that instead of our assets being equal to our liabilities we could not in all likelihoods of the case pay seventy-two cents on the dollar.[21]

Although Douglass had been assured that the financial condition of the bank was sound, he soon discovered that such assurances were indeed false, and reported the matter to the chairman of the Senate Committee on Finance. In response, Congress decided to liquidate the bank's affairs, officially closing the bank on June 28, 1874.

Despite Douglass's efforts to compel repayment to black depositors following the bank's collapse, by 1880 the return of such monies had not occurred in any coherent fashion. Urging Congress to recover and guarantee the savings

of the thousands of black depositors facing huge losses, in a speech at the
"Convention of Colored Men" on September 25, 1883, in Louisville, Kentucky,
Douglass asserted:

> The colored people have suffered much on account of the failure of
> the Freedman's [sic] bank. Their loss by this institution was a peculiar
> hardship, coming as it did upon them in the days of their greatest
> weakness. It is certain that the depositors in this institution were led
> to believe that as Congress had chartered it and established its head-
> quarters at the capital the government in some way was responsible
> for the safe keeping of their money. Without the dissemination of this
> belief it would never have had the confidence of the people as it did
> nor have secured such an immense deposit. Nobody authorized to
> speak for the Government ever corrected this deception, but on the
> contrary, Congress continued to legislate for the bank as if all that had
> been claimed for it was true. Under these circumstances, together
> with much more that might be said in favor of such a measure, we ask
> Congress to reimburse the unfortunate victims of that institution,
> and thus carry hope and give to many fresh encouragement in the
> battle of life.[22]

Such a speech was important as Douglass's reputation took a significant hit
due to the failings of the bank, which in large part had little to do with his
management of its affairs. Douglass intimated: "When I became connected
with the bank I had a tolerably fair name for honest dealing…but no man
there or elsewhere can say I ever wronged him out of a cent." As Douglass's
example demonstrates, at stake was black confidence in financial institutions
and black leaders of the time.[23]

By 1900 only $1,638,259.49 ($43,900,000 in 2010), or sixty-two percent,
of the total amount of deposits prior to the bank's failure had been paid. To be
clear, the repayment of sixty-two percent of the deposits did not mean that
sixty-two percent of the depositors were repaid. Rather, repayment was
piecemeal, leaving many without any sign that their savings would ever be
returned.

In the end, many black depositors lost their savings, receiving little to no
money back from the bank or the federal government. Soon general distrust
of banks set in among black Americans across the United States. Douglass
was not the only black leader disappointed and duped by the bank, as southern
black leader of economic self-sufficiency Booker T. Washington's comments

also reflect the psychological toll the bank's collapse took on black depositors:

> [Freedmen's] bank had agents all over the South, and coloured [*sic*] people were induced to deposit their earnings with it in the belief that the institution was under the care and protection of the United States Government. When they found out that they had lost, or been swindled out of all their savings, they lost faith in savings banks, and it was a long time after this before it was possible to mention a savings bank for Negroes without some reference being made to the disaster of the Freedman's [*sic*] Bank. The effect of this disaster was more far-reaching because of the wide extent of territory which the Freedmen's Bank covered through its agencies.[24]

W. E. B. DuBois, too, saw the financial collapse as distinctly tied to a collapse in black confidence in banking:

> Then in one sad day came the crash [of the Freedmen's Bank],—all the hard-earned dollars of the freedmen disappeared; but that was the least of the loss,—all the faith in saving went too, and much of the faith in men; and that was a loss that a Nation which to-day sneers at Negro shiftlessness has never yet made good. *Not even ten additional years of slavery could have done so much to throttle the shift of the freedmen as the mismanagement and bankruptcy of the series of savings banks chartered by the Nation for their especial aid.* [emphasis added][25]

Taken together, the statements of Douglass, Washington, and DuBois demonstrate that despite being treated like "market fools," black depositors had greatly bought into the mantra of frugality that the bank's leadership and materials promoted. Most striking, perhaps, is DuBois's comparison of the bank's collapse to "ten additional years of slavery," as such a comparison reveals the dispossession that took place in the wake of the bank's collapse. DuBois's juxtaposing of slavery and the Freedmen's Bank implicitly highlights the problems of racial exclusion and the racial injuries that persisted even as blacks were making socioeconomic gains. Not only were black depositors not being repaid, their money was given to mostly well-to-do whites, and mainstream banks continued to exclude them. In this way, the social boundaries that relegated the incomes and savings of freed blacks to a separate or "special" banking facility hardened, despite the clear interests and investment black depositors demonstrated throughout the Freedmen's Bank's short-lived history.

With the continued racial exclusionary practices of white banks, the need for a banking institution that would provide credit and loans to black Americans remained pressing. This lack of openness and access created what sociologists Melvin L. Oliver and Thomas M. Shapiro refer to as an "economic detour." As Oliver and Shapiro assert, the exclusion of black Americans from the local and national economy creates a detour for black consumers, wealth, and income, leaving them without a viable avenue to save, spend, and/or amplify their capital; thus it makes mobility for black Americans difficult despite emancipation.

According to Oliver and Shapiro, an economic detour can be characterized by the lack of power and conventional financial avenues for black consumers for shopping and buying goods and services, as well as the unwillingness of banks to give black Americans loans to create small businesses and to buy a home. Though the toll the collapse of the Freedmen's Bank's took on black confidence was profound, efforts to pursue economic self-sufficiency continued well after its doors were shuttered. In Philadelphia this effort took the form of the Brown & Stevens Bank, organized between 1920 and 1921.[26]

The Philadelphia Negro as Capitalist: Conflict, Banking, and Economic Collapse in the Black Seventh Ward

The first two decades of the twentieth century marked a period of significant growth in Philadelphia. With the expansion of railways and manufacturing, Philadelphia seemed an ideal place for migrants to seek new and promising economic opportunities. Besides seeking the potential for economic prosperity, southern black Americans, in particular, had additional motivations for migrating to Philadelphia. Many southern blacks came to Philadelphia seeking refuge: refuge from the formal and informal systems of racial oppression in the Jim Crow South; and refuge from the boll weevil infestation that destroyed cotton crops throughout the South, resulting in the destruction of a major economic resource for black Southerners, especially sharecroppers.[27]

Seeking such safety and economic advancement, southern black migrants arrived in Philadelphia in significant numbers. As a result, the black population grew dramatically from 39,371 in 1890, to 62,613 in 1900, to 84,459 in 1910. By 1915, black Philadelphians had gained significant economic ground (see Table 2.4). Indeed, the number of black professionals and laborers was on the rise. In March 1914, the *Philadelphia Tribune* lauded this shift. Noting the economic progress of black Philadelphians, the paper reported that among black Philadelphians were:

> 200 clergymen, 60 politicians, 32 dentists, 9 lawyers, 76 stenographers, 204 clerks and copyists, 117 musicians, 45 graduate nurses, 13 druggists, 297 retail merchants, 29 blacksmiths, 250 postal clerks, 10 wholesale merchants, 72 upholsterers, 6 roofers and slaters, 24 plasterers, 10 paper hangers, 57 painters, 308 brick and stone masons, 86 carpenters and joiners, [and] 5 electrical engineers.[28]

Due to its location and status as one of few predominantly black neighborhoods in Philadelphia, the Black Seventh Ward served as the major "port of entry" for blacks migrating into Philadelphia. As the maps show (see Figures 2.1–2.2), from 1890 to 1910 the distribution of the black population remained dense within and around the center of the city. Like those employed as maids, butlers, hotel workers, and nannies, blacks seeking employment also took up

Table 2.4 Occupational distribution of Philadelphians, 1890 and 1910 (%)

Occupations	All males	Black males	All females	Black females
1890[2]				
Agriculture	1.9	0.3	0.1	0.0
Professions	3.9	2.5	4.8	1.4
Domestic and service	17.3	61.5	37.9	88.5
Trade and transportation	29.5	28.0	11.4	1.3
Manufacturing and industries	47.4	7.7	45.8	8.8
1910[3]				
Agriculture	1.0	1.2	0.0	0.0
Professions	4.0	1.9	6.0	1.13
Domestic and service	7.1	28.1	36.2	92.02
Trade	18.7	12.2	9.1	0.35
Transportation	9.9	20.1	1.1	0.01
Clerical and public service	12.4	5.8	11.4	0.63
Manufacturing and industries	46.7	26.7	36.0	5.91

Notes: Percentages for Black Seventh Warders only. *Sources*: W. E. B. DuBois, *The Philadelphia Negro: A Social Study* (Philadelphia: University of Pennsylvania Press, 1899), 109; and V. P. Franklin, *The Education of Black Philadelphia* (Philadelphia: University of Pennsylvania Press, 1979).

residence in areas in close proximity to parts of the city offering such employment options.[29]

Such an influx, however, did not correlate with increases in the openness of the city politically, socially, and economically to black Philadelphians. With continued growth in size, the densely populated black areas of the city became important sites for the mobilization of indigenous resources. Neighborhoods like the Black Seventh Ward became key as sites upon which black residents, leaders, and activists negotiated, responded to, and organized around the needs of black Philadelphians. Given that the Black Seventh Ward was a prominent black area of the city, as well as the first place many southern migrants would stay upon arrival, the area seemed an ideal location for efforts targeting the economic development and improvement of black Philadelphia.

Initially many of the fraternal orders, such as the Knights of Pythias, and sociopolitical organizations such as the Citizen's Republican Club, responded by also functioning as ad hoc savings banks. Such organizations would use membership fees and donations it received to guarantee deposits and provide small loans. However, this practice and these institutions were unable to provide sizeable credit and loans for entrepreneurial endeavors and home buying; such were necessary functions if the development of black-owned businesses was to become a reality in the Black Seventh Ward. As a result, black business leaders sought to establish black-owned and -operated banks. The boycott of white businesses on South Street during the summer of 1916 perhaps best reveals the sociopolitical and economic environment preceding and facilitating the emergence of mobilization efforts to address the economic self-sufficiency and wealth accumulation of black Philadelphians.[30]

The Boycott of 1916: Black Philadelphia vs. the South Street Businessmen's Association

Although they were in a predominantly black neighborhood, the markets lining the streets of the Black Seventh Ward were owned and operated by white businessmen, who collectively formed the South Street Businessmen's Association. By 1916, relations between these businessmen and black Philadelphians were tenuous. Although black Philadelphians continued to patronize these businesses, there was growing frustration with the control white businessmen held over the goods and services provided to Black Seventh Warders. Given that many black individuals and families were experiencing unprecedented economic advancement, the control white proprietors wielded

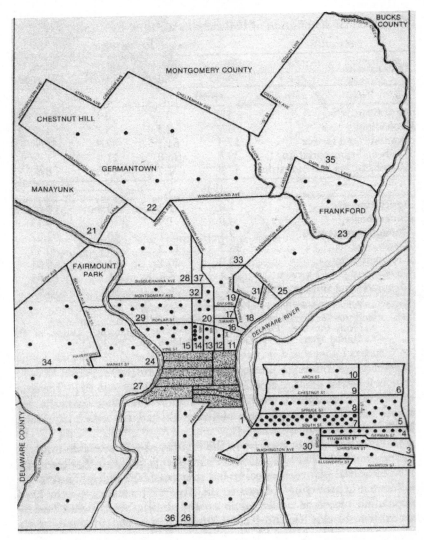

FIGURE 2.1 Distribution of black Philadelphians by ward in 1890. Each dot represents 250 blacks.

Source: John T. Emlen, "The Movement for the Betterment of the Negro In Philadelphia," *The Annals* 49 (September 1913): 83.

over them caused much anger and frustration. In addition, Black Seventh Warders complained that white proprietors along South Street were untrustworthy, accusing them of being unfair and of practicing racial exclusion in the operation of their businesses in the neighborhood. Such tensions came to a head during the summer of 1916.

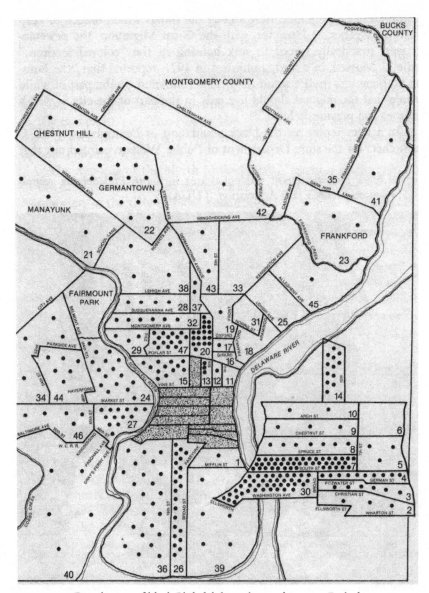

FIGURE 2.2 Distribution of black Philadelphians by ward in 1910. Each dot represents 250 blacks.

Source: John T. Emlen, "The Movement for the Betterment of the Negro In Philadelphia," *The Annals* 49 (September 1913): 86.

Despite the growing frustration and tension between black patrons and white proprietors, prior to the summer of 1916 black responses to the situation had been sporadic. However, when the *Philadelphia Tribune* reported that the South Street Businessmen's Association had called for the reassignment of black police officers patrolling the Black Seventh Ward, black Philadelphians threatened to boycott white-owned and -managed businesses on South Street. Specifically, the *Philadelphia Tribune* confirmed accusations of unfairness when it stated that white businessmen had targeted black police officers due to their role in thwarting attempts by white proprietors to swindle and take advantage of black customers.[31]

Initially, white proprietors disputed the *Philadelphia Tribune*'s claims. In response, *Philadelphia Tribune* reporters were sent out to further investigate the daily experiences of blacks that patronized white-owned businesses along South Street. These investigations revealed not only the pervasiveness of questionable business practices among members of the South Street Businessmen's Association, but also the growing racial tension between black customers and white proprietors. One reporter, for example, observed a conflict between a black female customer and the Jewish owner of a fish stand on South Street. While on South Street running errands, the black woman had stopped at the fish stand to purchase some fish. After picking the fish she wanted, the woman paid the owner a quarter and waited as he wrapped her purchase. As she waited, the owner took another order and when he returned to her with the wrapped fish, he asked for payment to which the woman responded, exclaiming: "I gave you a quarter." The proprietor disputed her claim: "No you didn't, if you don't pay me I'll have you arrested."

Seeing the proprietor's reluctance to give her the purchase and his possible attempt to swindle her, she rolled up her sleeves, put her bag down, and said: "Mr. Jew, you are at liberty to have me arrested if you wish, and I have enough to pay my way out, but I do not propose to be robbed by you. So if you don't give me my quarter, I am prepared to die and go to hell and take you with me for my 25 cents." Staring at the storeowner with eyes that seemed to dare him to deny her a refund, the woman stood at the fish stand until her quarter ($5.12 in 2010) was returned.

Just a few stores away, a black woman's attempt to return a pair of shoes also turned into a serious conflict. According to reports, the shoe salesman had swapped the new pair of shoes she tried on with a previously worn pair after receiving payment. After getting home, she noticed that the shoes were smaller than the pair she tried on and went back to the store to get the correct shoes. Initially, the shoe salesman denied her claims, instructing her that she would need to pay fifty cents ($10.24 in 2010) in order to change the shoes. In response, the woman called on a black police officer, on patrol outside the store; and together they insisted that the shoe salesman switch out the shoes to avoid making the situation bigger than necessary.[32]

In each of the cases, *Philadelphia Tribune* reporters also observed the important role of black police as protectors of black consumers on South Street. *Philadelphia Tribune* reporters found during their investigation that situations wherein blacks were mistreated occurred across the stores along South Street, and that black police played an important role as peacekeepers and on-site mediators of potential racial conflicts between black consumers and white proprietors. Concluding its investigation, the *Philadelphia Tribune* sought to empower and mobilize black Philadelphians:

> Colored people pay enough taxes in this city to be treated as citizens and [Police Commissioner] Robinson establishes a bad precedent by removing men because of their color to satisfy representatives of a few who desire to cheat their customers. Take all the colored trade off South Street and you will see a number of business places close up. If colored policemen are objectionable to Jew merchants on South Street, all colored people should go to the other side and do their trading and the same committee where we went to the front to have a colored patrolmen removed, will soon be seen going up to have them replaced.[33]

Despite the *Philadelphia Tribune*'s report, black police officers were reassigned to various areas of the city. In response, blacks across the city gathered in the Black Seventh Ward to determine how to counteract the decision to reassign black police officers and the less-than-honest business practices of members of the South Street Businessmen's Association. Held at O'Neil's Hall, located at Broad and Lombard Streets, the gathering was titled the "Indignation Meeting" and was "packed to the doors with over seven hundred on the pavement."[34]

Anxious to make a bold statement to the police department and the South Street Businessmen's Association, those in attendance insisted on immediate action. Organized by a variety of black leaders from across the city, the meeting provided a forum for black Philadelphians to voice their concerns and anger and to develop a plan to challenge the hegemony of the white businessmen along South Street. Black Republican leader G. Grant Williams presided over the meeting:

[W]e pay taxes enough to have more representatives than we get. Just think of it, only one councilman, and one fireman, and we have over 100,000 colored people, too. It is our duty to protect ourselves and resent this insult to the race. If it is lawful for them to remove our policemen because of their color it is just as lawful for us to find some other place to spend our money. So I hope the sense of this meeting will be to Stay Off South Street, so far as the white business places are concerned.[35]

Those in attendance were in agreement with Williams's argument, and it was soon clear that the removal of black policemen from the Black Seventh Ward was not the primary problem, but instead a symptom of a larger plight plaguing black Philadelphia—the economic marginalization of black consumers and capital.

Amos Scott, a black Republican leader and the primary political representative for black Philadelphians in local government, added to Williams's observation and again highlighted that the fundamental problem was the virtual exclusion of blacks from full participation in the local economy. Scott suggested that black Philadelphians move toward opening black-owned businesses that would allow more control over their money, a proposition in which he would gladly invest $1,000 ($20,500 in 2010) immediately.

Black residents, reverends, leaders, and politicians agreed with both Scott's and Williams's disposition, and it was resolved that changing the economic situation in the Black Seventh Ward required immediate and long-term action. Advocating a path toward the economic self-sufficiency of black Philadelphians, Williams concluded the meeting summarizing the agreed response:

> Therefore, it is resolved, that it is the sense of this meeting that we resent the wholesale discrimination practiced…at the request of the South Street Business Men's Association [to] remove the Colored Police Officers from South Street. It is further resolved that we the colored people, shall not patronize white South Street merchants until this wrong shall have been righted. It is further resolved that a copy of these resolutions be spread upon the minutes of the Indignation Meeting, a copy be sent to the Director of Public Safety, the President of the South Street Business Men's Association, to every Colored Church in the county of Philadelphia, and every Colored Organization: Fraternal, Political and Social.[36]

As was resolved, following the Indignation Meeting, black Philadelphians boycotted the white businesses on South Street for the duration of the summer of 1916. From their row homes and churches, black residents developed ways to avoid having to purchase goods and services from white-owned businesses along South Street. Pooling resources among themselves, many black residents shared their groceries with neighbors and family members in the area.

As important as the boycott was for black Philadelphians, it was a hard commitment for many, especially poorer Black Seventh Warders. Although there were few black-owned stores, their inventories paled in comparison to the white-owned markets, leaving many black residents without many options during the boycott. While some white businesses went into decline because of the boycott, others were dismissive and believed the black anger that fostered the boycott was unsustainable: "This talk will soon blow over...colored people will be found spending their money with us as...if nothing happened...wait and see."[37]

By the end of the summer, it appeared that the response of the local government was to do nothing, which meant that despite the efforts of black Philadelphians, whether or not black police officers would return to the Black Seventh Ward remained unclear. By September, the boycotting effort was fractured, as those who were poorer Black Seventh Warders were unable to hold out any longer. Perhaps the most important outcome of the boycott was that it revealed to black Philadelphians that white businessmen were invariably resistant to the needs and fair treatment of black consumers.[38]

As a result of the attempt to correct the bad business practices of white proprietors along South Street, the need for more fundamental change emerged. In the Black Seventh Ward, the strategy focused on the liberation of black consumers from the mistreatment they experienced at the hands of white businessmen, by building, developing, and maintaining a network of black financial institutions. Such a strategy of mobilization presented both a problem and an opportunity. The problem was not only black Philadelphians' inability to fully participate in the local economy, but also the mismatch between the limited choices in shops, markets, and restaurants and the increasing needs of a black population that was increasing in number and density.

To be sure, the boycott efforts confirmed for those involved that white leaders and businessmen were uninterested in black economic advancement. Mainstream banks and white leaders remained unresponsive to the needs of the growing black population, leading to the reasonable conclusion that, despite their best efforts, black Philadelphians were living in a separate city. The stifling economic climate did have some promise, particularly for those black Philadelphians who sought to take advantage of the growing, undervalued, and underserved capital of black consumers. For some, addressing this economic detour was financially wise and also in the best interests of black Philadelphians.

The boycotting effort during the summer of 1916 is representative of the social, political, and economic conditions of black Philadelphians. The lack of response from white leaders and businessmen to such boycotting efforts provides evidence of the political and economic marginalization of black Philadelphians, especially those residing in the Black Seventh Ward. Issues around transferring black police officers and price gouging were integral to black social and economic security, and the lack of change regarding such issues reflected the limitations of black–white power relations at the time.

Prompted by such limitations, an ideological shift occurred wherein there emerged a focus on an indigenous strategy to economic self-sufficiency. While banks were risky institutions and racial exclusion by mainstream banks was persistent, the need for such a financial institution for blacks remained. In turn, an indigenous bank emerged as a fruitful alternative. Whereas the boycott focused on compelling change from outside, the tactics to address the black economic detour in Philadelphia drew on intraracial strategies to solve black problems. In other words, after the attempt to compel white leadership to address the economic livelihood and safety of black Philadelphians failed, an indigenous network of institutions and leaders emerged as significant players in the effort to address the economic detour.

The shift to economic self-sufficiency was not just specific to black Philadelphians, as sociologists St. Clair Drake and Horace Cayton observed a similar disposition among black Chicagoans, referring to such ideology as the "doctrine of the 'Double-Duty Dollar'" in their classic *Black Metropolis*. For Drake and Cayton, the concept of the double-duty dollar referred to the ways in which black Chicagoans were *framing* their money as having two primary functions: "purchasing a commodity and 'advancing The Race.'" Attending a business exposition for black Chicagoans, Drake and Cayton observed this frame of the double-duty dollar being operationalized by a black pastor from Chicago's Black Belt:

> Tomorrow I want all of you people to go to these [black-owned] stores. Have your shoes repaired at a Negro shop, buy your groceries from a Negro grocer...and for God's sake, buy your meats, pork chops, and yes, even your chitterlings, from a Negro butcher. On behalf of the

Negro ministers of Chicago, I wish to commend these Negro Businessmen for promoting such an affair, and urge upon you again to patronize your own, for that is the only way we as a race will ever get anywhere.[39]

In this way, narratives of hopeful integration were supplanted by an ideology that situated the patronage of indigenous institutions as not only wise but also as a project of racial uplift.

Here, then, we see an example of what scholars such as Michael Dawson refer to as the "linked fate" framework, wherein black leaders and activists draw on presumed emotional ties and mutual experiences of blacks in order to frame an issue as a consensus issue while also generating consent and support in the process. However, as is the case here, such ideology can also supplant the needs of the individual in favor of an assumed black collective.[40]

This ideological shift is important in that it bespeaks the separation between white and black Philadelphia; between black interests and white interests during much of the first half of the twentieth century. Furthermore, the focus on economic self-sufficiency in the wake of the boycott was the result of a reframing of the rhetoric around the control white businessmen had over black consumers. In this way, black entrepreneurs were able to capitalize on the patterns of distrust in white-managed businesses and institutions vis-à-vis national events, such as the collapse of the Freedmen's Bank and local issues such as the mistreatment of black consumers. Such popular black sentiments and distrust regarding the business and political practices of some white Americans would prompt the creation of a network of black financial institutions.

Enter Edward C. Brown and Andrew F. Stevens

On the night of Monday March 4, 1918, two years following the boycott, W. E. B. DuBois returned to the Black Seventh Ward in a much-anticipated gathering at the First African Baptist Church, located at 16th and Christian Streets. "Oh, when I get to heaven, I'll take my seat / And cast my crown at Jesus's feet," sang Marian Anderson (famed contralto and Philadelphia native) at the packed gathering just a few blocks south of the Black Seventh Ward. Singing "Deep River," a popular Negro spiritual, Anderson's voice captivated the large crowd. As Anderson completed her moving rendition of "Deep River," the audience settled into the pews of the church, anticipating the start of this highly publicized social event. It had been advertised for weeks in advance, and black Philadelphians of various class backgrounds were anxious to hear DuBois's thoughts on the state of race in America generally and Philadelphia in particular.

Nearly twenty years after the publication of *The Philadelphia Negro*, DuBois's remarks revisited many of themes and arguments he made in his examination of the Black Seventh Ward at the close of the nineteenth century. DuBois, aware of the social realities and troubles of black Philadelphians, did not hold back on his critique of the power structure in Philadelphia: "The trouble with politics in Philadelphia is that you have no democracy." Adding: "[Black Philadelphians] have no democracy because the people who own the industries also control the politics and this makes politics in Philadelphia worse probably than any other city in the world."[41] Such comments surely reflected DuBois's assessment that the moral and political suggestions he offered in *The Philadelphia Negro* had been ignored by white Philadelphians, particularly his call to eliminate racial exclusion:

> There is no doubt that in Philadelphia the centre and kernel of the Negro problem so far as white people are concerned is the narrow opportunities afforded Negroes for earning a decent living. Such discrimination is morally wasteful, and socially silly. It is the duty of whites to stop it, and to do so primarily for their own sakes.... Again white people of the city must remember that much of the sorrow and bitterness that surrounds the life of the American Negro comes from the unconscious prejudice and half-conscious actions of men and women who do not intend to wound or annoy.[42]

To be sure, DuBois's words conveyed the sentiments of scores of blacks in many cities. However, for the black Philadelphians in the audience at the First African Baptist Church, his words affirmed that little had changed since his study. What had changed since DuBois's departure, though, was the rising prominence of a narrative of economic self-sufficiency.

Whereas DuBois's comments, both at the gathering and in *The Philadelphia Negro*, highlighted the important role whites would and should play in the uplifting of black Philadelphians, following the collapse of the Freedmen's Bank and the local boycott, narratives that amplified indigenous strategies for addressing discrimination resonated. Though in the wake of the collapse of the Freedmen's Bank DuBois and other black leaders asserted a loss of black confidence in banking institutions, the rise of black banks in Philadelphia reveal a more dynamic picture, wherein mistrust was associated with white-led institutions freeing up the possibility for their black-led counterparts to be successful and popular among the black masses. Such an emphasis on indigenous strategies for racial uplift and economic advancement provided the backdrop against which Edward C. Brown and Andrew Stevens developed their economic plans for Black Philadelphia.

Brown & Stevens Bank was established on the heels of the failure and subsequent collapse of two local black banks, the First Northern Colored Cooperative Banking Association of Philadelphia and the People's Savings Bank of Philadelphia. Having been chartered in July 1901, First Northern closed within the first year of its existence. Operating as an extension of a benefit society, the bank was plagued by mismanagement and poor banking procedures from its inception. The bank closed quickly and without serious damage to depositors and shareholders. Much like First Northern, People's Savings was a small organization. Organized in September of 1907, the small bank (with liabilities that never exceeded $11,000; $87,000 in 2010) closed in 1917, just a year before DuBois's return, demonstrating the limitations of benefit societies' ability to handle large amounts of deposits.[43]

Brown & Stevens Bank was founded through a partnership between two black business and political leaders in Philadelphia, Edward C. Brown and Andrew F. Stevens. As members of prominent black families in Philadelphia commonly referred to as "Old Philadelphians" or "OP's," Brown and Stevens were longtime associates. Stevens's father, also named Andrew, was one of the members of what DuBois referred to in *The Philadelphia Negro* as the "well-to-do" class of Black Seventh Warders. Writing of the elder Stevens, DuBois elucidated his huge success and prominence as a black caterer: "There are a large number of caterers in the Ward.... Of the principal caterers there are about ten, of whom the *doyen* was the late Andrew F. Stevens. These ten caterers do a large business, amounting in some cases probably to $3000 to $5000 a year" ($66,000 to $110,000 in 2010).[44] With this historical legacy and social capital in tow, Stevens was an ideal partner for Brown.

Brown, who returned to Philadelphia from Virginia around 1915, was experienced in the area of organizing and running a bank, having founded two banks in Virginia between 1900 and 1910: Brown Savings Bank in Norfolk and Crown Savings Bank in Newport News. Brown formed the Crown Savings Bank in partnership with two black porters who had amassed some capital through real-estate ventures. In order to develop his own bank Brown sold his interests in Crown Savings Bank and headed to Norfolk where he established the Brown Savings Bank in 1909. While initially the bank functioned primarily as a savings facility for black depositors in Norfolk, Brown soon began to use the money from banking deposits to pursue his own real-estate interests. As a result, the liabilities of the bank quickly began to outpace its assets. By 1915, Brown Savings was headed for ruin and was absorbed by Metropolitan Bank and Trust Company, the largest black bank in Virginia at the time, to prevent any serious losses to depositors.[45]

Having experienced both trials and triumphs in banking, Brown headed back to Philadelphia, where the black population had grown dramatically since his departure. Much like southern black migrants at the time, Brown headed north in search of fruitful economic opportunities and with the idea that the increasing black population of Philadelphia would provide the capital critical to achieving his financial goals and aspirations. Soon after his return to Philadelphia, he and Andrew Stevens entered into a business partnership and planned to develop an entertainment and financial district centered primarily within the Black Seventh Ward. This partnership was important not just in the material sense—as their lineage represented one of the more financially successful black Philadelphia families—but was also important in the symbolic sense as it represented a consolidation of social class and status, giving legitimacy to their entrepreneurial efforts and thus underscoring their efforts with an implicit indigenous quality, signaling a sort of "for us, by us" function and endeavor.

In their plans, Brown and Stevens sought to build a bank in the Black Seventh Ward with smaller branches located closer to emergent black enclaves in North and West Philadelphia. Additionally, Brown and Stevens were interested in making their institution a private bank outside of the purview of regulators. Drawing on the capital Brown had accumulated through real-estate holdings he managed in New York City, Brown and Stevens deposited the $100,000 ($1,220,000 in 2010) required by the State Banking Commissioner to establish a private banking facility. By 1921, the Brown & Stevens Bank was open for business, with its main office located in the heart of the Black Seventh Ward, at 427 Broad Street (Broad and Lombard Streets). While the branch in West Philadelphia was also open, the North Philadelphia branch was discontinued and later reopened as the Cosmopolitan State Bank.[46]

Whereas the Brown & Stevens Bank was a private bank outside of the purview of the state banking commission, Cosmopolitan Bank was organized through a state charter on June 18, 1923. Although a state-affiliated bank, in practice and organization Cosmopolitan Bank operated as a branch office of Brown & Stevens Bank, with the banking duo functioning in their respective roles as president and vice president. This lack of distinction played a critical role in the later collapse of the two banking institutions as, unbeknownst to depositors, the two institutions were indeed the same, despite differences in name and affiliations with the state. The omission of a clear distinction on the part of Brown and Stevens would later play a critical role in the economic livelihood of the Black Seventh Ward, shaping subsequent patterns of neighborhood change.[47]

Before the Collapse: Brown & Stevens Bank, 1920–1925

Brown & Stevens Bank opened to much acclaim and rapidly achieved success. Given the growing need for a bank that would support and advance the economic interests of black Philadelphians, the black press and black sociopolitical and cultural institutions characterized the bank's emergence as both timely and necessary. Additionally, while black Philadelphians had not had positive experiences with banking, the pressing need for a financial institution that catered to them outweighed their understandable skepticism. Stories of the successes of Brown and Stevens in business and real-estate ventures covered the pages of the *Philadelphia Tribune*, prompting many to seek the services of the bank. Such positive reports also helped curb some of the residual skepticism black Philadelphians had about black banks. Indeed, Brown, in particular, had been successful in the area of real estate, owning a series of apartment buildings called the Peyton Apartments in New York City. One of the earliest black businessmen to own and manage large real estate in a big city such as New York, Brown was seen by many as a financial "wizard" whose economic designs for Black Philadelphia and the Black Seventh Ward would yield incredible results.[48]

Together, Brown and Stevens developed a financial plan that sought to achieve their own personal economic aspirations and targeted the socioeconomic needs of black Philadelphians at multiple levels. While Brown was interested in real estate and entertainment, Stevens sought economic means to support his political aspirations. Appreciating one another's personal interests, the banking duo took on interdependent roles based on their individual strengths and aspirations. Given their interests, Brown operated more as a behind-the-scenes manager of their various business ventures and of the day-to-day business of the bank. Stevens, on the other hand, was more the public-relations specialist of the duo, spending time at gatherings and in the community to encourage black Philadelphians to deposit money at the bank and seek out its services for credit and loans, particularly for home mortgages.[49]

Keenly aware of the economic detour experienced by black Philadelphians, Brown and Stevens took an approach that emphasized the interconnected nature of black socioeconomic needs. In an attempt to address the exclusion of blacks from participation in the local economy, Brown and Stevens sought to develop their black business/financial and entertainment district centered in the Black Seventh Ward. To accomplish this goal, Brown and Stevens made three important and interconnected choices. First, they bought property centrally located in the Black Seventh Ward. Such property was designated for the construction of the Brown & Stevens Bank, a black theater, and apartment buildings similar to those Brown managed in New York City. Located on both the east and west corners of Lombard and Broad Streets, the properties purchased by the banking duo initially left many Black Seventh Warders uneasy. Whatever fears or skepticism Black Seventh Warders dissipated after Brown made clear his plans for the area:

> The three houses at 422–24–26 South Broad Street (which are directly opposite of the bank) are to be torn down, probably beginning next month, and upon this splendid site, which has frontage of 60 feet on Broad street, and with a depth of 80 feet extending way back on Lombard street are to be erected beautiful modern apartment houses such as those we have in New York.[50]

Second, Brown and Stevens invested heavily in the entertainment sector, seeking to establish a network of institutions that would cater specifically to black audiences and patrons. To reach their goal of establishing an entertainment district within the Black Seventh Ward, Brown and Stevens organized three different businesses that would oversee the development and management of black entertainment in the Black Seventh Ward: (1) the Dunbar Amusement Corporation, (2) the Elite Amusement Corporation, and (3) the Clef Club Singers and Players. The Dunbar Amusement Corporation was the financial umbrella for the Dunbar Theater established by Brown and Stevens. Erected on the southwest corner of Broad and Lombard Streets and named after famed poet Paul Laurence Dunbar, the Dunbar Theater was established to provide a black-owned and -operated venue for concerts and shows for black spectators. Both the Elite Amusement Corporation and the Clef Club were responsible for recruiting, nurturing, and providing the talent that the Dunbar Theater would feature. While the Elite Amusement Corporation was charged with providing and financing theatrical productions, namely vaudeville shows, the Clef Club was a talent agency of sorts, charged with finding and developing black musicians and singers who would be showcased at the Dunbar Theater in various concerts throughout the year.[51]

Third, the banking duo worked closely with black leaders, press, and social and political organizations to encourage black Philadelphians to seek out the bank's financial services. Here, Stevens's political aspirations were an asset for the financial duo, as he used his status and connections to get black leaders, reverends, residents, and well-to-do families to invest in their business ventures and make deposits (large and small) at the bank. As a result of these three choices, by 1922, only a year after it was officially established, Brown & Stevens Bank held the savings of nearly 11,000 black depositors, totaling nearly $1,000,000 ($[2010]13,000,000). Just as Brown & Stevens Bank was an early success, so too was the Dunbar Theater. Hosting plays and concerts produced by local and national black artists, the Dunbar Theater emerged as the preeminent entertainment venue for black Philadelphians. The Clef Club was also a success, becoming a major entertainment resource providing amateur and professional musicians and singers for a variety of events targeting black audiences in Philadelphia.[52]

Collectively, the three major financial decisions the banking duo made significantly altered the social landscape of the Black Seventh Ward. Due to the popularity of the Brown & Stevens Bank, the Clef Club, the Dunbar Theater, and the soon-to-be built apartments located at Broad and Lombard Streets, the Black Seventh Ward was transformed from a purely residential enclave into an emerging business and entertainment destination for black Philadelphians. In particular, the creation of banks, clubs, and a theater generated a source of employment for indigenous blacks and southern migrants that relied on the relationship between black patronage and black wealth accumulation. Others, seeking to benefit from or match Brown's and Stevens's early successes, also set up shop in the Black Seventh Ward. By 1924, many of the offices and headquarters of emerging black professionals and entrepreneurs were located on and around Broad and Lombard Streets; thus solidifying the prominence of the area as the predominant black enclave in Philadelphia.

Additionally, the banking duo managed to recruit residents and entrepreneurs to the area by extending loans and property to black Philadelphians interested in the location. In effect, then, within a span of five years, the banking duo incentivized the Black Seventh Ward by developing a series of financially successful enterprises based in the Lombard/South Street area. Indeed, their efforts amounted to a significant indigenous revitalization movement. Despite such success, white banks and business leaders remained unwilling to change their discriminatory practices, leading to the expansion of black institutions such as those owned and managed by Brown and Stevens. As a result, the banking duo's affairs extended beyond the day-to-day management of their bank and various business enterprises. Serving as the major financial brokers for black Philadelphians in and outside of the Black Seventh Ward, Brown & Stevens Bank became the primary home for many of the loans and mortgages funding the development of black Philadelphia, with the Lombard/South Street area emerging as a financial and entertainment black district.[53]

Taken together, the banking duo's economic approach resulted in a profoundly interconnected black financial and entertainment network. The economic development of black Philadelphia relied heavily on their financial decisions, and the capital of their two banks. Further, the initial success of the bank was predicated on the combined efforts of indigenous black institutions to relieve black Philadelphians of the fear they had about banks and financial institutions. In an effort to reassure black Philadelphians about the security of banks, little attention was paid to the overlap between larger black economic needs and the banking duo's aspirations.

Given the racially segregated economic conditions of the city, the need to support indigenous black institutions was great and, as in the case of Brown and Stevens, prompted many residents and leaders to be less critical of black entrepreneurs whose efforts seemed poised to advance black interests. While such interconnectedness initially helped black Philadelphians thrive in spite of their exclusion and incentivized the Black Seventh Ward, the subsequent collapse would reveal the true cost of the interdependent relationship between black economic advancement and the financial decisions of Brown and Stevens, as their banks, the Brown & Stevens Bank specifically, crucially held together the newly emergent black business and entertainment district based in the Black Seventh Ward.

The Collapse and Beyond

Despite very rainy conditions, on Wednesday, February 4, 1925, black depositors urgently gathered in the Black Seventh Ward awaiting the opening of the Brown & Stevens Bank located at Broad and Lombard Streets. This gathering was by no means in anticipation of a grand opening. Rather, black Philadelphians waited at the entrance of the Brown & Stevens Bank hoping to receive their deposits back in full. During the day-long run on Brown & Stevens Bank, Brown spoke with the local press to convey his confidence in the bank and assure interested parties: "We will weather the storm, unless the run is too heavy on us tomorrow. We are solvent, but of course you know the strongest bank in the world cannot hold up under some conditions." Within the first three hours of business on February 4, the bank paid out more than $20,000 ($249,000 in 2010) to depositors, exhausting the amount of cash the bank had on hand. While Brown had been able to convince some depositors of the bank's solvency, most who arrived, particularly those with large deposits, were unconvinced and sought the full amount of their deposits.[54]

Initially, Brown believed that his efforts to convince the morning crowd that their savings were secure had been successful. In the afternoon, however, depositors who remained unconvinced by Brown's claims arrived at the bank in large numbers, refusing to leave until their money was returned. As the end of the business day neared, Brown began to instruct depositors to return on Thursday because the bank no longer had enough cash on hand to repay savings in full. However hopeful and confident Brown may have seemed, the fact remained that in one day more than 300 depositors had withdrawn their savings.

Repeatedly assuring all in line and inside the bank that their money was safe, Brown announced that there would be a meeting at the Knights of Pythias Meeting Hall (located at 19th and Lombard Streets) to discuss the bank's solvency and the security of deposits, loans, and credit managed by the bank. Providing details about the meeting, Brown remarked to the press:

> We are going to have some of our preachers give assurances to our depositors in their churches, and we are planning meetings at which the financial conditions of the bank will be thoroughly discussed. We are also going to print advertisements and statements in some of our newspapers. The rumors about the bank have been in circulation for about a year. There have been anonymous telephone calls to some of our depositors. The run started this morning almost as soon as the doors were opened. We are going after the people who have been doing this work. We know the names of some of them, and we are going to have detectives find out who the rest are.[55]

Although Brown's claim that rumor was responsible for Wednesday's unexpected bank run may seem surprising or dubious, news reports at the time suggest that rumors indeed played a significant role. By all accounts, two connected rumors played a significant role in the suddenness of the run on the bank—a sad series of events all too reminiscent of the factors leading to the collapse of the Freedmen's Bank. The first was tied to the collapse of

Marcus Garvey's pan-African movement, following collective attacks of local and national authorities, which subsequently led to Garvey's imprisonment. When rumor spread that Brown & Stevens Bank had heavily invested in the Black Star Steamship Company, Garvey's project, fear that Garvey's failure was tied to their savings spread rapidly. Adding to this account, the *Evening Bulletin* reported: "When word of Garvey's sentence spread through the section [where most of the black depositors live] his name was linked up with the affairs of the bank, and it is said that some of the larger depositors became panicky and started the run."[56]

A second rumor resulted from the experience of one of the bank's biggest depositors, who unsuccessfully attempted to collect his entire deposit of $20,000 ($249,000 in 2010) on Monday February 2, 1925. When told he would have to wait a day or two for the return of his money, the depositor was said to have gone through the Black Seventh Ward spreading word about his experience with the bank, asserting that deposits held at the Brown & Stevens Bank were endangered. Rumors mattered for the livelihood of the bank since its inception, as black leaders and institutions had used stories of Brown's successes elsewhere to convince black Philadelphians to participate in and support the banking duo's various enterprises. Just as positive stories had constructed the banking duo's success, negative rumors surely facilitated the reemergence of black skepticism of banking institutions. Indeed, research on rumors by sociologist Gary Alan Fine illustrates that individuals use rumors despite their relative validity to guide decisions and behaviors.[57]

Like its predecessor the Freedmen's Bank, Brown & Stevens was plagued by failed financial ventures, particularly the rising and well-publicized debt of the Dunbar Theater. Although their early investments and enterprises were profitable, Brown and Stevens did not use those profits to reinvest in their existing properties. Instead, as Tables 2.5–2.7 indicate, early profits were used to support new ventures, such as black theaters in New York City and Baltimore and real estate in Pennsylvania and Virginia.[58]

In an effort to restore public trust in the bank, the banking duo and a number of black elites arrived at the meeting at the Knights of Pythias Hall to reassure depositors. Initially the nearly one thousand depositors in attendance were clearly angry and hostile. However, after Tanner Moore (former dean of Howard University's School of Education) spoke about the important work Brown and Stevens had accomplished with the bank and the critical role of the trust and savings of depositors, anger began to dissipate. Moore's appearance, in particular, suggested an unbiased perspective and signaled the national/regional importance of such black financial institutions.

Table 2.5 Discounts and loans of the Brown & Stevens Bank listed in the names of Edward C. Brown and Andrew F. Stevens or of their business enterprises (Auditor's report, February 11, 1925)

Date	Due	Maker	Collateral or endorser (initials)	Amount ($)	Estimated equivalent, 2010 ($)
12-30-24	Demand	E. C. Brown	ECB	37,000.00	460,000
		A. F. Stevens	AFS		
06-30-24	Demand	E. C. Brown	ECB	20,000.00	249,000
		A. F. Stevens	AFS		
03-04-21	12-02-22	Brown and Stevens	ECB	1,300.00	16,200
		By E. C. Brown			
11-20-24	02-20-25	Brown and Stevens	AFS	1,000.00	12,400
		By A. F. Stevens			
12-04-23	Demand	E. C. Brown	ECB	21,000.00	261,000
		A. F. Stevens	AFS		
02-24-23	04-25-23	E. C. Brown	ECB	37,500.00	466,000
12-05-23	Demand	E. C. Brown	ECB	37,500.00	466,000
01-22-23	01-29-23	Brown and Stevens	AFS	5,000.00	62,200
		By A. F. Stevens			
12-01-22	03-01-23	E. C. Brown	ECB	3,000.00	37,300
		A. F. Stevens	AFS		
09-06-23	11-06-23	Hillman Realty Co.	ECB	800.00	9,950
		By E. C. Brown			
12-11-24	03-11-25	A. F. Stevens	AFS	500.00	6,220

Date	Due	Maker	Collateral or endorser (initials)	Amount ($)	Estimated equivalent, 2010 ($)
12-05-23	Demand	A. F. Stevens	5,000 shs. Com. and 1,000 shs. pf. Bankers Finance and Discount Corp.	50,000.00	622,000
12-02-24	02-20-25	A. F. Stevens	AFS	1,836.00	22,800
12-24-24	03-01-25	A. F. Stevens	AFS	605.00	7,530
12-29-24	03-29-25	A. F. Stevens	AFS	500.00	6,220
12-20-24	03-20-25	A. F. Stevens	AFS	181.00	2,250
11-23-24	02-23-25	A. F. Stevens	AFS	150.00	1,870
11-10-24	02-10-25	A. F. Stevens	AFS	260.00	3,230
12-05-24	02-10-25	A. F. Stevens	AFS	37,500.00	466,000
12-05-23	Demand	A. F. Stevens	AFS	37,500.00	466,000
11-26-22	02-26-25	E. C. Brown A. F. Stevens	ECB AFS	3,000.00	37,300
09-26-23	Demand	Brown and Stevens By A. F. Stevens	AFS	2,200.00	27,400
01-12-22		E. C. Brown & Co. By E. C. Brown	ECB	3,500.00	43,500
02-05-24	Demand	E. C. Brown & Co. By E. C. Brown	ECB	20,000.00	249,000
02-06-24	Demand	E. C. Brown & Co. By A. F. Stevens	AFS	23,808.45	296,000
06-30-23	Demand	E. C. Brown A. F. Stevens	ECB/AFS	60,000.00	746,000

(continued)

Table 2.5 continued

Date	Due	Maker	Collateral or endorser (initials)	Amount ($)	Estimated equivalent, 2010 ($)
02-07-23	Demand	E. C. Brown & Co. By E. C. Brown	ECB	1,000.00	12,400
12-22-22	03-22-23	E. C. Brown & Co. By E. C. Brown	ECB	3,000.00	37,300
12-14-22	02-14-23	E. C. Brown & Co. By E. C. Brown	ECB	3,500.00	43,500
09-28-23	12-28-23	Dunbar Amusement Co. By E. C. Brown	ECB	1,600.00	19,900
03-14-24	06-14-24	Dunbar Amusement Co. By E. C. Brown	ECB	3,500.00	43,500
12-10-21	Demand	Dunbar Amusement Co. By E. C. Brown	ECB	15,000.00	187,000
02-19-24	Demand	Dunbar Amusement Co. By E. C. Brown	ECB	7,600.00	94,500
12-04-23	03-24-24	Elite Amusement Co. By E. C. Brown		4,500.00	56,000
		Total	ECB	460,340.45	5,730,000

Source: Walter L. Fleming, *The Freedmen's Savings Bank: A Chapter in the Economic History of the Negro Race* (Westport, CT: Negro Universities Press, 1970) 50; U.S. Senate, 46th Cong., 2nd sess., 1880, Rep. 440; U. S. Senate, *The Freedmen's Bank Bill,* 46th Cong., 3rd sess., 1881; U.S. Senate, 62nd Cong., 2nd Session, 1912, Rep. 759. 4.

Moore made an explicit link between the bank's livelihood and that of the black community:

> You must realize that Brown is a Negro.... If we don't get behind him with all of our strength we shall not be getting behind our own race. He has done much to better the condition of the Negro in Philadelphia. We can't go back on him now! If there is one movement you should back up with all of your resources, it is the movement to save this man and the bank.

Moore, like other black leaders at the time, privileged the need for such institutions over a critical discussion about the questionable business practices of the banking duo. In this way, Moore's framing referred back to the double-duty dollar ideology by situating the bank (and its leadership) within the rhetoric of racial uplift and collective responsibility. Further, Moore's appearance was a reflection of the broader interdependency between the livelihood of the bank and black economic advancement within and beyond Philadelphia, as the banking duo had heavily invested in the Howard Theatre in Washington DC and the Douglass Theater in Baltimore. Given the context of racial exclusion and the national economic detour impacting black Americans, the potential demise of the Brown & Stevens Bank compelled leaders such as Moore to construct the bank as "good for all."

Brown followed Moore's comments with a moving and tearful plea: "I've always worked for the Negro.... I've done my best for our race. I'm proud to have you doing your best for me now. I'm not crooked. If I had been I would be on a train now. You give me time and we will pay back dollar for dollar." As Brown visibly wept, audience members began to stand up to display their solidarity with the bank and Brown. Others went further, making pledges of monetary support for the bank. George Harris, a florist at 17th and Kater Streets, for example, pledged to sell his business and turn the money over to the bank. Harris was not alone in his pledge, as several pastors from black churches in the Black Seventh Ward made monetary pledges that collectively totaled $150,000 ($1,870,000 in 2010). Much like the work done to quell black fears about banking, again black leaders and institutions rallied to support the banking duo.

Black leadership's support of Brown and Stevens reveals the larger importance indigenous black financial institutions had given the social and political conditions. Black Philadelphians were not alone in their economic detour, as black Americans across the country lived under similar conditions. Reluctant to question the banking duo's business practices, those rallying continued support for the banking duo emphasized the shared experience of exclusion and marginalization among blacks in order to frame the need for black banks such as those managed by Brown and Stevens. Indeed, leaders, such as Moore, and indigenous institutions, such as the Knights of Pythias, amplified the linked-fate ideology to frame the bank's problems. Here, however, such ideology, while seemingly uniting the black masses, supplanted individual needs or issues in favor of what was perceived to be the collective needs of all black people.[59]

Such efforts seemed to quell the fears of depositors, until word spread that Cosmopolitan Bank (located at Ridge Avenue and Master Streets in the Uptown/North Philadelphia area) was in financial trouble too. Initially the financial troubles of Brown & Stevens and Cosmopolitan Banks appeared to be unrelated, although seemingly similar in cause. The explanation provided by E. H. Vaughan, acting manager of Cosmopolitan Bank, mirrored Brown's: "Much of our assets are in real estate. The depositors are protected, as all the money can be recovered, some of it immediately, as we have $30,000 ($373,000 in 2010) on deposit with a bank at Broad and Chestnut streets, and another substantial deposit with another bank." Given Cosmopolitan's position as a state-commissioned bank, an investigator was quickly assigned by the state to assess the causes of the bank's sudden failure (see Tables 2.5–2.7).[60]

The investigation revealed a series of discrepancies in banking records and reports of the bank's manager. While auditing the bank's records, it was found that Brown and Stevens were the principal stockholders in the bank and virtually ran the bank, although Vaughan appeared to oversee the bank's daily operation. Further, the state investigation revealed that Brown had received more than $20,000 ($249,000 in 2010) in cash from the bank using a bad check, and that a $38,000 deposit ($473,000 in 2010) Cosmopolitan made with Brown & Stevens Bank remained frozen due to that bank's financial troubles. When local newspapers reported these facts, depositors at both banks were sent into a frenzy of anger and distrust. Such frenzy also gripped black leaders and businessmen who were heavily invested in the bank, many of whom also publicly pledged to support Brown and Stevens and their bank.[61]

By February 14, 1925, a little over a week after the initial run on Brown & Stevens Bank, both banks were forced to close due to their inability to repay depositors and the mounting evidence of questionable management practices. In response, William R. Smith, deputy secretary of banking in Pennsylvania, was appointed as receiver for both of the banks. Having been

Table 2.6 Stocks and bonds of Brown & Stevens Bank (February 11, 1925)

Date of entry	Item	Amount ($)	Estimated equivalent, 2010 ($)
12-31-20	Dunbar Amusement Corporation	16,250.00	202,000
	Clef Club, Singers and Players, 2 shs. at $10	20.00	249
	Hotel Dale Company	225.00	2,800
	Brown's Savings and Bank Co., 50 shs. at $125	6,250.00	77,700
	Elite Amusement Corporation	28,600.00	356,000
	Service Company	500.00	6,220
	Quality Amusement Corporation	11,600.00	144,000
	Hillman Realty Corporation	800.00	9,950
03-05-20	Dunbar Amusement Corporation, 400 shs. at $10	4,000.00	49,800
03-27-20	Brown's Savings and Bank Co., 50 shs. at $125	6,250.00	77,700
04-01-20	Dunbar Amusement Corporation, 1,500 shs. at $10	15,000.00	187,000
08-02-20	Hotel Dale Company, 5 shs. at $10	50.00	622
11-19-20	Dunbar Amusement Corporation Eleven (11) $1,000 6% Gold Notes	11,000.00	137,000
12-24-20	Dunbar Amusement Corporation Ten (10) $1,000 6% Gold Notes	10,000.00	124,000
02-14-21	Dunbar Amusement Corporation	730.00	9,080
02-23-21	Dunbar Amusement Corporation Six (6) $1,000 Mortgage Ctfs.	6,000.00	74,600

(*continued*)

Table 2.6 continued

Date of entry	Item	Amount ($)	Estimated equivalent, 2010 ($)
02-28-21	Dunbar Amusement Corporation Nine (9) $1,000 Mortgage Ctfs.	9,000.00	112,000
05-17-21	Citizens and Southern Banking Company	10.00	124
06-01-21	Dunbar Amusement Corporation, 1,500 shs. pfd.	15,000.00	187,000
06-01-21	Dunbar Amusement Corporation, common	3,000.00	37,300
06-23-21	Dunbar Amusement Corporation, 221 shs. at $10	2,210.00	27,500
06-30-21	Dunbar Amusement Corporation	50,000.00	622,000
07-25-21	Dunbar Amusement Corporation	50.00	622
11-09-21	Dunbar Amusement Corporation Bonds	4,000.00	49,800
12-17-21	Dunbar Amusement Corporation Stock	2,300.00	28,600
12-03-21	Dunbar Amusement Corporation Stock	630.00	7,840
07-01-21	Dunbar Amusement Corporation	90,000.00	1,120,000
09-07-22	Dunbar Amusement Corporation, 10 shs.	15.00	187
	Dunbar Amusement Corporation (sold to cover)		
	Peyton Apartments Corporation (past due notes)	1,601.00	19,900
09-29-22	Dunbar Amusement Corporation, 27 shs. at $10	270.00	3,360
12-02-22	Dunbar Amusement Corporation, Geo. A. Jeter, 5 shs.	40.00	498
12-07-22	Bonds owned	99.50	1,240
01-09-23	Cosmopolitan State Bank	394.00	4,900

02-06-24	Cosmopolitan State Bank	18,750.00	233,000
	U.S. Government Liberty Bonds	3,301.72	41,100
	Total	317,982.22	3,960,000

Source: Walter L. Fleming, *The Freedmen's Savings Bank: A Chapter in the Economic History of the Negro Race* (Westport, CT: Negro Universities Press, 1970) 50; U.S. Senate, 46th Cong., 2nd sess., 1880, Rep. 440; U.S. Senate, *The Freedman's Bank Bill*, 46th Cong., 3rd sess., 1881; U.S. Senate, 62nd Cong., 2nd Session, 1912, Rep. 759, 4.

appointed, Smith's major responsibility was to assess the financial status of both banks, and develop a procedure to repay depositors as quickly as possible. While some sought legal means of their own to get back their savings, most awaited the announcement that they could come down to the bank and receive their money.

After reviewing the records of both banks, Smith found that both Brown and Stevens had used the liquid assets of the two banks, namely the savings of nearly 13,000 depositors, to fund personal expenses and business endeavors connoted by a series of questionable withdrawals. As Tables 2.1–2.4 demonstrate, Brown and Stevens withdrew varying amounts (usually) under the auspices of various business enterprises such as the Dunbar and Douglass Theater endeavors. Like their white counterparts charged with running the Freedmen's Bank, the banking duo had used the deposits to the detriment of those who entrusted the bank to protect their savings and incomes.[62]

Attempts by Black Seventh Ward leaders to provide temporary assistance to depositors, particularly to those depositors who were poor and had families, were unsuccessful. Again, the continued discriminatory practices of the white business community made black relief efforts difficult as the capital needed to support needy families relied on the same pool of black money paralyzed by the banking collapse. The unsuccessfulness of such efforts can also be attributed to the fact that much of the financial security of black Philadelphians across class and neighborhood was directly or indirectly linked to the success or failure of the two banks. The economic detour that provided the socioeconomic conditions that facilitated Brown's and Stevens's prosperity and failure also fostered a codependent relationship between black wealth accumulation and savings, and black patronage.

In particular, black businesses established following Brown's and Stevens's efforts in the Black Seventh Ward relied upon the patronage of blacks living in and commuting to the Black Seventh Ward. Practically overnight black Philadelphians were thrown into an unanticipated economic depression due to the profound link between the two banks, black patronage, and the *special monies* (i.e., savings and incomes) of black depositors. With little disposable income available, black merchants who had built shops and stores to cater to black consumers began to close.[63]

By 1928, nearly all depositors remained unpaid. That same year, Brown, who fled the Black Seventh Ward as reports about his mismanagement mounted, died in New York City. Further, whatever money had been received from the sale of the real estate owned by Brown and Stevens (including the two banks) had been paid only to creditors. In May of 1933, the state banking commission announced that the banking affairs had concluded, and that claims of six dollars ($74.60 in 2010) or less would be paid out. Financial and news media reports indicate that the receiver was able to salvage only "about $100,000" ($240,000 in 2010) "out of the $1,000,000 resources" and pay back approximately 2,000 depositors; such reports also revealed that even those "who did not have a quarter in [the bank] ... 'lost' [significant] amounts," illustrating that the financial damage caused by the banking collapse was far reaching. In addition to shrinking the already fragile wealth of black Philadelphians, the banking failures precipitated the loss of jobs for those employed by the banking duo, the demise of the black Dunbar, Douglass, and Standard Theaters, and the Clef Club. In the end, at least 8,000 depositors never received repayment, and many were left in dire straits. Such an economic collapse was only amplified by the tremendous economic depression caused by the Great Stock Market Crash of 1929.[64]

And Then There Were None?

Black Americans have experienced various racial injuries, such as slavery, Jim Crow, and racial residential segregation (to name just a few). Accordingly, such injuries have been the impetus for many within this group to seek other strategies and solutions, through alternative institutions. However, existing debates have focused more on the cultural and adaptive strategies black Americans have employed following such injuries, with significantly less attention paid to historical periods preceding the development and implementation of emergent black cultural and social practices.

In this way, there are several lessons to draw from the story of the Brown & Stevens and Cosmopolitan Banks. First, the social history of black economic development in the Black Seventh Ward reveals that the interdependent relations between black neighborhoods is in some ways a direct product of

Table 2.7 Discrepancies between amount counted in vault and stock and bonds carried on the books (February 11, 1925)

Name of Issue	On books ($)	In vault ($)	Estimated equivalent, 2010 ($)
Brown's Savings and Bank Company	12,500.00	...	155,000
Capital Petroleum Company	...	20.00	249
Citizens and Southern Banking Company	10.00	...	124
Clef Club Singers and Players	20.00	20.00	249
Cosmopolitan State Bank of Philadelphia	19,144.00	...	238,000
De Lux Brush Company	...	100.00	1,240
Douglass Amusement Corporation	90,000.00	90,000.00	1,120,000
Dunbar Amusement Corporation	149,531.00	64,680.00	1,860,000
			850,000
Peyton Apartments Corporation	1,601.00	...	19,900
Elite Amusement Corporation	28,600.00	33,400.00	356,000
			415,000
Hillman Realty Corporation	800.00	800.00	9,950
Homer Oil and Leasing Co.	...	2,500.00	31,100
Hotel Dale Company	275.00	...	3,420
Nevada Union Copper Mines Co.	...	500.00	6,220
Pontotoc Petroleum Company	...	250.00	3,110

(continued)

Table 2.7 continued

Name of Issue	On books ($)	In vault ($)	Estimated equivalent, 2010 ($)
Quality Amusement Corporation	11,600.00	11,600.00	144,000
			144,000
Service Company	500.00		6,200
		1,000.00	12,400
United Auto Stores, Inc.	...	100.00	1,240
U.S. Government Liberty Bonds owned	3,401.22		42,300
		1,200.00	14,900
Total	317,982.22	206,170.00	3,960,000
			2,560,000
Summary			3,960,000
As carried on books		317,982.22	
As counted and seen		206,170.00	2,560,000
Net discrepancy of shortage		111,812.22	1,390,000

Source: District Court of the United States, Eastern District Pennsylvania, Equity No. 9330, No. 14078; Format adapted from Abram L. Harris, *The Negro as Capitalist* (New York: Negro Universities Press, [1936] 1969).

the marginalization of black Americans. In this case, the economic exclusion of black Philadelphians provided the conditions necessary to develop an entertainment and financial district based in the Black Seventh Ward. While such conditions helped to incentivize entrepreneurship and development in the Black Seventh Ward, they also fostered a precarious and fragile relationship between black patronage and the black Philadelphians' ability to sustain and accumulate wealth.

Although banks are institutions that allow for depositors and investors to sustain or accumulate wealth, black banks such as Brown & Stevens and Cosmopolitan Banks were overextended. While an economic detour can provide a structural opportunity for entrepreneurs, the overreliance on a singular racial consumer base creates a dilemma—the dual pursuit of a racial uplift project and wealth relying upon the same politically and economically marginalized population. As Brown and Stevens began to extend their interests, the likelihood of collapse only increased because mainstream financial opportunities remained closed to black entrepreneurs. However unfortunate the collapse was, the truly lasting damage was perhaps to black confidence in banks and banking generally. In the contemporary context it is commonly believed that a culture of distrust is a primary reason for lower rates of savings and investment by blacks, especially poorer blacks.[65] This case, however, reveals a more complicated picture.

Second, this case reveals that many black Americans once operated with some level of trust in banking institutions, so much so that Brown & Stevens and Cosmopolitan Banks held the savings of nearly 13,000 depositors. Those who managed to have savings or money to invest in the two banks were fortunate survivors of the closure of and fallout from the Freedmen's Bank, the First Northern Colored Cooperative Banking Association of Philadelphia, and the People's Savings Bank of Philadelphia. This case, then, points to a significant juncture in the origins of distrust for both mainstream and black businesses and financial institutions.[66]

Confronted by an economic detour, mistreated by white proprietors along South Street, and unable to move the local government to respond, black Philadelphians endeavored to become economically self-sufficient. During this endeavor, Black Seventh Warders benefited from increased development and the growing density of goods and services. Such development also provided money and services to blacks in other neighborhoods also excluded from full participation in the local economy.

Last, an examination of this critical juncture in the history of the Black Seventh Ward, reveals that changes in and across neighborhoods were the product of a series of interdependent relationships: the interdependent relationship between the development of one black neighborhood and the shift of resources from another black neighborhood; the interdependent relationship between the exclusion and marginalization of blacks and the growth of indigenous black institutions and neighborhoods. Although the critical juncture explored here perhaps implicitly connects with economic losses of black Americans during the Great Recession, research that explicitly investigates and ties together the role of race, risk, and other mechanisms that at the time drove informal economic institutions is still needed. As historical and contemporary economic crises continue to ravage communities of color, our attempts to understand and seek solutions are better served if informed by the social history of banking from 1865 to 1929 that placed black Americans on a path of economic loss and disenfranchisement.

While the black economic depression sparked by the banking collapse of 1925 was devastating, it provided an equalizing force of sorts diminishing intraracial class divisions. As a result of the banking collapse and subsequent events, class interests among black Philadelphians converged around issues of housing reform, and the Black Seventh Ward was a focal point yet again.

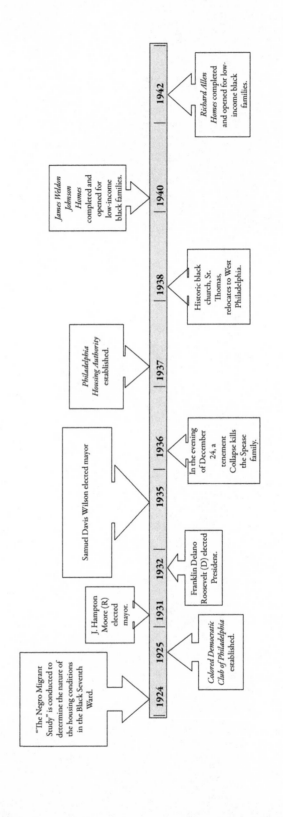

"The Negro Migrant Study" is conducted to determine the nature of the housing conditions in the Black Seventh Ward.

J. Hampton Moore (R) elected mayor.

Samuel Davis Wilson elected mayor

Philadelphia Housing Authority established.

James Weldon Johnson Homes completed and opened for low-income black families.

| 1924 | 1925 | 1931 | 1932 | 1935 | 1936 | 1937 | 1938 | 1940 | 1942 |

Colored Democratic Club of Philadelphia established.

Franklin Delano Roosevelt (D) elected President.

In the evening of December 24, a tenement Collapse kills the Spease family.

Historic black church, St. Thomas, relocates to West Philadelphia.

Richard Allen Homes completed and opened for low-income black families.

3

The Night the Roof Caved In

ON SATURDAY JANUARY 2, 1937, the city of Philadelphia was in mourning. On that cold morning, countless mourners gathered at the Shiloh Baptist Church, a staple in the Black Seventh Ward; many recalled the tragic event that claimed the lives of the Spease family. Lucy Spease (age forty-two), a recent widow, and her three children—Bernice (age thirteen), Samuel (age six), and Helen (age five)—lost their lives in a horrific scene just a week before Christmas.[1]

While preparing for the holiday season, on Saturday, December 19, 1936, Spease was likely eating dinner with her children in their small but homey second-floor apartment at 519 South 15th Street. The disrepair of Spease's apartment was noticeable, especially as the cracks along the walls gave way to the wintry air from outside. Indeed, it was common practice in the winter for residents to cook, eat, and sleep in their winter coats. Spease's apartment was not unique; in fact all of her neighbors, including those in the next-door apartment building 517 South 15th Street, had complained about property conditions to the landlord, a white man by the name of Abraham Samson (age twenty-seven), many times.

At the same time, Raymond Blackwell, Spease's neighbor at 519, frustrated with the state of the building and his apartment, decided to voice the concerns of the residents to the landlord, perhaps hoping to see repairs made as families readied for the impending Christmas holiday. Having waited until the early evening, Blackwell left his second-floor apartment hoping to convey his concerns and the urgent need for repair. When he arrived, Blackwell handed Samson his rent while repeating to the landlord the repair issues that he and others, including Spease, had noted for countless months. In his plea to Samson, Blackwell described the disrepair of the building exclaiming: "the walls on the second floor front room [are] bulging at least a foot and a half [and] the paper in the kitchen [is] falling off and the walls [have] begun to crack."[2]

As Blackwell hoped to convince Samson of the dire nature of the apartments, Spease tucked Bernice, Samuel, and Helen into bed. Soon after, Spease and other residents began to feel the walls shake and see the ceiling plaster fall down in huge chunks. Suddenly, the floor beneath their feet caved in as they rushed to the children. This, too, was the case for others in the building, including Blackwell's cousin, Alberta Richardson, who lived on the third floor. Richardson, who welcomed her cousin Hattie Bouy (age twenty-five) and Buoy's two sons Luther (age four) and Hubert (age five), was preparing to give her children a bath when the walls began to crack. Hattie Buoy, a resident of another Philadelphia neighborhood, decided to arrive early on Saturday in order to spend part of her weekend with Richardson and her children. Somewhat more fortunate than the Spease family, Richardson was already heading out as the wall shook, but fell through the floor as she and her young daughter Norma reached the hallway. Blackwell, walking with the hopes that his words had finally pushed Samson to action, arrived at 519 to find that the entire building had collapsed. A pile of ruins more than a story high, with nearly thirty-five people scattered within them, was all that was left of the two buildings located at 517–519 South 15th Street (see Figure 3.1).

Barely alive, Lucy Spease could be faintly heard calling out "Hurry please; Hurry please." Unfortunately, by the time rescuers found her she had succumbed to her injuries and died. Rescuers found Lucy Spease lying dead not too far from her children Bernice and Samuel, and Richardson's cousin Hattie, all of whom also died in the collapse. Though Buoy's sons, Luther and Hubert, escaped the collapse alive, they were left orphaned by the death of their mother, Hattie. Helen, Spease's youngest daughter, died the following day at Frederick Douglass Memorial Hospital. The site of collapse, littered with dismembered body parts, took several days to clear. In the end, multiple people had been killed, and more than a dozen were injured.[3] On December 24, 1936, the front page of the *Philadelphia Tribune* carried a list of the names and some of the photos of the victims:

> **Dead**: Hattie Buoy, 25, 2630 W. Gordon St., Lucy Spease, 42, 519 S. 15th St., Bernice Spease, 13, 519 S. 15th St., Samuel Spease, 12, 519. S. 15th St., Helen Spease, 6, 519 S. 15th St., Vivian Jones, 5, 519 S. 15th St., Odessa Jones, 7, 519 S. 15th St.
>
> **Injured**: Luther Buoy, 4, 2630 W. Gordon St., Hubert Buoy, 5, 2630 W. Gordon St., Hattie Williams, 34, 519 S. 15th St., Edna Richardson, 7, 519 S. 15th St., Susan Dorman, 72, 517 S. 15th St., Wardell Brown, 55,

FIGURE 3.1 Police officers, firemen, and other rescuers surveying the site at 517–519 South 15th Street following the collapse that occurred in the evening on December 19, 1936. Temple University Libraries, SCRC, Philadelphia, PA.

517 S. 15th St., Thomas Williams, 12, 519 S. 15th St., William Taylor, 29, 519 S. 15th St., Thomas Seldon, 40, 309 S. 20th St., Patrick Shields, 2533 Ellsworth St., Alberta Richardson, 28, 519 S. 15th St., Helen Jones, 26, 510 S. 15th St.[4]

Within the context in which it occurred, this event accelerated an unprecedented period of housing reform and construction in Philadelphia, prompting two of the first three housing projects built to supply affordable housing to poor and working-class black residents.[5] While this outcome provided tremendous resources to black Philadelphians, the designation of race-specific public housing had serious implications for black residents specifically and Philadelphia more generally. With respect to the problem of resource allocation and urban development, issues of housing reform and public housing have been central to discussions of urban black life and urban inequality. Whereas existing scholarship and debates emphasize the role of exogenous factors in understanding such disparities and change, this chapter focuses on questions regarding the political agency of urban black residents. That is, how did black residents frame such a tragedy? Did black residents call for state, federal, and local intervention? If so, how were such calls framed and how were indigenous resources mobilized and/or impacted by such narratives and action?

Using the tenement collapse as a critical juncture, this chapter explores these questions. I begin first with an examination of housing reform efforts occurring before the tenement collapse, particularly during the 1920s and early 1930s, foregrounding the sociopolitical climate within which the collapse occurred. Here, I detail intraracial factionalism and cultural divisions that made housing reform difficult. Next, I explore the response of city officials and black leaders to the tenement collapse, illustrating the varying debates and protests aimed at housing reform. I conclude the chapter by examining the effects of the housing reform efforts of black Philadelphians.

Altogether these sections chart how housing reform, public housing, and state intervention with respect to housing moved from a *cross-cutting* issue to a *consensus* issue. Essentially, I use the political agency of black Philadelphians such as secondary marginalization and framing to examine the causes and consequences of housing reform and public housing construction. Ultimately, this chapter considers the costs and benefits of black responses to the poor housing conditions in which many of them lived, while also demonstrating how black political agency facilitated and frustrated urban and neighborhood change.

On the Margins: The Black Seventh Ward, Black Politics, and Housing Reform in the 1920s

Heading into 1920, the black population of Philadelphia was growing, especially in the Black Seventh Ward. Increases in the black population were a product of the growth of three major groups: indigenous blacks, southern black migrants, and West Indian black immigrants. While increases occurred across these three major groups, the largest increases were by far among the southern black migrant population. Philadelphia's black population, much like several other northern urban destinations such as New York and Chicago,

FIGURES 3.2 AND 3.3 Homemade plumbing used by Seventh Ward blacks (*c.* 1920). These outhouses were common features in the tenements of the Black Seventh Ward as many buildings were without adequate plumbing. Temple University Libraries, SCRC, Philadelphia, PA.

grew significantly up to 1920—increasing from 62,613 in 1900, to 84,459 in 1910, to 134,229 in 1920. The Black Seventh Ward's population grew consistently from 1900 to 1920, from roughly 9,000 to 12,241.[6] Indeed, the neighborhood remained predominantly black well into the early 1920s. Although the Black Seventh Ward's population continued to grow during this period, the housing options and residential space they occupied did not.

In fact, the only housing options open to black residents in the neighborhood were on two major streets, South and Lombard Streets. As a result, life in the Black Seventh Ward was a congested one. It was common practice for landlords

FIGURES 3.2 AND 3.3 Continued

to refashion tenements and rooming houses, increasing the number of rooms provided by dividing existing rooms or apartments into several "new" rooms or apartments. Additionally, many of these apartments and rooms were without bathrooms, heating, and major plumbing. Many Black Seventh Ward residents built outdoor plumbing facilities which would be shared by all residents in a given building, while others littered the streets of South and Lombard, especially the myriad alleys in between, with their waste (see Figure 3.2 and 3.3).

Daily life was, indeed, a struggle for families and individuals who occupied these residences and those who lived in neighboring homes. Many, namely black elites and middle-class blacks, were anxious to leave such congested conditions, especially as rates of tuberculosis rose among Black Seventh Warders as the population continued to increase in number and density. While some were fortunate enough to move outside of the Black Seventh Ward, others were met with severe racism and violence when attempting to move elsewhere. Cases of violent attacks covered the pages of the *Philadelphia Tribune*, showing that even when blacks attempted to move onto blocks neighboring Lombard and South, racially motivated violence ensued.

George Graham was not exempt from such violence. A member of the black middle class, Graham purchased a home just a few blocks north of the Black Seventh Ward, at 2535 Pine Street. Having moved from the more congested area of the Black Seventh Ward, Graham celebrated with family and friends as he moved his final box into his home in late April of 1919. Aware of the racial violence and aggression that besieged black residents as they moved out of the South/Lombard Street area, Graham was not naïve about his white neighbors adoring him upon his arrival. Unlike some black Philadelphians that moved into predominantly white areas, Graham prepared his home for possible attack. Graham's home, rife with guns and ammunition, was prepared for his possible self-defense.[7]

On April 27, 1919, shortly before 1 a.m., Graham awoke to the sounds of windows shattering in the front room and loud thumps at his door. Rushing downstairs with shotgun in hand, he crept toward the front door to look outside to see who had attacked his home. To his dismay, Graham saw a crowd of more than thirty whites, mostly men, screaming a "shoot to kill" slogan with many having guns in hand. Walking cautiously over the broken window glass on the floor, Graham moved quickly to figure out a way to buttress the front door, anticipating an escalation in the violence of the crowd outside.

Before he was able to secure the front door, the crowd rushed his home and Graham began to fire his shotgun. As the incident rose in intensity, many Black Seventh Warders came to the aid of Graham. As he continued to fire, friends, family, and other concerned blacks from all classes were out front beating on the attackers who continued to push their way into Graham's home. By the time the police arrived, whites and blacks were in the street fighting one another. Upon arrival, all of the black people involved, including Graham, were taken into custody receiving no treatment for their injuries. Of the more than thirty white attackers, only four boys were held: Joseph McLoughlin (age 17), Lawrence Stanton (age 18), Andrew McCloskey (age 18), and Charles McCloskey (age 16). While initially held on $400 bail, each was later released with little admonishment.[8]

Graham and his experience at 2535 Pine Street are representative of a long-standing battle between blacks and whites that W. E. B. DuBois documented in his early study of the Black Seventh Ward in *The Philadelphia Negro*. Also representative is how in many of these racially violent residential-based conflicts, blacks across class aided in support. While such an episode suggests a united black front against racial violence, beyond such moments of racial aggression within group divisions characterized intraracial relations at the time. Without question, distinctions between homeowners and renters, and between northern and southern, remained important markers among black Philadelphians and underscored competing perspectives about how to advance black interests and challenge the status quo. Such distinctions are important in that they also highlight the heterogeneity of black perspectives on housing inequality. The safety and security of black homeowners, who were members of a fragile black middle class, were often privileged above those of working-class and poorer black renters.

Whereas scholars such as William Julius Wilson and Elijah Anderson have emphasized the historical role of black middle-class residents as social buffers often protecting (and policing) poorer blacks, this example demonstrates that poor and working-class blacks also functioned as a buffer of sorts for their middle-class and elite counterparts.[9] Coming to the aid of middle-class black homeowners as they moved out of the Black Seventh Ward into predominantly white areas of the city, poor and working-class blacks provided an important buffer of protection and defense against the racial violence precipitated by the "encroachment" of the black residents. Despite such consensus around the safety and security of black homeowners, little agreement existed about how or whether to address the inequality endemic to black housing across class.

Racial violence, while significant, was not the only source of housing strife. Issues of cost inflation also plagued those seeking to venture away from the dense Black Seventh Ward. White realtors were in the practice of increasing the cost of housing to interested black Philadelphians by hundreds of dollars, forcing many to contend not only with subsequent racial aggression but also with exorbitant rental and mortgage costs. Such issues took a backseat to the focus on political enfranchisement by black leaders. Comprehensive housing reform, then, was situated as a cross-cutting[10] issue prior to the collapse, situated as a need for a segment of the black population, namely poor, working-class, and newly arrived southern blacks. Paying little attention to the inequality in housing impacting blacks across social class, black leaders, instead, focused on gaining entry into the ranks of the city's leadership. Given this goal, black leaders tended to shy away from outright conflict with white political leaders, often quieting black discontent in order to achieve black political representation. Perhaps the best example of such behavior is in the controversy around the naming of a newly constructed community center and playground in the Black Seventh Ward.

The Phyllis Wheatley Community Centre: A Snapshot of the Climate of Intraracial Relations

When Mayor J. Hampton Moore arrived to the Black Seventh Ward on October 31, 1920, to deliver a speech at the groundbreaking ceremony for the Phyllis Wheatley Community Centre at Lombard Street between 10th and 11th Streets, black leaders and residents gathered in large numbers. The site was not too far from the local black and popular political group, the Citizens Republican Club (CRC) located at 15th and Lombard Streets, and Moore's appearance was especially supported by black Republican leadership. Clenching his fist, Moore declared that the Black Seventh Ward was unfit and a virtual disaster area, exclaiming that he would burn down the area to rebuild it, with his own political headquarters at the center. Focusing on old Equity Hall, a dilapidated unused facility located near 10th and Lombard Streets, Moore declared that R. R. Wright, a leading black preacher, politician and major in the armed forces, would be his guiding executive in this effort.[11]

The response of blacks in attendance was mixed. While middle-class and elite blacks overwhelmingly supported Moore's measure, recently arrived southern black migrants and poorer indigenous blacks were confused and worried. Although for well-to-do blacks the removal of blight would facilitate new possibilities for black leadership, disadvantaged blacks were sure that such a massive demolition of housing in the South/Lombard Street area would mean that they would be homeless. Unfortunately for the working-class, poor, near-poor, and southern black residents, black Republican leadership of the Black Seventh Ward focused less on the idea of the massive decimation of black housing in the neighborhood, and more on the possibilities emergent from the incorporation of Wright by Moore into his administration, if only in a peripheral capacity. Invigorated by Wright's appointment, black leadership sought to add more blacks to the ranks of local political officials. Backing Amos Scott, notable local black Republican leader and lawyer, for magistrate, leadership in the Black Seventh Ward sought to mobilize the black masses to support the nomination and election of Scott in the upcoming elections. In the November elections of 1921, Scott was overwhelmingly supported by blacks across the city and received the backing of Charles B. Hall, white city councilman for the Seventh Ward, and Moore. Amos Scott was elected the first black magistrate in Philadelphia. Yet, this victory was not without sacrifice for Black Seventh Warders.[12]

Seeking to mobilize the black populace to support further enfranchisement in the local political structure, black Republican leadership did little to

preserve the culture of the Black Seventh Ward; this fact would be most evident in the dispute over the proposed Phyllis Wheatley Community Centre.
While leadership in the Black Seventh Ward elevated Scott as nominee for
magistrate, Mayor Moore wavered on the naming of the public facility built
in the heart of the Black Seventh Ward. It was originally promised as the
Phyllis Wheatley Community Centre, but Moore later decided to consider a
different name, Charles Seger.

Responding to an ordinance introduced by Hall to name the location after
Hall's friend and political associate Charles Seger, Moore decided to forgo the
previous name for the community center. Seger, recently deceased, had been
for most of his life a key political voice in Philadelphia and leader for
Philadelphia's Jewish community. In fact, the newly built community center
had been placed on the grounds of properties that Seger had owned that had
been condemned. Arriving at the ceremony with R. R. Wright and Edward
J. Henry, president of the CRC, Moore announced that he was unsure about
the name of the new community center, to which some of the blacks and Jews
in attendance jeered. Wright stepped forward with his concerns, informing
the audience:

> Someone has suggested that we give a [different] name to this recreation
> centre. The Mayor has indicated from the beginning that here in this
> district where the colored men and women predominate the centre
> should have the name of someone who has rendered distinguished ser-
> vice to the colored race. I suggest the name of one who stands for the
> colored race, a slave child brought to this country and kept here in
> slavery, who despite all obstacles became an educated woman—a writer
> and a poet, a woman who wrote of her people and who sang their
> songs.[13]

Wright, turning to blacks in the audience, then asked those in attendance to
raise their hands if they agreed with naming the center after Phyllis Wheatley,
to which a majority raised their hands.

Sensing the discontent and possible embarrassment of the mayor, Henry
exuded his influence over Black Seventh Ward residents, announcing his
strong support of the mayor and afterwards asking blacks in the crowd if any
disagreed with the possible naming of the center after Seger. Calling for a
show of hands again, Henry looked out into the crowd to see no hands in the
air "Does anyone disagree with the mayor?" With that, the matter was settled
and after a small meeting held by Moore on the topic, which no blacks

attended, the community center in the heart of the Black Seventh Ward was named the Charles Seger Playground. In the end, the community center and the official acknowledgement by the city of Philadelphia of the black presence in the larger Seventh Ward was sacrificed for the procurement of Scott's seat as magistrate. Within the next three years after Scott's victory, prominent black Republican leaders, John Asbury and Andrew Stevens, were elected to state house of representatives.

Though a seemingly small historical event, this snapshot illustrates the ways in which existing black leaders quieted black discontent in an effort to achieve what was deemed a more important need or consensus issue, that of increased black political representation. As a result, the naming of the playground was supplanted by political aspirations, sacrificing the existence of black cultural markers within the Seventh Ward. Given that the playground was situated in the Black Seventh Ward, losing a battle over the naming of such an institution reveals the tension confronting black residents and leaders. Indeed, the racial climate of the city led many black residents and leaders to avoid direct confrontation and sacrifice seemingly smaller political victories for those deemed larger in importance. The playground episode is emblematic of the intraracial negotiations that made housing reform tenuous and highlights the tactics of black leadership of the time.

The Negro Migrant Study of 1924 and Housing in the Black Seventh Ward

By 1923, conservative black Republican leadership, under Henry's direction, generated significant political success at least in terms of increasing the representation of blacks in public office. Yet, Black Seventh Warders continued to be plagued by serious housing issues. Such issues were only magnified by the tremendous influx of southern black migrants. Believing that the influx of southern black migrants lay at the problems of black housing in Philadelphia, many of the black Republican leaders such as Henry, Wright, and their supporters paid little attention to housing issues. Distinguishing themselves and their leadership, black leaders often spoke in unkind terms about their southern migrant counterparts. For the most part major black leaders were convinced that housing conditions would improve if indigenous blacks and black churches in Philadelphia worked to assimilate and teach southern black migrants how to behave and live in a northern urban environment such as Philadelphia.[14]

While the voices and beliefs of Henry, Wright, Asbury, and Stevens dominated black political discourse, other blacks, namely those involved in the
interracial organization the Armstrong Association (the Urban League),
thought differently. Forming an interracial committee to survey southern
black migrants in the Black Seventh Ward and neighboring areas, the
Armstrong Association joined local white-led housing advocacy organizations
the Octavia Hill Association and the Housing Association of Delaware Valley
(HADV),[15] and the Traveler's Aid Society to investigate the influx of black
southern migrants from 1923 to 1924. Using volunteers, the Committee on
Negro Migration in Philadelphia went door-to-door gathering information on
housing conditions, labor, and health. Research volunteers using short ques-
tionnaires assessed the causes of southern migration and determined that divisions between indigenous and southern blacks led to the mistreatment of
migrants upon their arrival into the city. Such treatment was then compounded
by the opportunism of white landlords and realtors who charged even more in
rent to southern black migrants than to their indigenous black counterparts.

The final report, written by the primary researcher of the study, William
D. Fuller, was delivered to the committee on June 1, 1924. Titled *The Negro
Migrant in Philadelphia*, Fuller's report extended the findings of an earlier
study conducted by the HADV in 1917, emphasizing the prominence of the
southern black presence in Philadelphia. Fuller reported that from 1922 to
1924 more than 20,000 southern blacks had migrated into Philadelphia.
Upon arrival, southern migrants tended to reside in previously established
black centers, such as the Black Seventh Ward and thus crowded into already
limited housing. Among the list of housing violations found the following
were most prominent: (1) insufficient water supply: (2) insufficient toilet
facilities; (3) defective sanitary equipment; (4) overcrowding: (5) leaky roof;
(6) paper or plaster falling off walls; and (7) windowless rooms. Despite the
deplorable housing conditions, the study found that black Philadelphians
paid the rates often associated with the more elite housing costs whites paid,
approximately $20 and $30 monthly, for room-sized apartments. Based on
the study findings, the Armstrong Association, HADV, Octavia Hill
Association, and Traveler's Aid Society (as well as several other local organizations) concluded that existing housing must be renovated and new housing
built. Indeed, such conditions were not new as W. E. B. DuBois also observed
and reported such conditions in *The Philadelphia Negro*, writing:

Of the 2441 families only 334 access to bathroom and water-closets....
Even these 334 families have poor accommodations.... Many share the

use of one bathroom with one or more families.... Most of these houses have to get their water at a hydrant in the alley, and must store their fuel in the house.[16]

Here, then, given the similarity between DuBois's and the Migrant Study's findings, we can see that these housing problems were not new, but instead recurring. Even with such compelling data, both the city and the black leadership paid little attention.[17]

As historian Vincent P. Franklin notes in *The Education of Black Philadelphia*, by the mid-1920s black leadership focused much of its attention on discrimination, and began laying the groundwork for education reform later realized during the civil rights movement. Adding to this point, the continued distinctions made among black residents and leaders made housing reform difficult, as many indigenous black Philadelphians believed the problems of housing were the by-product of the in-migration of southern black migrants. While key leaders such as John Asbury and Andrew Stevens worked to introduce an Equal Rights Bill to the Pennsylvania General Assembly, and Isadore Martin, president of the Philadelphia branch of the NAACP, pushed the Philadelphia Board of Education to create more black "normal"[18] schools, housing issues continued to plague black Philadelphians, especially those in the Black Seventh Ward; an area that became commonly referred to as Hell's Acre during this period.

Running a series of investigative reports, the *Philadelphia Tribune* spent much of 1925 documenting the ills of housing for black Philadelphians. With headlines like "Dying Like Flies," the *Tribune* exposed the increasing death rate and exposure to smallpox that plagued Black Seventh Ward residents due to dilapidated housing and unsafe tenement overcrowding. Describing the conditions, the *Philadelphia Tribune* reported:

> In 1921, only 15 Negroes died out of every 1000 in the city. This was 3 per 1000 more than the death rate for whites who had 12 deaths out of every 1000. But in 1922 the number of Negro deaths had increased to 17 per 1000.... But the worst is yet to come. In 1923 the Negro death rate had increased to 21 per 1000 while the white death rate was a fraction over 13, making the difference between the number of Negroes and whites per 1000 who died, 8....Do the figures cited mean that the Negro is less healthy in this city than elsewhere? Why is it that when fewer and fewer Negroes are dying annually in other cities that for the last few years the situation has been just the opposite in Philadelphia?...The

answer is quite simple.... The housing conditions of the Negro in this city are responsible for high death-rates...instead of these conditions improving they are becoming worse. It has been conservatively estimated that 40,000 Negroes have come to Philadelphia ever since the census of 1920. To properly take care of these people 2000 new houses should be built yearly. As a matter of fact out of 35,000 new houses built during the past year in Philadelphia not one was available for a Negro tenant.

Similar to the response the Negro Migrant Study of 1924 received, neither the mayor nor city officials seriously considered the *Philadelphia Tribune*'s call to action. The contrary disposition of existing black Republican leadership is perhaps most telling. In response to such findings, black Republican leaders attributed these deplorable conditions to the supposed "backwardness" of southern black migrants, suggesting that outhouses were vestiges of rural living and that such problems would fix themselves once southern black migrants were taught how to live in a city. As a result, the ills of poor housing continued to plague the Black Seventh Ward, becoming a commonplace expectation among blacks when searching for housing options in the city. However, some were moved to action on behalf of working-class and poorer Black Seventh Ward residents and the larger city as new voices began to emerge and were aligning themselves with the Democratic Party.

By 1924, the city's Democratic Party was working to undo its image as a party for white ethnics. Much like Democrats in other cities, during the mid-1920s the Democratic Party in Philadelphia began attempts to form an alliance with the city's black population with hopes of shifting the black voting bloc away from the Republican Party. Many Black Seventh Warders critiqued black Republican leadership as representing an older and more highbrow voice, remiss in its attention to the plight of poorer blacks whose problems would benefit from serious state intervention. The most vociferous contention against the older black Republican leadership of Henry, Wright, Asbury, and others came from a young group of black organizers and professionals in the Black Seventh Ward. Led by attorney Austin Norris and physicians Lionel Francis and Charles Craft, discontented Black Seventh Warders formed the Colored Democratic Club of Philadelphia (CDCP) in the summer of 1924. Conducting a series of informational sessions and meetings throughout the summer, the CDCP garnered support quickly.[19]

During a warm summer night in June of 1924, Norris rallied Black Seventh Warders against the dominant Republican leadership that controlled the city and the black political agenda. Norris, standing before a crowd of concerned Black Seventh Warders, described the failures of black Republican leadership. Asserting connections between discrimination against blacks and Republican success with the support of blacks, Norris called for a new day and new faces in black political leadership. He concluded his speech calling for blacks to divide their vote and make use of the resulting political power. To rousing applause, Norris concluded his remarks:

> So ladies and gentlemen … it seems to me that our friends to whom we have been so loyal and whose victories can be directly attributed to our vote have treated us as badly as our enemies from whom we have no right to expect anything. Certainly from all indications by changing our allegiance there is no chance of hurting our interest from what has happened in New York, Chicago and New Jersey, the chances of benefit for our race is very probable. In taking this step we are even acting on the advice of ex-President Harding in his Birmingham, Alabama, speech, who advised the Negroes to divide their vote.[20]

While Norris's sentiments resonated for black Philadelphians across class, his message and the mission of the CDCP, especially in its call for state intervention and support, struck a chord with southern migrants and poor and working-class Black Seventh Warders. Much like black workers, youth, and leaders in Birmingham, Alabama, depicted by historian Robin D. G. Kelley, Norris's sentiments sought to build a new constituency of black leadership by drawing on black *infrapolitics*, or the black political advancement emerging from "below" as a result of the efforts of working-class and poor blacks.[21]

Here, Norris was seeking to empower working-class and poor blacks, both indigenous to Philadelphia and from the South, to challenge the hold black elites had on local black politics and political involvement. By the close of the 1920s, the CDCP had gathered a membership that rivaled the CRC. In response, the CRC attempted to rework its image, and build a new coalition by focusing on generating a new and younger generation of black Republican leadership.

In the election of new officers in December of 1928, Henry, the perennial favorite, was convinced by the membership to step down and withdraw from the race for club president. In turn, William S. Hagans, a young upstart conservative leader, was selected president of the CRC. With Hagans's election came the selection of several other young Republican leaders, namely John W. Harris, Jr., Herbert Brown, and Harry Duplessis who were elected as first vice-president, second vice-president, and financial secretary respectively. By 1930, it was clear that the members of the CRC and the CDCP were not only competitors within local black Philadelphia politics, but also representative of the class and cultural cleavages emergent among Black Seventh Warders during the 1920s. Additionally, the financial ruin of the latter part of the 1920s (see chapter 2) was only intensified by the need for affordable and equal access to housing that underscored the lives of Black Seventh Ward residents throughout the 1920s.[22]

In sum, during the 1920s housing reform never took shape in Philadelphia either at the mayoral level or within the political agenda of leading black politicians and organizers. Operating as a cross-cutting issue, housing reform was thwarted by intraracial divisions. Indeed, during the 1920s divisions based upon social class and culture marred black politics. In essence, major black leaders paid little attention to housing issues, as those black Republicans who aligned themselves with the conservative leadership of Moore sought continued black representation and distanced themselves from their poorer and (often) southern counterparts. This lack of attention by black Republican leaders gave way to an emergent youthful and new black Democratic coalition based out of the Black Seventh Ward, and led to a bifurcated black political constituency that would critically shift discourse on housing reform during the 1930s.

From Margin to Center: Black Politics and Housing Reform in the Early 1930s

Through the 1920s, Philadelphia's black population continued to dramatically increase. Between 1920 and 1930 the city's black population rose 63.5 percent, from 134,229 to 219,559, outpacing the growth of the city's white population, which grew by only 2.4 percent during the same period (see Figure 3.4). However, the Black Seventh Ward population declined significantly during this ten-year period, from 12,241 in 1920 to 8,430 in 1930. Many of the residents who exited were contained in the neighboring Thirtieth Ward as many blacks often moved just one to three blocks south of the South/Lombard Street areas. Some of the decrease was also the result of middle-class blacks making use of the advent of the streetcar to move into previously unavailable housing in West Philadelphia and of whites moving deeper into South and Northeast Philadelphia. The secondary migration of whites further south into Philadelphia made way for the black population to solidify its presence across the Seventh and Thirtieth Wards. Together these two wards

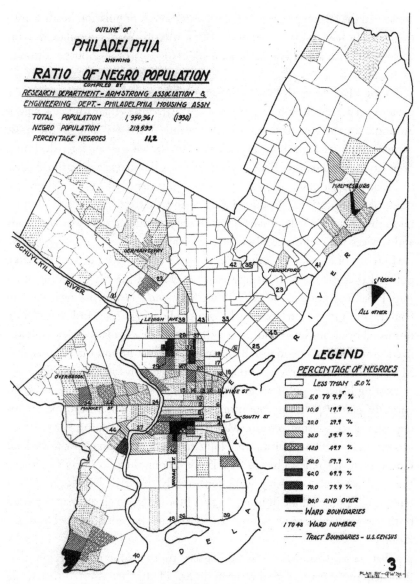

FIGURE 3.4 Distribution of black Philadelphians, 1930. By 1930 three major black areas in the city were discernible, south of Center City, and North and West Philadelphia.

Source: Temple University Libraries, SCRC, Philadelphia, PA.

contained the largest portion of the increased black population heading into the 1930s. Indeed, the decrease in the Black Seventh Ward's populace did not correspond with a decrease in the population density of the South/Lombard Street area.

In the Black Seventh Ward, the density of the area was estimated at 164 persons per acre, well above 111.21 per acre, the overall average for black neighborhoods in the city; thus the Black Seventh Ward was one of the most densely populated black neighborhoods in the city despite its declining population. Further, the Black Seventh Ward still remained the primary hub of black political and cultural life, containing many of the key churches, political organizations, produce markets, and theaters. As a result, despite relocating, black Philadelphians across the city continued to rely on the goods and services situated in the Black Seventh Ward.[23]

In terms of housing reform, the early 1930s began with much of the same political rhetoric about housing that characterized the 1920s. As historian John F. Bauman notes in *Public Housing, Race, and Renewal*, during his tenure from 1931 to 1935 Moore continually ignored housing issues, and consistently dismissed poor housing conditions within which most black Philadelphians lived.[24] Somewhat outside of Bauman's focus, but important here, is that Moore's dismissive opinion of housing reform was only furthered by the focus of existing black Republican leadership, which offered quiet consent in an effort to garner political appointments in Moore's administration. In his opposition to housing reform, Moore argued: "Philadelphia is a City of Homes....A thousand cities and industries are appealing to the Federal Government for relief. Philadelphia is not among them." Efforts to provide new and affordable housing were consistently thwarted by Moore. In his crusade to oppose public housing, in 1933 Moore vetoed an ordinance passed by the city council to vacate several streets to build the proposed Carl Mackley Homes.[25]

That same year, Moore would assert to the American Legion that Philadelphia "was too proud to have slums." He further asserted that while "there may be some dilapidated houses...that does not constitute slums." By Moore's estimation people were "merely living within their means." While Moore's comments resonated with some, namely white realtors, bankers, and small builders, his comments likely frustrated Black Seventh Warders, particularly working-class and poor blacks.

With the financial ruin that came with the failure of Brown & Stevens and Cosmopolitan Banks and the advent of the Great Depression, housing woes underscored a collective black experience in spite of existing divisions based on region and social class. As such, Moore's comments struck many black Philadelphians as out of touch and dismissive. For influential black leaders who had aligned themselves with Mayor Moore in the early 1920s, such an allegiance, given Moore's continued position on housing reform and denial of slums emergent from poor housing conditions, was a politically dangerous one to maintain.[26]

By 1933, the limited housing options and the larger economic depression disrupted the hold the Republican Party had on the Black Seventh Ward voters. Those who managed to escape the financial ruin, which hit many of the Black Seventh Ward's middle-class and elite black families, continued to be plagued by price-gouging and racial violence in their attempts to purchase homes in predominantly white areas of the city. Working-class and poorer Black Seventh Ward residents watched as their homes and the Black Seventh Ward every day turned more and more into an uninhabitable and dangerous neighborhood. As H. Viscount Nelson observes in his historical examination of black leadership during the Great Depression in *Black Leadership's Response to the Great Depression in Philadelphia*:

> Decreased income and depleted savings, coupled with the reluctance of banks to grant black people loans, not only prevented blacks from migrating into white areas, but also prevented many African American homeowners from maintaining their property. Distinctions between middle and lower class therefore narrowed, as it became difficult to determine the resident's class from the façade of a home.

Thus black Philadelphians had likely become weary of a number of things: they were weary of Moore's conservative Republican leadership; they were weary of the racial violence that ensued when attempting to move out of the over-crowded poor housing in the Black Seventh Ward; they were weary of black leadership's blind allegiance to the Republican machine and Mayor Moore; they were weary of the high rents white landlords and realtors charged; they were weary of living in one-room apartments with no plumbing and heating.

As a result, many of the older black political establishments had begun to experience significant membership decreases. This fact was most obvious in the CRC. Once the most powerful and significant black political group in Philadelphia, by 1932 the CRC was on the verge of collapse. Plagued by a battle between a new generation of black Republicans and the older genera-tion that rose to prominence at the dawn of the twentieth century, the CRC was in the midst of an identity crisis. With the election of Hagans, many in the organization believed that his presidency would usher in a new groups of leaders who would be more in touch with the issues and concerns of the black masses. This, however, had not been the case. Instead of ushering in a new generation of black Republican leadership, Hagans's presidency was a time of turmoil for the organization with ambivalence and infighting characterizing the climate of the CRC well into the 1930s.[27]

In 1932, a general meeting, called to consider endorsing Republican presidential incumbent Herbert Hoover for reelection, revealed such tension. While for many decades the discussion of endorsing a Republican incumbent was short and simple work, with a decreasing membership and a rival black Democratic organization rising in popularity, such a discussion was no longer an easy task. Some, mostly those who were seen as stalwarts of the CRC, contended that such an endorsement was obviously in the interest of the CRC and black Philadelphians generally; others vehemently disagreed. Many who disagreed asserted that endorsing Hoover would signal to blacks in the city that the CRC was not evolving and instead stubbornly tied to a blind allegiance to the Republican Party, a party that to many continued to turn a blind eye to the social realities of black Philadelphians. This disagreement turned ugly, with some engaging in an actual brawl. In the end, the CRC decided to support Hoover, who was later defeated handily by Democrat Franklin Delano Roosevelt.

The decision to back Hoover would haunt the CRC, and generate an onslaught of embarrassing critiques from Norris and the CDCP for many years; much of the critique contended that the CRC failed to adequately represent the interests of the city's black population. By December 1933, the CRC was on the verge of bankruptcy and had watched its membership dwindle to dismal numbers. The political battle, however, was not over.[28]

Although the failure of the CRC in its endorsement of Hoover was a significant blow to the organization and black Republican leadership, the Democratic presidential victory did not necessarily mean that black Republicanism was dead. The battle for mayor in the 1935 elections revealed that Republicanism was still very much alive and viable at least at the local political level. S. Davis Wilson, Republican nominee for mayor, met with serious competition in Democratic nominee John B. ("Jack") Kelly. Kelly, a vocal supporter of New Deal politics and reform under the Roosevelt administration, centered housing reform as a critical aspect of his political platform. Having witnessed the powerful voting bloc blacks provided in the election of Roosevelt for president, Kelly took aim at the Black Seventh Ward's deterioration and housing reform to garner black support. Kelly, situating the Black Seventh Ward slums as a symbol of Republican failures, argued that progressive rather than conservative politics must be adopted.[29]

The *Philadelphia Tribune* capitalized on the attention Kelly's mayoral bid brought to the housing realities of Black Seventh Warders. Running a series of investigative reports on the poor housing conditions in the Black Seventh Ward, the *Philadelphia Tribune* called for state intervention to change the conditions in Hell's Acre. Whereas the *Philadelphia Tribune*'s report in 1925 focused on the health-related issues that resulted from living in dense and dilapidated conditions, the series of reports in 1935 focused more on the neglect of city inspectors, price-gouging by white landlords, and substandard facilities within which Black Seventh Warders lived.

Describing the substandard housing conditions, the *Philadelphia Tribune* reported: "Living conditions in the Acre are not based on the house or apartment unit. Here the basis of any examination is the single room...you find whole families living in ONE room, not two or three or four rooms." In a subsequent article, the *Philadelphia Tribune* proclaimed: "The slums of Philadelphia are no accident. They are planned slums. Neither was the invasion of better class homes in North and West Philadelphia in recent years an accident. It was planned by property speculators too and the Negro, as in the slums, paid the price and acted knowingly as the pawn in a game of millions."[30] The *Philadelphia Tribune* and mayoral candidate Kelly were not alone in their efforts, as white housing advocates became vociferous proponents of housing reform. Despite the growing importance of housing reform, black Philadelphians remained divided about which persons were best suited to represent and advocate for black residents, as evidenced in the attempt to appoint blacks to the HADV and the activism of black residents preceding the tenement collapse.

The Advisory Committee and Housing Reform

Like Jack Kelly, Bernard Newman, a white activist and executive secretary of the HADV, acknowledged the importance of the issue of housing reform for the city's black population. Building on the attention to housing issues generated by Kelly in his quest to become mayor and developing a plan for using funds from the Public Works Administration (PWA), Newman put together an advisory committee that would advocate and oversee the development of affordable housing in Philadelphia. Newman, anticipating "slum clearance," thought it ideal to select a potential site for building new homes that would house displaced black residents. Convinced that the time was ripe for housing reform,

Newman met with a variety of black leaders and citizens to determine the best black candidate to take up a post on the newly formed committee. Several names were given, but Crystal Bird Fauset's rose to the top of Newman's list.

Born in Maryland in 1893, Fauset, née Bird, was the daughter of educators, Benjamin Oliver Bird and Portia E. (Lovett) Bird. Following the death of her parents, she lived with relatives, moving to Boston where she attended high school. After completing high school, Fauset earned a BA from Columbia University's Teacher College, worked as an administrator for the YMCA, and married into the Fausets, one of Philadelphia's oldest black elite families. One of the emergent voices of a new black Democratic contingent, Fauset became a heavy favorite to be selected as the only black member of the HADV's advisory committee. Newman found in his early discussions with black residents and leaders that for many the appeal of Fauset was the fact that she represented a new cohort of black leaders who were elite, and also concerned about and advocated for working-class and poorer black Philadelphians. But as the time to make the official appointment neared, black Republican leaders criticized Newman's choice, and advised that Wright, an older conservative and more established member of the black elite, would be a better choice.

In the end, Newman elected to officially appoint both Fauset and Wright, and in May 1935 black Philadelphians had two representatives on the advisory committee. Newman's experience was emblematic of the continuing friction among black Philadelphians and the competing interests of established black elites and middle-class leaders and those invested in black infrapolitics.[31] Indeed, Fauset represented both a different cohort of black leadership and also a differing political approach, one that relied on the mobilization of poor and working-class black residents and on more direct confrontation with the status quo. In other words, Fauset's political disposition favored an approach that combined the capital of the black elite with the infrapolitics of the disenfranchised black masses advocated by Austin Norris just a few years earlier. Further, the contention between Fauset and Wright's appointments signaled that although housing was becoming more of a consensus issue there was intraracial competition around who should represent black interests and have power over the measures taken to address such problems.[32]

However, Black Seventh Warders, refusing to leave the solution to their housing woes in the hands of Fauset and Wright, spent much of the spring and early summer in a letter-writing campaign. Initially a spontaneous occurrence, black residents later organized the letter-writing campaign by soliciting letters from Black Seventh Warders and sending them in bulk, with hopes that the sheer volume of letters would spark action. Sending letters to secretary of the federal PWA, Harold Ickes, black residents called for federal funds to be designated to provide black Philadelphians with low-income housing, particularly those in the Black Seventh Ward.

Backed by Newman, the letter-writing campaign, along with the *Philadelphia Tribune*'s investigative reports managed to get the attention of Secretary Ickes. By June, it appeared that efforts to bring attention to Philadelphia's growing slum problem had been successful, as the *Philadelphia Tribune* reported that the PWA had designated ten million dollars in federal funds to Philadelphia for slum removal and the building of new housing. Timing mattered for the success of the writing campaign, as cities across the country were lobbying federal officials to designate funds to address similar issues.

Given the recent interest the federal government had been taking in urban housing and development, cities like New York, Chicago, and Philadelphia were realizing what resources there were at the federal level and beginning to take advantage of them. Clear that the Black Seventh Ward should be the target for such funds, the *Philadelphia Tribune* predicted that because the neighborhood represented "the mathematical center of the very worse housing in the city of Philadelphia it is more likely that most of the 40-block clearance will take place in this area." With Kelly as mayor, many black leaders were convinced that Black Seventh Warders would finally receive the attention they desperately needed.[33]

Although Newman expected that Fauset and Wright would be invigorated by such an announcement, neither gravitated to his idea of building affordable housing for the city's black population. This was due in part to the fact that Fauset and Wright came to the advisory committee with their own political ends in mind. Fauset sought to solidify her potential as a possible state representative in an upcoming election and bolster black support of the local Democratic Party, while Wright, who was much older, used the position to try to give new life to his waning public image. Additionally, Wright and Fauset were cautious about aggressively pursuing ideas of housing reform as Newman conceptualized it, as Newman's ideas were predicated upon an assumption that Wilson would not win the mayoral election.

Given the track record of the Republican response to housing over the years, Fauset and Wright were ambivalent and in turn seemed ineffective. Newman, disappointed with Fauset and Wright, pressed on with his mission to develop new housing. He set his sights on the old Glenwood cemetery, located in North Philadelphia on 25th Street between Glenwood and Ridge Avenues, and sent Fauset and Wright to evaluate its potential as possible sight for a new housing project. Although Fauset and Wright did go out to look at the site, their lack of interest in the advisory committee led to little discussion about the Glenwood site. By 1936, the advisory committee was seen by black and white Philadelphians as a failure, merely a symbolic organization and not one of action or reform as Newman had promised.[34]

In the end, the CDCP and many progressive black Philadelphians rallied behind Kelly and the CRC, and more conservative black Philadelphians supported Wilson. Although Kelly received significant black support in his bid to be mayor of Philadelphia, Republican Samuel Davis Wilson won in November of 1935. Though Wilson was triumphant, Kelly's tremendous black support signaled to him and other leading Republicans that housing reform was emerging as one of the most critical political issues in the city, especially among its black population. With the failure of the advisory committee and the defeat of Jack Kelly, it seemed housing reform in Philadelphia was at a standstill. Even though it had become a key issue, actual reform had not yet seen the light of day, and Black Seventh Warders continued to suffer in overcrowded, dilapidated, and unsafe housing.[35]

In sum, the persistence of housing problems and differing rhetoric used by black Philadelphians around housing issues, reveals that housing, even among blacks, was a cross-cutting issue, circumscribed and defined by intraracial divisions. Reminiscent of the process of *secondary marginalization*, to prevent any discontent among white Republican officials, some black elites and leaders backed away from housing concerns by accentuating supposed intraracial cultural and regional difference to temper any uprising among black residents. Such framing reverberated throughout the city. In this case, dissension around housing facilitated the rise of the Democratic Party in Philadelphia and shifted the allegiance many black Philadelphians had to the Republican Party.

With the shift in opinion toward compelling local, state, and federal officials to redress black housing conditions, competing black attitudes around housing helped provide the conditions for the subsequent rise in the importance of the Democratic Party, and even provided some of the means that would later be used to address housing issues in the form of ten million dollars of federal funding. Having provided the context preceding the tenement collapse, I now turn to a discussion of the sociopolitical history of the Black Seventh Ward in the wake of the tenement collapse. Following this discussion, I will elaborate upon the impact of the actions and attitudes of black Philadelphians following the collapse.

A New Deal for Housing Reform: The Politics of the Tenement Collapse and the Rise of Racialized Housing in Philadelphia

On Sunday December 20, 1936, Fauset, heading a committee of black Philadelphians who sought to investigate the collapse of 517–519 South 15th Street, toured the site. Inviting leading Democratic figure Kelly along, Fauset and her committee made sure to ask neighbors and former residents about the condition of the building prior to the collapse, inquiring into the landlord's malfeasance. During their tour of the site, it became clear to Fauset and Kelly that the collapse was avoidable and the result of years of neglect by black and white Republican leadership. Kelly, reflecting on his tour of the site, asserted: "This catastrophe is plainly due to the neglect of some city department...where human lives are endangered the safety of human lives takes precedence over property rights."

Both Kelly and Fauset argued that the progressive politics of the New Deal were the appropriate alternative to years of Republican inaction on the issue of housing. Fauset, in an editorial for the black newspaper the *Philadelphia Independent*, argued:

> Time after time, these housing needs have been pointed out to us. Several years ago, [the Committee on Negro Migration (1924) and the Philadelphia Housing Association (1927)] surveyed these places and reported that something need to be done, and be done quickly...but the houses crashed and killed several women and little children. What does this mean for all of us? It means that we women who make the homes of the land, who revere the home, must act as well as merely observe or voice an opinion. Once sensing a situation, we must not wait on others to meet the need, whether they be officials or other [black] people...we must pitch in and compel action.

Whereas Kelly's message sought to compel white officials into action, Fauset took to the black press to ignite a powerful black response, particularly calling on black women to rally for housing reform. Both Kelly's and Fauset's comments targeted old leadership and held Mayor Wilson culpable, and they foreshadowed a renewed focus on housing reform—one which would rely on the combined efforts of black residents and concerned white leaders.[36]

Fauset's commentary, in particular, is significant for several reasons. First, her comments are representative of the gendered politics and rhetoric that precipitated the rise of black female-led groups and activism targeting domestic issues such as housing after World War II, recently described by historian Lisa Levenstein.[37] Second, her use of the tenement collapse to forge a collective black narrative is illustrative of the manner in which previously contentious or cross-cutting issues are reframed to express a collective black reality. In this case, for instance, we find in Fauset's commentary an absence of place. That is, we find no mention of the Black Seventh Ward. In this way, by removing place from her discussion of housing, Fauset, like other black leaders at the time, reconfigured the existing narrative of black housing from earlier years by using the tenement collapse to compel local, state, and federal officials to redress black housing. Positing housing reform as a consensus issue, Fauset's commentary is representative of the ways in which ties among black neighborhoods and residents are played up or downplayed for particular political ends.

Crystal Bird Fauset, however, was not alone in her call to redress poor housing conditions following the Spease family deaths. Just a few days after the collapse and the printing of Fauset's commentary, Philadelphia newspapers were flooded with letters from concerned citizens across the city:

> This is a very serious situation for the City of Philadelphia. To let things like this exist is criminal. These houses have been condemned and the responsibility rests upon the City officials. The fault lies in the fact that the tenement house business has not been properly regulated. Some drastic new arrangements should be put in force. The newspapers can render a valuable service by bringing this situation to the attention of the public. (Richard A. Cooper, 1732 Christian Street)

> The collapsing of the buildings…show[s] strong indication of the need of careful inspection of the dwellings of which the poorer classes of colored people are compelled to occupy. There should be in Philadelphia, the demolition of such structures and at the same time, City officials should see that proper arrangements are made for the kinds of dwellings that human beings are living in. (Robert J. Nelson, 1214 N. 57th Street)

> Just such a catastrophe as has happened was predicted by me and my late wife, Madeline B. Rainey, over a year ago. Both of us were vitally interested in housing problems, my wife serving as head of a city-wide housing group prior to her death. However, in the face of this terrible calamity I would like to point to the necessity of persons or agencies forgetting political capital, working together toward a common end. In the past, whenever housing problems have arisen various political

factions have disagreed concerning where a definite housing project should be located. I don't think we should tolerate such pettiness from now on. (Joseph H. Rainey, state athletic commissioner)

Upon hearing of this terrible disaster, I feel that it was a terrible thing to befall our people at this time. Something should be done by the city to compensate these people in some way or other. If needed, I will do all I can to help in the burial of unfortunates who were trapped. (William Allmond Jr., Democratic member of state legislature, 17th and Christian Street)

The condition of the building is the condition of many others in the same neighborhood. The responsibility lies upon the inspectors of the city. A few years back a careful survey was made, in which I took part, in order to condemn these houses which were unfit. Our newspapers wrote of it and pictures of these houses were published. People are permitted to live in these houses in order that the owners may collect rent, someone should be responsible for these slums. (Walter K. Jackson, 1743 Christian Street)

The occurrence itself was deplorable. The action of authorities in taking steps could have prevented such a thing. No one who has been interested in the housing conditions of this city should be surprised at this disaster. If action is neglected, we may look forward to a series of similar occurrences. Condemning houses is a minor action, the demolition of these houses should be the major action. (Wayne Hopkins, Armstrong Association of Philadelphia)

This tragedy ought to serve to arouse the people of Philadelphia to action in the interest of better housing. It is a serious reflection on the law enforcement body of our city. It constitutes a challenge to the coming session of the Legislature, which I am quite sure it will meet. At the last session of the legislature, a bill for adequate housing was passed by the Democratic controlled House of Representatives, but it was killed in the Republican controlled Senate. With both Houses Democratic, in the new legislature, the people have a right to expect and get proper relief. (Rev. Marshall Shepard, Member of State Legislature)[38]

These letters reveal several themes that emerged from the collapse for citizens, leaders, and organizations, including the development of a housing authority, holding city officials accountable, and condemning and/or demolishing uninhabitable properties in the Black Seventh Ward. In each of the comments the themes are asserted as possible panaceas to prevent future disasters. As evidenced by the commentary above, the Democratic Party was also situated as a key solution to the housing problems as was slum clearance.

Sitting Republican mayor Wilson, however, needed little prodding. He too was outraged. While touring the site (see Figure 3.5), Wilson determined three actions were necessary: (1) arresting and charging Samson, the landlord, with homicide: (2) razing the slums of the Black Seventh Ward; and (3) building new housing. Wilson personally handled Samson's arrest and bail hearing, publicly announced his disapproval of the treatment of countless Black Seventh Warders, and created a mayoral housing commission overnight. Having charged Detective Richard Anderson, a black Philadelphia police officer, with the investigation into the collapse, Wilson soon discovered that Samson also managed two other properties in the Black Seventh Ward; much like 517–519 S. 15th Street, these properties were also in a dangerous state of disrepair. Detective Anderson's investigation led Wilson to serve as magistrate for the case against Samson and issue a bail of $10,000 ($157,000 in 2010). For his part, Samson adamantly denied any guilt or responsibility for the collapse.[39]

Wilson seemed determined to combat the decline of black neighborhoods with an unprecedented focus on slum clearance and housing reform. Commenting on the disaster, he confessed that Black Seventh Warders "can't live the way they are now...it is impossible for humans to live in the squalor I saw this morning." This confession by Wilson was quite a departure from Mayor Moore's contention just four years earlier that there were no slums in Philadelphia.[40]

Within a week of the tenement collapse, Wilson had already begun to raze dilapidated housing near the site of the collapse. Using the ten million dollars given to Philadelphia due to the earlier writing campaign of black Philadelphians, Wilson quickly took to the Black Seventh Ward, removing residents from properties and placing "Condemned, Unfit for Habitation" signs on the condemned properties. Despite Wilson's intentions, such actions appeared to many as an additional attack on Black Seventh Warders. In response, Black Seventh Warders took to the streets, openly protesting the actions of the mayor, black leadership, and housing conditions in the neighborhood. Furious with Wilson's lack of planning, residents asserted that the mayor had no plan for rehousing displaced residents, and was instead more focused on the superficial aspect of the problem, expending his energies solely on removing properties that looked bad.

FIGURE 3.5 Mayor S. Davis Wilson (right), photographed as he toured the site of the tenement collapse. Temple University Libraries, SCRC, Philadelphia, PA.

In response, Barnes and Wilson suggested housing displaced Black Seventh Warders in a local armory, to which residents angrily responded. One group of tenants argued: "They still haven't told us where we can move…we positively will not live like pigs in an armory. If they want us out of here they'll have to come and drag us out." Another resident of the Black Seventh Ward, a young black women, asserted: "we have a right to a home…we have household furnishings, children and pets. What would we do with them in an armory?" The response of Black Seventh Warders intimidated Wilson, and he soon changed his policy on slum clearance. Subsequently, Wilson allowed police to condemn properties but decided against evicting residents, instructing police that they were not allowed to force residents out of their homes.[41]

Wilson's response signaled a victory for Black Seventh Warders. By actively voicing their concerns and protesting in the streets, black residents managed to shift the mayor's approach to fixing their housing problems. Much like the letter-writing campaign a year earlier, initial protests of Black Seventh Warders were spontaneous events. Differing from conventional wisdom regarding black protests and resistance, in this case these protests were spontaneous acts of resistance that then spawned organizations to maintain pressure. This relationship between black protests and the subsequent development of organizations to sustain political resistance echoes the divide in political approaches foreshadowed by the tenuous appointments of Fauset and Wright to the HADV's advisory committee, and Norris's emphasis on infrapolitics. Whereas established black leaders relied on organizations such as the CRC to rally and organize residents, in the wake of the tenement collapse newer organizations depended upon the success of spontaneous protests of black residents and the dissent of working-class and poor blacks.

Black residents capitalized on this victory by forming and enhancing two groups that would play a significant role in housing reform policy, the Tenants League and the Philadelphia affiliate of the National Negro Congress (NNC). As historian James Wolfinger notes in *Philadelphia Divided: Race and Politics in the City of Philadelphia*, the Tenants League, led by executive secretary Bernard Childs, became one of the most powerful voices of housing reform for black Philadelphians especially in the late 1930s. The Tenants League, which drew support from the Workers' Alliance, the Armstrong Association, and the Communist Party's International Labor, utilized the emergent interracial alliance to push conservatives and Republican leaders to act with urgency and produce results immediately.

The NNC echoed the Tenants League's call to action. Led by Fauset along with her husband, Arthur Huff Fauset, the Philadelphia branch of the NNC often provided venues for the Tenants League to voice their concerns and directives. In his capacity as leader of the Philadelphia branch of the NNC, Fauset seized on the collapse to propose institutional changes with respect to black housing in Philadelphia:

> The National Negro Congress has repeatedly pointed out the need of slum clearance and decent housing conditions for Negroes in the city of Philadelphia. Delegates have been sent to Washington, to the Philadelphia Housing Committee and to Mayor Wilson, urging speedy drastic action. The National Negro Congress again points out to the citizens of Philadelphia the need of pressing for the following, immediately: 1. Legislation [to create a] housing authority by the city. 2. Appropriation of at least $10,000,000 for slum clearance in Negro areas in Philadelphia. 3. Rigid inspection—physical and sanitary, of all housing in Philadelphia. 4. Immediate demolition of untenable houses in Philadelphia. 5. Rigid sanitary and inspection codes, rigidly applied. The National Negro Congress is calling a Legislative Conference

Saturday, January 16, 1937, at the Y.W.C.A., at which time plans will be matured for a thorough legislative program on housing. Delegates from all organizations are urged to attend.[42]

In this way, then, black citizens and housing advocates facilitated the development of housing bureaucracies in Philadelphia. During much of 1937, as Fauset promised, the NNC held rallies that often ended with memorials for victims of the tenement collapse. Deploying the memory of the Spease family and others who were affected the by tenement collapse, the NNC sought to ignite working-class blacks using housing reform as a means of generating a new generation of black political leadership that would be rooted in the Democratic Party.[43]

While attempts were made by the police to disrupt the influence of the Tenants League, the organization, in concert with the NNC, remained influential with large memberships. Further, the response of black residents forced Wilson to consider broader policies on housing reform. Realizing the scope of the problem and the need for a formal city entity to supervise housing reform, city officials under Wilson's leadership formed the Philadelphia Housing Authority (PHA). The PHA, created in August 1937, was charged with the mission of clearing, reconstructing, and replanning "the areas in which slums exist" and of providing "safe and sanitary dwelling accommodations for persons of low income." A board of five unpaid members, James McDevitt, Roland Randall, Frank Smith, Joseph Greenberg, and W. Harry Barnes, headed the PHA; Mayor Wilson personally selected both Greenberg and Barnes. Barnes's appointment, in particular, signaled Wilson's commitment to black interests in housing reform. Barnes, a prominent black physician and Republican leader, also took time to speak at gatherings, to assure black residents that providing housing for Black Seventh Warders and other low-income black Philadelphians was the PHA's top priority. The funding for the PHA came from the Wagner-Steagall Act. The Wagner-Steagall Act, passed in 1937, was the federal law that created the United States Housing Administration (USHA) and contained a provision for low-interest loans that local authorities could use to cover up to ninety percent of costs associated with slum clearance and building housing projects.

That same year, the trial of Abraham Samson was under way. Raymond Blackwell, who had complained to Samson just hours before the collapse, and his cousin Alberta Richardson testified at the trail. Like Blackwell, Richardson testified that she had complained to Samson on numerous occasions but had been rebuffed by the landlord: "[Samson] would pat me on the back and say he would do something about it." Recounting the moments before the collapse occurred Richardson offered:

> We had a late supper and I was getting ready to give the children their bath, when I heard the walls cracking in the front room. Seeing that the house was getting ready to fall down I picked up my youngest child and was reaching for the other one, and that is all I remember until I woke up in the hospital... The saddest part of it all was that my cousin, Hattie Buoy, who was killed, had come to visit me and after we had put the children to bed we were going out to do some shopping... I noticed a week ago that plaster was falling from the walls and I had planned to move right after Christmas. Now I don't know what I will do as everything has been lost.[44]

In addition to Richardson's and Blackwell's testimonies, two affidavits from victims unable to leave hospital were also read aloud at the trial. Testimony from those visiting loved ones the night of collapse also affirmed Richardson's account, such as comments from William Taylor (age twenty-nine), who was with his girlfriend at the time:

> I had noticed the walls cracking before when I was in the house. But this time when I mentioned that the building was going to fall I hardly gotten the words out of my mouth when the floor fell from under us and all the walls started falling... While I was under the wreckage I saw the bed had caught on fire and was burning me so I pushed my way out and then helped Mrs. Jones out.

Samson was found guilty on June 23, 1937, of multiple counts of involuntary manslaughter, one for each death resulting from the collapse. Samson, in his testimony, blamed Frederic C. Wheeler, vice president of real estate for the Fidelity-Philadelphia Trust Company, from whom he had leased the dilapidated properties. Wheeler, however, was found not guilty and Samson was immediately jailed for defaulting on his $50,000 ($787,000 in 2010) bail pending a new trial.[45]

Meanwhile, by 1938, the USHA had approved twenty million dollars for Philadelphia, with which the PHA was to build upwards of fifty thousand homes over the next five years. The PHA, however, would never reach that level of construction and development.[46] There was an issue with the funds the PHA received from the USHA; the Wagner-Steagall Act made it difficult to build new housing on clearance sites located in densely populated areas, containing as it did a provision that limited the costs per square foot for areas used to build new housing. Given the costs associated with clearing occupied land, already vacant or abandoned areas emerged as ideal locations. Board members, along with Newman, who was often invited to planning meetings, debated the location of a housing project for displaced blacks.

Walter Thomas, an official on the City Planning Commission, made a pivotal suggestion that would influence the framework within which public housing in Philadelphia would be built; Thomas suggested to the board that the housing project be built in an area already heavily black. Thomas suggested the North Philadelphia area would be ideal, as the area had become predominantly black over the last twenty years. In his estimation, designating particular areas for blacks would solidify a place for black people in the city to live and would also "have a wholesome effect on" the property values of whites.

Taking up Thomas's suggestion, the PHA developed an informal rule that the housing projects built should reflect the "prevailing racial composition of the surrounding neighborhood." This racial formula for public housing construction is significant in that it foreshadows a similar custom used by the PWA in later years. The formula for housing construction advocated by the PHA is similar to that employed by myriad cities in the postwar period. As scholar Roger Biles demonstrates in his analysis of postwar housing policy, city housing agencies such as the Chicago Housing Authority also built public housing with a focus on preserving the racial composition of neighborhoods slated as sites of housing construction.[47] Also known as the "neighborhood composition rule," the racial formula used by the PHA anticipates similar racially motivated public housing policies adopted in cities throughout the United States.[48] Here, then, housing reform in Philadelphia should be read as in conversation with larger national patterns, and it should also be instructive for thinking about why and how racialized housing manifested itself in the United States.

Newman, having worked to build a housing project for many years, brushed the dust off his previous plans for the no-longer-used Glenwood cemetery and passed them along to board members who quickly approved the location. The Glenwood cemetery was seen as an ideal location as it met both the criteria of low-use space and the informal rule of preserving the racial composition of the targeted area. As the PHA was deciding how to use the federal funds, remaining Black Seventh Warders were beginning to migrate into other parts of the city. In response, on the one-year anniversary of the collapse black residents held a meeting at the Wesley AMEZ Church at 15th and Lombard Streets, a block from the tragic site. The meeting featured representatives from citywide organizations and Black Seventh Warders immediately began to voice their concerns. Reverend C. A. Roach, rector of the black St. Peter's Claver Catholic Church, warned residents against the "political ballyhoo and political bluffs" that city leadership often employed, and argued: "We don't want Mayor Wilson going through the streets telling what he's going to do. Nothing has been done since these buildings collapsed, carrying to their deaths 7 persons. Now we want some thing done." The audience shouted in agreement.

Others added to Roach's comments, namely labor leader E. Washington Rhodes, who suggested that black Philadelphians continue to challenge Mayor Wilson and other leaders calling for black residents to "test the white man's sincerity."[49]

Much like many of the formal and informal gatherings of black residents and leaders following the tenement collapse, in this meeting black Philadelphians called for tangible outcomes and they centered conditions that caused the collapse (such as price-gouging, discrimination, inadequate plumbing/construction, and general landlord malfeasance) as emblematic of a larger issue that united black Philadelphians. This meeting is also important because it is representative of how black Philadelphians spoke about housing reform. In many of these gatherings, the site of the collapse, the Black Seventh Ward, was not situated as a direct beneficiary of housing reform efforts such as the construction of affordable housing. Instead, as shown in this meeting, the tenement collapse was operationalized as a collective narrative and consensus issue, legitimating calls for housing reform by black residents in areas outside of the Black Seventh Ward.[50]

Reverend Roach's claim that nothing had been done was not unfounded. By 1938, nearly two years after the tenement collapse, Black Seventh Warders had still not seen actual changes in the housing stock in the neighborhood or their residences. Even though for some, this posed a significant problem, most were hopeful due to the promise that the new housing would be primarily for black Philadelphians. Reports by the HADV, the PHA, and local newspapers suggested that the potential for new housing in North Philadelphia had prompted many black residents to move into the area, while others moved a few blocks south of the Black Seventh Ward, joining the growing ranks of the black population in the neighboring Thirtieth Ward. In these reports, many black residents cited the continued neglect of white landlords in the Black Seventh Ward as a central factor that contributed to their secondary migration.

Such neglect was a clear product of the combined responses of Wilson and black-led housing advocacy groups. Wilson's response, the Tenants League, and the NNC made landlords uneasy and angry, often feeling unjustifiably targeted as the sole culprits. As a result, many landlords were cruel to residents, continuing to leave residences in disrepair; it appeared that following the tenement collapse, many landlords cared even less about the quality of the existing housing. Letting the disrepair continue, many land-lords sought to sell the property and distance themselves from the Black Seventh Ward and the tenement collapse altogether. The response of Black Seventh Warders, to move out, had serious implications for the cultural and sociopolitical viability of the Black Seventh Ward.[51]

As residents continued to move out of the Black Seventh Ward, cultural and political institutions began to experience crises in their finances and their memberships. Although black residents had from 1920 to 1939 migrated out of the neighborhood into areas in South, West, and North Philadelphia, the dense population that remained provided key resources to black institutions that helped preserve the cultural and sociopolitical prominence of the Black Seventh Ward. In fact, though black residents had migrated to other parts of the city, many still received their goods and services from and were members of institutions in the Black Seventh Ward. These institutions included Mother Bethel AME Church, St. Thomas PE Church, Wesley AMEZ Church, the CRC, the Frederick Douglass Memorial Hospital, the Durham Normal School, the *Philadelphia Tribune*, and the headquarters of many of the lodges and social clubs for blacks in Philadelphia. Yet, in the wake of the tenement collapse these institutions watched their memberships and attendance dwindle, and their finances become nearly depleted. In 1938, key Republican and Democratic leaders in the Black Seventh Ward experienced huge political loses. While a diminished CRC hoped the reelection of Henry would invigorate black conservatives and Republicans in the city to reestablish ties with the orga-nization, black Democratic leader and one of the founders of the CDCP, Austin Norris, was ousted as the Black Seventh Ward's representative on the City Democratic Executive Committee. Norris had been the only black person on the committee, and his exit meant black Philadelphians no longer had direct representation on the committee, a problem that would have lasting effects.

The turn of events for St. Thomas African Episcopal Church (see Figure 3.6) following the tenement collapse perhaps best reveals the latent implications of the battle for housing reform that ensued following the Spease family deaths. Founded in 1793 by black reverend and leader Absalom Jones, St. Thomas had been a key institution in black Philadelphia from its inception. Following the collapse the institution, like others, fell on hard times. With many black Philadelphians refusing to come to the impoverished Black Seventh Ward, and residents moving to other areas, St. Thomas was without

FIGURE 3.6 A Sunday Morning View of the African Episcopal Church of St. Thomas in Philadelphia—taken in June 1829.
Source: Balch Institute, Historical Society of Pennsylvania.

the robust membership it had come to expect. As mortgages began to mount, the foreclosure of the church loomed. Congregants and church leadership searched for ways to deal with this problem. Unable to rely on the financial stability a larger congregation once afforded, members and church leaders decided that a move to West Philadelphia would be in the church's best interests.

West Philadelphia, had over the first thirty years of the twentieth century, become the premiere destination for middle-class blacks as they migrated within Philadelphia, and many of those families and individuals formed the basis of St. Thomas's congregation during its heyday. In the end, the building near the Black Seventh Ward, located at 12th and Walnut Streets, was sold to cover outstanding debts, and the church joined with a newer one in West Philadelphia, the Church of the Beloved Disciple at 57th and Vine Streets. Holding its first combined service in June of 1938, St. Thomas bid farewell to its home just a few blocks north of the Black Seventh Ward.[52]

Although many were saddened by the move, Reverend Robert L. Bagnall, rector for St. Thomas, assured congregants the move was in the church's best interests, commenting: "I believe that the steps taken in this direction will give this, the oldest Negro church organization in America, an opportunity to build a larger, strong and useful parish among the 70,000 colored people of West Philadelphia.... The church at 12th and Walnut streets was removed from its congregation and had no community in which it could effectively work." St. Thomas was not alone in its struggle as a historic black institution rooted in and near the Black Seventh Ward, as Frederick Douglass Memorial Hospital (see Figure 3.7), experiencing similar financial woes, joined with Mercy Hospital in West Philadelphia by the early 1940s. Here, as in the case of the Phyllis Wheatley Community Centre, a black cultural institution was forsaken in an effort to address what appeared to be a larger black issue.[53]

Ultimately, the decline of key institutions in the Black Seventh Ward received little attention from city officials and much of the black leadership. The focus instead was on the provisions for public housing and the location of new construction. Such news came in May of 1938. The PHA had decided to

FIGURE 3.7 Frederick Douglass Memorial Hospital (*c.* 1930).
Source: The African American Museum in Pennsylvania.

build a new housing project on the Glenwood cemetery, and assured black Philadelphians that the new homes would primarily house low-income black families. Choosing to name the new project the James Weldon Johnson Homes (see Figure 3.9), after the noted black activist, the PHA's choice received overwhelming approval from blacks and whites alike. The ground-breaking of the Johnson Homes was a cultural event. Local black musicians provided entertainment as thousands of black Philadelphians celebrated the construction of the new housing project. Many brought completed applications with them, as others sought out Barnes and other officials for housing applications inquiring about the requirements the PHA imposed for those interested in living in the homes.

During the groundbreaking ceremony, PHA officials announced that two more housing projects would be built as well. The second housing project would also be in North Philadelphia and would primarily house low-income black families. It would be called the Richard Allen Homes, named for the historic black activist and minister who founded the African Methodist Episcopal denomination and Mother Bethel AME church in the Black Seventh Ward. The third project, named the Tasker Homes, would be located in the primarily white area in South Philadelphia near 28th and Tasker Streets, and primarily house low-income white families. These announcements represented real success in the battle for housing reform. In fact, the PHA's race-based housing policy and approach was favored by blacks and received little opposition from white Philadelphians. By the end of 1940, the Johnson Homes were completely occupied, and in February of 1940 the PHA broke ground for the Allen Homes.[54]

When applications for the Allen Homes began to come in, the PHA quickly assigned families and soon the project was completely occupied. Rejected black families were upset, and began to send applications in to the PHA for occupancy in the Tasker Homes that had been designated as primarily for white families. When the black families were rejected, they sought help from the Tenants League and the NAACP, who were able to accomplish little. As a result, many low-income black families in need of affordable public housing continued to live with relatives and friends in overcrowded living arrangements. PHA officials denied charges of discrimination and reminded black residents of their commitment to supporting black families, namely the Johnson and soon-to-be-completed Allen Homes. The officials and some black leaders, such as PHA official Barnes, pushed for many to wait for other housing, as pressing the PHA to shift the racial dynamic of the Tasker Homes could potentially backfire and lead to the Johnson and Allen Homes changing from predominantly black housing projects. As a result, little debate occurred among black Philadelphians and legal disputes were resolved in favor of the PHA's approach. However, when the PHA decided to turn over the Allen Homes to the Defense Housing Administration, the backlash from black residents, leaders, and activists was tremendous.

The Last Battle: The Allen Homes and Housing Reform

Seeking to garner more federal money for its shrinking budget, in late 1941 the PHA decided almost overnight to give the Allen Homes to the Defense Housing Administration. The Defense Housing Administration, charged with providing affordable housing to war workers, had been struggling to find appropriate housing sites in Philadelphia. Unable to broker the construction of sites because of the work of the PHA, the Defense Housing Administration could not make use of the federal funds budgeted to fully house all war workers in Philadelphia. By 1940, the PHA, aware of this struggle, sought to exchange the Allen Homes, which had been assigned to low-income black families, for a portion of the Defense Housing Administration's federal funds. Black residents, especially those who had been assigned to the Allen Homes, openly disapproved the actions of the PHA and Defense Housing Administration. Citing the PHA's actions as a violation of an agreement with black Philadelphians, black leadership rallied constituents across class and neighborhoods to compel the PHA to follow through on its promise to make the Allen Homes a predominantly black low-income housing project.[55]

Black leadership along with black press encouraged black residents to openly protest and even suggested that all blacks put in applications for a residence in the Allen Homes. It was also suggested that black Philadelphians should solidify their place in North Philadelphia by moving in large numbers into the area surrounding the Allen Homes. Local mainstream press was outraged too. The *Philadelphia Inquirer* and the *Evening Bulletin* ran opinion columns on the issue often emphasizing the promise of the city to the victims of the tenement collapse. These homes were created to "rid the city of a squalid slum district and to give the evicted families and other low income groups decent living accommodations at a small cost...the latter objective now goes up in smoke. The poor are turned away. Others are to get their promised homes," one columnist wrote in the *Philadelphia Inquirer*.[56]

Black residents across class and political lines took once again to a writing campaign, targeting President Roosevelt with their calls to action. In a letter to the president, composed by a committee consisting of leading reverends E. Luther Cunningham and Marshall L. Shepard, along with influential black attorney Raymond Pace Alexander, black leaders made clear their position and the issues surrounding the Allen Homes:

> We, the undersigned, representatives of the quarter million Negro residents of Philadelphia, make this appeal in behalf of the low income group of people for whom the Richard Allen Homes Project in Philadelphia was planned, intended and constructed. We share the growing fear of this entire city as expressed by the unanimity of the daily and weekly press in this area, and insist that you, Sir, take immediate cognizance of the fact that the United States Housing Authority has diverted the use of these homes from their original purposes at the expense of the low income group, who are least able to obtain decent housing even in normal times and not able at all in these times. We urge you to act in the interest of these persons who cannot obtain decent housing within their capability to pay. This is equally a defense measure, which will sustain and insure the morale of a large percentage of the citizens of our country. We pray your deepest consideration to this plea and your early action and reply.[57]

In February of 1942, the official announcement was made that the United States Housing Administration agreed with black Philadelphia residents; thus making efforts to preserve the Allen Homes as housing for low-income black families a success.

That same month the Edwards family (see Figure 3.8) became the first family to move into the new Allen Homes. More than 5,000 other black residents joined the Edwards family, and, with that, all of the units in the Allen Homes were occupied (see Figure 3.10). As the moving of black residents into the Allen Homes came to an end, so too did the era of housing reform born out of the tenement collapse, as a new conservative agenda took over. Led by Republican Robert Lamberton, who had been elected as mayor in the fall of 1939, the city quickly abandoned the progressive housing reform of the New Deal era. Returning to the dismissive rhetoric espoused by Wilson a decade earlier, Lamberton denounced the public housing program, asserting, "Slum areas exist...because some people are so utterly shiftless that any place they live becomes a slum." While some blacks protested Lamberton's position, many likely decided that such confrontation would end in the evisceration of existing housing and chose to remain silent; thus the New Deal era of housing

FIGURE 3.8 The Edwards Family moving into the Richard Allen Homes in 1942.
Source: Temple University Libraries, SCRC, Philadelphia, PA.

for black Philadelphians faltered and ultimately ended. Tenant League leader Bernard Childs's observation best characterized this shift in progressive housing reform: "The period of agitation when everyone was concerned about housing is over…and apathy has set in." Childs's observation was correct, as housing reform efforts in the postwar years would not operate with the same political fervor and urgency as that which characterized the period following the tenement collapse.[58]

The Beginning of the End for the Black Seventh Ward?

In the wake of the tenement collapse we see population and institutional shifts in the Black Seventh Ward. In this case, black residents and indigenous institutions shifted to other black areas of the city as a consequence of public housing construction. Such secondary migration, or within-city migration, led to a shift in the city's racial geography and the institutional makeup of black Philadelphia. In an effort to maximize their portion of the limited resource of public housing, black Philadelphians quietly consented to the racial formula employed by housing officials. In times when there was dissent among black Philadelphians, black leaders actively worked to address the intraracial friction to preserve the status quo.

FIGURES 3.9 AND 3.10 Both the James Weldon Johnson Homes (top) and the Richard Allen Homes (bottom) were well received by black Philadelphians. By 1942, black residents had fully occupied both housing projects. Temple University Libraries, SCRC, Philadelphia, PA.

When the shift in the status quo was seen to negatively impact black Philadelphians, black residents and leaders implored federal intervention on their behalf to preserve their piece of the public housing pie as it had been originally promised by PHA officials. In this way, black Philadelphians mobilized to hold local officials accountable for their promises to working-class and poor black families in Philadelphia. However, by framing black housing concerns amplified by the tenement collapse in a general way, black Philadelphians deemphasized the Black Seventh Ward and facilitated the

FIGURES 3.9 AND 3.10 Continued

appropriation and relocation of cultural symbols such as Richard Allen and James Weldon Johnson Homes to emergent black neighborhoods elsewhere in the city.

Although the tragic death of the Spease family, the overcrowding, and the dilapidated housing that sparked such housing reform were rooted in the Black Seventh Ward, the approach black leaders and residents took emphasized the issue of housing and not the place in which the tenement collapse occurred. In other words, the framework within which black Philadelphians operated to compel state and federal intervention to address housing reform was not a ward-specific or place-based argument, and as such did not hold officials accountable for rebuilding and sustaining the Black Seventh Ward; thus it facilitated the racial organization of public housing in Philadelphia. While at a cursory level having city officials cater specifically to the housing needs of black families gave way to new housing opportunities, the choice to build new housing in North Philadelphia as opposed to the Black Seventh Ward shifted the black population culturally, politically, and socially, as evidenced by the relocation of prominent black institutions such as St. Thomas Church and the Frederick Douglass Memorial Hospital.

The trajectory of housing reform in Philadelphia shows the importance of the intraracial politics and choices made over time by Black Seventh Warders. The tragedy of the tenement collapse forged a series of powerful black responses that critically shaped the manifestation of housing reform in Philadelphia, and altered patterns of secondary migration by black and white residents. To be sure, compelling the conservative leadership that controlled Philadelphia to utilize federal funds in order to intervene on behalf of low-income and poor blacks was a significant accomplishment, and one that would have been virtually unthinkable during the 1920s.

Despite the successes of the New Deal era for black progressivism, there were serious costs. Much of these costs began and ended with the Black Seventh Ward. In their quest for housing reform, black Philadelphians inadvertently participated in a process by which the Black Seventh Ward was gradually depoliticized. Black residents actively participated in the race-based public housing program informally advocated by the PHA. With the departure of such institutions, those black residents who remained in the Black Seventh Ward became more isolated, even as the black population was beginning to extend its presence across Philadelphia.

An examination of the sociopolitical history of the Black Seventh Ward and its place in the fight for housing reform in the New Deal era provides an opportunity to analyze and understand the interdependent relationship between neighborhoods within local black politics. Most often, urban black neighborhoods are examined and understood as distinct densely populated areas of a given city. This case, however, reveals a more complicated picture. The tragedy of the tenement collapse politicized the Black Seventh Ward in ways that detracted from other black neighborhoods in the city. Situated as the principal site of overcrowding and poor housing, attention to the Black Seventh Ward prior to the collapse overshadowed the fact that such a problem transcended most all black neighborhoods in Philadelphia at the time. As the housing reform battle ensued, however, black protestors and leaders began to mobilize the narrative of the tenement collapse by separating the tragedy from the neighborhood in which it occurred to achieve their political ends.

By the time that the Johnson Homes and Allen Homes were occupied, it did not matter where the tragic event that provided the impetus for building public housing had occurred. Essentially, when black leaders and residents removed place from their discussion of housing reform, soon the neighborhood itself faded from public memory. As a result, the residents, the organizations, the social clubs, the churches, the markets, and the hospitals of the Black Seventh Ward never directly benefited from the funds and construction that resulted from housing reform. As the city entered into the postwar period, urban renewal efforts further threatened the preservation of the Black Seventh Ward. With a shrinking black population and the flight of key businesses and organizations to North and West Philadelphia, Black Seventh Warders would indeed feel the latent and lasting effects of the sociopolitical decisions blacks made during the New Deal period of housing reform.

Much like the research of urban historians Martha Biondi and Rhonda Y. Williams, this chapter reveals that black residents were not passive recipients or spectators of public housing.[59] However, an important distinction between this research and existing discourse is that this research also suggests that local housing efforts were frustrated and facilitated by events in urban black enclaves and debated among urban black residents. Indeed, this case reveals that black residents actively shaped narratives about shared housing problems and the ways in which local and federal officials should address such issues.

As this chapter demonstrates, changes in and across black neighborhoods were the product of a series of interdependent relationships; the interdependent relationship between the decline of one black neighborhood and the development of another black neighborhood; the interdependent relationship between the deterioration of one black neighborhood and the allocation of resources to another black neighborhood; the interdependent relationship between the marginalization of blacks and the development of race-based policies aimed at mitigating the effects of poverty and urban decay. As a result of the out-migration of residents and resources from the Black Seventh Ward, efforts to protect the shrinking black enclave in the postwar period would rely on the combination of intra- and interracial alliances across neighborhoods in the midst of the bulldozers accompanying urban renewal. In turn, the following chapter engages and analyzes the postwar period in the Black Seventh Ward.

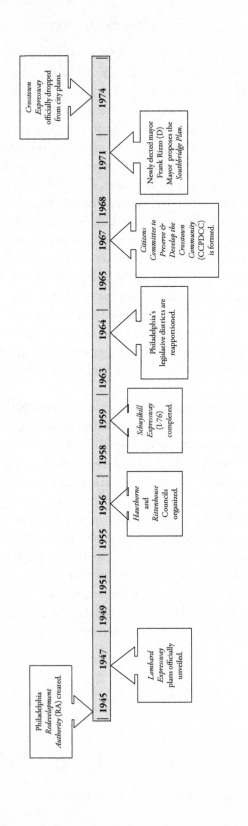

Philadelphia Redevelopment Authority (RA) created.

1945 | 1947 | 1949 | 1951 | 1955 | 1956 | 1958 | 1959 | 1963 | 1964 | 1965 | 1967 | 1968 | 1971 | 1974

Lombard Expressway plans officially unveiled.

Hawthorne and Rittenhouse Councils organized.

Schuylkill Expressway (I-76) completed.

Philadelphia's legislative districts are reapportioned.

Citizens Committee to Preserve & Develop the Crosstown Community (CCPDCC) is formed.

Newly elected mayor Frank Rizzo (D) Mayor proposes the Southbridge Plan.

Crosstown Expressway officially dropped from city plans.

4

Philadelphia's "Mason-Dixon" Line

IN DECEMBER OF 1968, just a year short of its fiftieth anniversary, the Royal
Theatre located at 16th and South Streets was forced to close its doors.
Established in 1919 and black-owned and -operated from its inception, the
Royal Theatre was one of few institutions that featured both theatrical and
movie productions for black audiences. Describing the decay within and
demise of the Royal Theatre, manager Henry "Paul" Lawn was not short on
words: "The floor, by the way, is so soaked with urine that there is no getting
the stench out of the place. The kids also toss lighted cigarettes at each other,
and that screen up there—look at it. It costs $1400 and another $400 to
install. See all those slash marks, the holes, the stains? Now do you understand [why] we've closed?"[1]

Abraham Oritsky, owner of Scotty's Men's Shop at 1449 South Street,
echoed Lawn's sentiments. Highlighting the rising violence in the wake of
such decay in the Lombard/South Street area, Oritsky exclaimed: "The hold-
ups and muggings are what's driving people out of here. The street is going to
look like a ghost town in a prairie soon. I know four or five businesses here
that are planning to get out as soon as they can. And we've all been here for
forty or more years." While clear about the role of looting and violence in the
decline of their businesses, both Lawn and Oritsky believed a bigger scheme
by the local government was truly responsible for the decline of the neighborhood. When asked by *Philadelphia Tribune* reporters, Lawn and Oritsky, as
well as other business owners (white and black) and residents, identified the
city's urban renewal plans as the "vast conspiracy by the city" that led to the
area's decline.[2]

The decline that prompted the Royal Theatre to close its doors was the
result of the city's decison in the late 1940s to build an eight-lane expressway
through the Black Seventh Ward. Referred to initially as the Lombard
Expressway and later as the Crosstown Expressway, the planned highway
was set to replace South Street with an interchange connecting interstate

highways I-95 and I-76, running North–South and East–West respectively. As a result of the proposal to build the Crosstown Expressway, massive disinvestment and abandonment took place across the Seventh Ward. Although the actual Crosstown Expressway was never built, the anticipation of such construction led many to forgo property maintenance and to sell their businesses and properties in the area at wholesale prices. While some residents with means were able to move out of the declining area to neighboring wards, nearly 6,000 black residents were left behind in dilapidated housing with no idea if, when, and where they would have to move.[3] After more than two decades of debate and protest, the Crosstown Expressway was officially jettisoned from Philadelphia's formal urban development plans in 1974.

Using the rise and fall of the Crosstown Expressway as a window into the decades following housing reform, this chapter reveals the unanticipated consequences of urban renewal in Philadelphia, made visible through an examination of the political agency exerted by black Philadelphians during this period of urban (re)development. To analyze the convergence of the political agency of black residents and government intervention, I rely on two interrelated concepts emergent from scholarship on postwar urban America. First, I draw on the work of political economy scholars such as John Logan, Harvey Molotch, and John Mollenkopf on the emergence of "growth coalitions," wherein the interests of civic, corporate, and political leaders overlap significantly, producing an alliance concerned with revitalizing the city through extensive redevelopment and federal involvement aimed at urban America. As Logan and Molotch suggest, such alliances led to urban growth across the United States and relied upon a precarious alliance between competing interest groups.

This postwar marriage of civic, corporate, and political leaders set into motion the period of urban renewal in Philadelphia that envisioned a revitalized Center City as key to local economic prosperity and targeted the seemingly vulnerable Black Seventh Ward. The second concept I rely upon is what historian Arnold Hirsch terms "the second ghetto," or the type of disadvantaged urban minority neighborhoods emergent in the wake of increased government intervention during the postwar period. As I will show, in an effort to shape postwar urbanization in Philadelphia, the Black Seventh Ward, like Chicago's South Side in Hirsh's recent examination, became the site upon which federal and local intervention and the activism of residents converged. In my view these two concepts—growth coalition and second ghetto (while emergent from different disciplines)—complement one another greatly. If we think of the second ghetto as a structural consequence of growth coalitions, then we can more directly gauge the relationship between structural shifts and political agency over time.[4]

In what follows, I examine the social history of the Black Seventh Ward in the postwar period with a focus on the impact of urban renewal in the area. Focusing on the Crosstown Expressway, I analyze the Black Seventh Ward's shift from its days as "Hell's Acre" in the prewar period to the impoverished and abandoned urban neighborhood emergent as a result of urban renewal in the postwar era. I begin by detailing the sociopolitical context that gave rise to urban renewal in Philadelphia, leading to the proposed Crosstown Expressway. In this discussion, I describe the development of the growth coalition in postwar Philadelphia, and its impact on urban renewal plans for the Black Seventh Ward.

After providing the sociopolitical history that gave rise to the Crosstown Expressway, I then detail the debate that ensued. Organized around the mayoral administrations from 1950 to 1974, my discussion reveals a more complicated picture regarding urban renewal and political agency. Just as this struggle against urban renewal was occurring in the Black Seventh Ward, black Philadelphians were participating in the larger civil rights movement by taking to the streets of North and West Philadelphia and calling for changes in education and economic opportunity. Whereas the better-known organizations, such as the Urban League and National Association for the Advancement of Color People (NAACP), loom large in existing discussions of this historical period, I focus on the activism of those in the Black Seventh Ward who sought to bring attention to the issues of urban renewal locally.

In particular, this chapter augments the urban renewal battle not to *discount* the broader civil rights movement, but instead to bring attention to other battles and organizations during this period to demonstrate the layers and limitations of black protest in the city, with especial focus on activism against urban renewal. As historian Robin D. G. Kelley reminds us, "some of the most dynamic struggles take place outside—indeed, sometimes in spite of—established organizations and institutions."[5] As we will find, activism in the Black Seventh Ward relied on new organizations developed with a singular focus on urban renewal, relying on a support network of affluent and ethnic whites.

Here, then, I situate the understudied Crosstown Expressway battle as a part of the larger civil rights and postwar-era struggles of urban black Americans to take control over policies impacting urban life and change. Whereas existing research on urban renewal has privileged "successful" cases such as the redevelopment of Chicago's Lakefront and New York's Lower

East Side and Harlem, I focus on the failed plans to build the Crosstown Expressway to demonstrate the less visible or latent effects of urban renewal and political agency.[6] I argue that an important consequence of urban renewal was that it made neighborhoods inhabited by urban minorities visible and thus targets of government intervention, creating a disincentive for community-based and private (re)development in such neighborhoods.

The Birth of an Expressway

Heading into the postwar period, Philadelphia's black population continued to increase, growing from 219,599 in 1930, to 250,880 in 1940, to 376,041 by 1950. With continued migration into the city by southern black migrants, blacks had established a strong presence in three major areas of the city: South-Central (which included the Black Seventh Ward), West, and North. By 1950, North Philadelphia contained the city's largest black population with 164,801 black residents—due in large part to the recent construction of predominantly black public housing in that district. Two other areas of the city, South-Central and West Philadelphia, accounted for the remaining majorities of Philadelphia's black population with 80,754 and 101,556 respectively. As a result of such population increases and secondary migration of blacks over time, North, West, and South Philadelphia contained eighty-nine percent of total nonwhite households. As the map indicates (see Figure 4.1), by 1950 black Philadelphians were concentrated in a triangular area of the city with a proximal relationship to the city's downtown area.[7]

Just as blacks were concentrated in these areas, so too were the social problems that plagued them, particularly with regard to housing. In fact, surveys conducted by the Philadelphia Housing Authority (PHA) on the quality of the city's housing stock in 1949 found that black households contained the most deficiencies. According to the survey, the most pervasive deficiencies included poor plumbing, poor heating, and poor water supply.[8] With many manufacturing firms leaving the city, continued overcrowding in and around the downtown area, a growing black population, and a pressing housing shortage, following World War II, Philadelphia was in a state of flux. Although the severity of such housing problems was particularly intense for black Philadelphians, most all Philadelphians were in need of a revitalized local economy and renewed and expanded housing stock.

In response, local businessmen, developers, and elected officials sought to develop a postwar Philadelphia that would thrive despite the out-migration of the manufacturing firms that had for so long been key to local economic

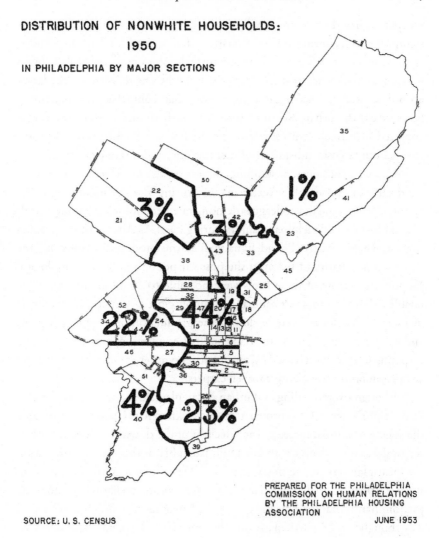

DISTRIBUTION OF NONWHITE HOUSEHOLDS:

1950

IN PHILADELPHIA BY MAJOR SECTIONS

PREPARED FOR THE PHILADELPHIA
COMMISSION ON HUMAN RELATIONS
BY THE PHILADELPHIA HOUSING
ASSOCIATION

SOURCE: U. S. CENSUS   JUNE 1953

Figure 2

FIGURE 4.1 Distribution of nonwhite households by regional area within Philadelphia in 1950. It should also be noted that at this time in Philadelphia the term "nonwhite" was basically synonymous with "black," as other nonwhites (namely Hispanics) accounted for approximately one percent.

Source: Commission on Human Relations, "The Housing of Negro Philadelphians," City Archives.

prosperity. The loss of the textile industry in Philadelphia was especially significant. Accounting for "one-quarter of the city's total manufacturing employment in 1947," costs and advances in technology rendered Philadelphia's textile manufacturing firms obsolete. Such a shift was reflective of the larger economic and technological competition that compelled manufacturing bases across the urban North to shift "to southern and western states that attracted investment with lower wages, free or subsidized sites and plants, cheaper utility costs, subsidized worker training, and forgone taxation."[9]

National trends notwithstanding, there were also local factors that caused the decline of Philadelphia's textile manufacturing base. As urban geographer Carolyn Adams and her colleagues demonstrate, technological advances dealt a fatal blow to Philadelphia's manufacturing base. As Adams and colleagues suggest, whereas many "Philadelphia textile firms produced silk hosiery," the increased popularity of nylon in the postwar period required technological support that many of these firms were not able to establish and thus were unable to "convert to new products and simply closed." Other manufacturing firms in Philadelphia "were leaders in the production of wool carpet yarns and wool carpeting," and were "viable industries until the invention of tufted carpeting in 1950, which used nylon and other synthetics and took the market away from far more expensive woven carpets."[10]

Although overcrowding and urban decay plagued many parts of the city, Philadelphia's central downtown area, better known as Center City, became the source of mutual interest. The selection of the downtown area for urban renewal was not a decision unique to Philadelphia, as this was the convention for local planners in the postwar period. Describing a similar situation in Boston, sociologist Herbert Gans wrote of the same scenario regarding the predominantly Italian-American West End neighborhood: "The West End was thought to be particularly suitable for redevelopment. Because of its central location adjacent to Beacon Hill and near the downtown shopping area, real estate men had long felt that the area was 'ripe' for higher—and more profitable—uses.... Some businessmen believed that the decline of the downtown shopping district could be ended by housing 'quality shoppers' on its fringes."[11] The Black Seventh Ward, like Boston's West End, was seen by early proponents of urban renewal as an ideal site to rebuild Philadelphia. Viewed for decades as a "slum" or "Hell's Acre," it seemed to be an obvious site for urban renewal, especially given its gradual decline. Such decline suggested that resistance from Black Seventh Warders would perhaps be minimal or at the very least easier to manage than that of larger black populations in North and West Philadelphia.

However agreeable the redevelopment of Center City Philadelphia appeared, there were two significant obstacles to revitalization efforts in the downtown area. The first obstacle was the control conservative Republicans in Philadelphia had over city politics. In the prewar period many local businessmen and developers had supported the Republican stance against federal involvement in urban development, particularly due to the additional constraints federal government often attached to federal dollars. Yet, in light of population increases, the severely weakened local economy, and the subsequent increasing rates of unemployment, federal involvement was seen as key to a revitalized and redeveloped Philadelphia.

The second obstacle was the increasingly dilapidated Black Seventh Ward located in Center City. Following the construction of the Richard Allen and James Weldon Johnson Homes in North Philadelphia, those who remained in the Black Seventh Ward tended to be low-income renters occupying the oldest and most substandard housing in the city. Given the focus on a revitalized Center City, public and affordable housing for the city's low-income and poor residents emerged as a key aspect of revitalization plans in Philadelphia. Such problems were not unique to Philadelphia, as cities such as Washington DC, Detroit, Chicago, New York, Newark, and Atlanta also experienced rapid growth in their black populations, giving rise to housing shortages and the need for additional funds to supplement a local tax base reduced by suburbanization.

As a result, local political and corporate stakeholders across urban America sought new alliances and power relations that were amenable to accepting federal funding and intervention, which in the case of Philadelphia meant a concerted shift in political allegiances away from Republican toward Democratic leaders and candidates. The process of changing the dominant political party in Philadelphia from Republican to Democratic would have to contend with the long history the GOP had in controlling local politics. We can look to W. E. B. DuBois's *The Philadelphia Negro* again for insights:

> In the period before the [Civil W]ar the city was ruled by the Democratic Party, which retained its power by the manipulation of a mass of ignorant and turbulent foreign voters, chiefly Irish. Riots, disorder, and crime were the rule of the city proper and especially in the surrounding districts. About the time of the breaking out of the war, the city was consolidated and made coterminous with the county. The social upheaval after the Civil War gave the power to the Republicans and a new era of misrule commenced. Open disorder and crime were

repressed, but in its place came the rule of the boss, with its quiet manipulation and calculating embezzlement of public funds. To-day the government of both city and State is unparalleled in the history of Republican government for brazen dishonesty and bare-faced defiance of public opinion.

DuBois's assertion is key as it demonstrates that the power of the Republican Party was across local and state levels. Further, DuBois also observes that the prominence of the Republican Party was distinctly tied to the rise of Philadelphia from a single city to both a city and a county. The above excerpt also highlights that, unlike that of its Democratic predecessor, the Republican model in Philadelphia of governing the city and state was rooted in the notion of a "boss" or a singular and hegemonic power structure with little in-fighting and internal discordance. DuBois's comments, then, demonstrate that Philadelphia's Republican Party would not be an easy one to remove from power, while it also highlights its historical roots as a ruling political regime in Pennsylvania politics.[12]

DuBois's comments, highlighting the political corruption of Philadelphia's Republican Party, foreshadow the attacks that proponents of the postwar growth coalition would make to unseat Republican leadership. Whereas DuBois's comments reveal that both political parties operated with some level of corruption, in the postwar period the stance on federal intervention between Republicans and Democrats became a defining difference between the two political parties. The preoccupation with urban growth and acquiring the funding necessary to redevelop Philadelphia and make it competitive with the growing suburbs on its periphery led to a strategic shift away from the Republican Party and a fragile growth alliance. The social and political history behind the development of the Crosstown Expressway plans reflects this shift. Briefly revisiting this history sets the stage for the Crosstown debate, while also revealing the various and precarious ties that bound together the growth coalition that led to the Black Seventh Ward's selection as the site for highway construction.[13]

Turning away from the Elephant, Embracing the Mule

Organized informally as the Young Turks, Philadelphia's growth coalition included planner-architects Edmund Bacon and Oscar Stonorov; emergent Democratic leaders (and lawyers by trade) Joseph Clark, Abraham Freedman, Walter Phillips, and Richardson Dilworth; housing advocates Dorothy Schoell Montgomery and Henry Beeritz; and G. Holmes Perkins, dean of the school of Fine Arts at the University of Pennsylvania (home to the university's Department of City Planning). Phillips, Freedman, Montgomery, Stonorov, and Bacon were all also associated with housing advocacy organization the Housing Association of Delaware Valley (HADV); thus from the start this growth coalition had a keen awareness of the importance of housing and saw its virtues as critical to urban revitalization.

By 1942 the city council approved legislation to establish a new planning commission, and the new mayor, Bernard Samuels, provided a substantial budget for it. With the approval of a new planning commission, Phillips transformed the City Policy Committee into the Citizen's Council on City Planning (CCCP). As its founder, Phillips asserted that the purpose of the CCCP was "to criticize or praise from the citizen's standpoint, proposals of the City Planning Commission." Sharing office space with the HADV, the Phillips-led CCCP began to put its redevelopment plans in motion. The proximal relationship of the CCCP and the HADV was no accident; it indicated the shared investment in the construction of new housing as key to redeveloping Philadelphia.[14]

By 1945, the legislation known as the Pennsylvania Redevelopment Act led to the establishment of Philadelphia's Redevelopment Authority (RA). Organized by Mayor Samuels in 1946, the RA was headed by five men— John P. Crisconi, Joseph McDonough, Kevy Kaiserman, Earl Barber, and Irwin Underhill. All except Underhill, a prominent black missionary/theologian and manager of the Richard Allen Homes, were realtors.[15] The new development law required the City Planning Commission to identify and then certify neighborhoods for redevelopment. Following such certification the RA would then work to relocate residents in targeted areas to new housing (usually outside of the redevelopment zone). The CCCP, with Phillips at the helm, worked virtually in tandem with the newly created local planning organizations, working specifically with community leaders to increase the appeal of and involvement in redevelopment plans for Philadelphia. With a primary goal of reestablishing Philadelphia as a "bright, [and] clean city" by 1947, the CCCP established a membership base that included more than 100 community organizations.

Raising more than $400,000 from Philadelphia-based firms and corporation, the CCCP and the City Planning Commission presented the "Better Philadelphia Exhibition," a public event hosted by the Gimbels department store to provide Philadelphians and interested parties with an opportunity to look at a diorama of a redeveloped Philadelphia—representative of their plans to turn Philadelphia into a modern, clean, and desirable urban space.

Alongside the windows and displays showcasing the latest fashions, city planners publicized the newest image of Philadelphia. Just a few feet away from makeup and fragrance counters, city planners unveiled an intricately redesigned Philadelphia that incorporated a new transportation infrastructure. Such infrastructure building required the development of a series of new highways to address the problem of traffic congestion emergent due to increased commuting between Philadelphia and outlying suburbs like King of Prussia and Levittown, Pennsylvania.[16]

Included in the plans were a riverside promenade, a revitalized Independence Mall, and a series of highways/expressways, notably one through Lombard Street tentatively titled the Lombard Expressway. Proposed by Robert B. Mitchell, executive director of the City Planning Commission, the Lombard Expressway was lauded as a key component of the massive highway construction integral to the successful redevelopment and revitalization of Philadelphia. The exhibit proved extremely popular, and those willing to pay the $1 entrance fee were seemingly impressed with the redeveloped version of Philadelphia exemplified in the diorama.[17]

Although the PHA identified a significant housing shortage across the city, which could be solved only with the construction of nearly 50,000 new homes over five years, it was more than conservative in its approach to allaying the problem, scheduling to build just 19,500 over a six-year period with hopes that such construction would "trickle down" to needy families.[18] With a deteriorating downtown area, out-migration of local industry and manufacturing jobs, and flight of white residents to outlying suburbs, the local business community believed action was necessary, and given the limited funds of the local government federal assistance was deemed critical. Together with the CCCP and the HADV, downtown businessmen launched a concerted effort to rout the city's Republican leadership.

At the same time, Mayor Samuels and the local Republican leadership were in the midst of a crisis of their own. Initiated at Samuels's behest, a blue-ribbon Committee of Fifteen was established in 1948 by the city council to investigate possible misconduct by Republican officials. During its investigation, the committee found that corruption and mismanagement among city officials were pervasive. When the findings of the committee were made public, anger mounted and talk of reform united those in opposition to the Republican leadership. To be sure, such findings were only confirmation of a history of corruption in Philadelphia's Republican leadership highlighted by W. E. B. DuBois in *The Philadelphia Negro* nearly fifty years earlier. However, the anger prompted by the blue-ribbon committee's findings helped to

generate enough negative sentiment toward Republican leadership that proponents of the growth coalition could chip away at the various offices and
resources Philadelphia and Pennsylvania Republicans controlled.[19]

In response to the committee's findings, local corporate leadership formed
the Greater Philadelphia Movement (GPM), and worked in tandem with the
CCCP and the HADV to reform the local government and begin revitalization efforts, particularly in Center City wherein much of their economic
interests lay. Center City was seen as ideal as it already contained many major
institutions such as city hall, the art museum, Independence Hall, and the
Franklin Institute. Much like the HADV and the CCCP, the GPM believed
public housing was a necessary component of downtown revitalization especially to eradicate decrepit areas of the Center City such as skid row and the
increasingly dilapidated Black Seventh Ward.[20]

Here, then, proponents of the emergent growth coalition had a mutual
interest in housing. However, the understanding of the role of housing differed and perhaps foreshadowed later friction between the corporate and
housing contingent of the coalition. As redevelopment would cause the
displacement of residents, for business leaders in the coalition such as the
GPM housing was situated as more of a tool of redevelopment. Housing
advocates such as the HADV, on the other hand, envisioned housing as an
important redistributive tool to compensate for decades of local officials
neglecting to address the continued housing needs of poor and working-class
Philadelphians.

Through collaborative efforts, by 1949 the GPM–HADV–CCCP alliance rallied social and political reformers to elect to public office founding
members of the Young Turks, namely Richardson Dilworth as city treasurer
and Joseph Clark as city controller. Here, the alliance forged between the
GPM, HADV, and CCCP benefited in particular from the existing
Democratic opposition, as its pro-federal assistance and pro-public housing
positions resonated with these constituencies who had grown tired of the cor-
rupt Republican regime. As city controller, Clark had the power to appoint
two members to Philadelphia's Housing Authority, and upon election he
wasted little time appointing Walter Phillips, another founding member of
the Young Turks and leader of the CCCP.[21]

Such change in the ranks of local officials was timely as by July the federal
Housing Act of 1949 was passed. This legislation contained provisions that
provided federal funding for slum clearance and urban renewal. In addition,
it provided federal funds for extensive development of public housing as well.
Capitalizing on this sweeping legislation the GPM–HADV–CCCP began a

campaign to unseat Republican Mayor Samuels and to provide the city with more control over redevelopment. Although Philadelphia, due to its large size, had significant political powers in the state legislature, all local legislative and executive decisions needed to pass through the state legislature first.

In order to maximize revitalization and redevelopment in Philadelphia, the GPM–HADV–CCCP believed that a Home Rule Charter was necessary, as it would allow Philadelphia to in effect govern itself. Together with reform Democrats led by chairman James Finnegan, the GPM–HADV–CCCP drafted the charter just before the spring of 1951. On April 1, 1951, city voters approved the charter; the new charter provided the mayor's office with significant administrative, fiscal, and appointive power, and maintained the City Planning Commission as an independent body charged with developing a strategic redevelopment plan, adding to its responsibilities the preparation of zoning ordinances and the development of an annual capital budget and program. That same year, the GPM–HADV–CCCP, along with James Finnegan, local Democratic chairman, successfully organized Joseph Clark's campaign for mayor of Philadelphia.[22]

Clark's election and the Home Rule Charter represented the rise to prominence of the newly emergent growth coalition, within which the interests shared between civic leaders, downtown businessmen, housing advocates, and local politicians determined the scope of and process by which urban renewal in Philadelphia would occur. Clark's election represented a significant shift in the political landscape of Philadelphia, as he was the first Democratic mayor since Daniel Fox's election in the fall of 1861. Further, the rise of the growth coalition is representative of the shifting social and political conditions throughout the United States that gave rise to many cities seeking large amounts of federal assistance to address issues of urban decay and redevelopment.

The growth coalition's effort to wrest control of local affairs from the state is emblematic of the efforts of local and state political and corporate leaders to shift the role of local governments nationally in the postwar period, especially regarding housing and urban redevelopment. The series of events giving rise to the prominence of the growth coalition in Philadelphia are paradigmatic of similar processes occurring in cities across the United States, including New York, Chicago, Washington DC, and St. Louis, wherein during the postwar era local agencies, like housing authorities, and legislation such as home rule charters, were developed and/or retooled to facilitate the revitalization of the central city.[23]

By 1953, officials certified sixteen areas of the city for redevelopment. Although these included neighborhoods across the city, the powerful growth alliance focused in particular on what had been termed the South-Central area of the city. The South-Central area was an agglomeration of the Black Seventh Ward, the neighboring predominantly black Thirtieth Ward of South Philadelphia, and the predominantly white Eighth Ward to the northeast. Returning to their original plans for the South-Central area, officials announced that not only would renewal efforts mean that residents and businesses would be relocated but that also the city planned to build an expressway, referred to as the Lombard Expressway, through the Black Seventh Ward. Moreover, officials announced that redevelopment in the Lombard/South Street area had three purposes: (1) "removing the slum areas in that section"; (2) "providing a location for new development"; and (3) "providing a badly needed east-west highway in the area that would, among other things, speed up traffic within the center city." The expressway in the area was, perhaps, the linchpin of redevelopment plans for the area, as city officials were convinced that "a high capacity roadway will be needed between the projected Schuylkill Expressway and the proposed Delaware Expressway, running east and west along the southern edge of the central business district of Philadelphia."[24]

The City Planning Commission designated the Lombard/South Street area as a "combination highway and re-development project" and called for the Redevelopment Authority to begin to relocate the area's residents and businesses. Although the city was initially unsure about the source of the total funds needed to construct the highway project, the passage of the Federal Highway Act in 1956 provided it with the federal assistance necessary, with a projected cost of $60 million. With the assurance of federal assistance for the project, the city conducted preliminary studies to select the best route for the area. After considering "six locations between Lombard and Bainbridge Street," which were two blocks apart, city officials and engineers recommended the predominantly black South/Bainbridge Street area for the site of the expressway.

Having moved from its original location of Lombard Street, the name of the expressway was then changed from the Lombard Expressway to the Crosstown Expressway, as the proposed roadway would allow traffic to move crosstown between I-95 and I-76 (see Figure 4.2). With the preliminary report concluded and federal assistance assured, in 1960 the city formally adopted redevelopment plans for the area highlighting the newly dubbed Crosstown Expressway as a top priority. With extensive construction and displacement looming, the Black Seventh Ward again became a critical site upon which both reform and change in the city converged.[25]

Essentially, the growth alliance forged in the postwar period successfully unseated Republican leadership and, in turn, shifted the local political stance on redevelopment, housing, and federal assistance. While this shift helped to

FIGURE 4.2 Map of the expressway plans.
Source: Philadelphia City Planning Commission (1960), City Archives.

center the importance of housing and attempted to account for the city's housing needs, the probusiness disposition of some of the growth proponents, namely the GPM, was at odds with the pro-public-housing stance of HADV leaders also comprising the growth coalition. This shift, it would seem, addressed a major concern DuBois had had regarding local politics, corruption, and the marginalization of the Philadelphia's black electorate. As we will see however, the shift away from the Republican Party would not necessarily mean that black residents were actively integrated into the emergent Democratic-based coalition. The growth coalition's goal of redeveloping Center City into a commercial and upper-middle-class residential district relied heavily on relocating the area's predominantly low-income black residents elsewhere.

Over the course of roughly ten years, Philadelphia's postwar growth coalition accomplished several key victories in the pursuit of renewing and rebuilding the city, namely the change in the dominant local political party from Republican to Democrat, the establishment of a home rule charter, and an urban renewal plan that sought to facilitate more efficient travel for residents and commuters by developing a more pronounced highway system through the city. However successful the coalition was during the postwar period, its origins were fraught with setbacks, disagreements, and tenuous arrangements regarding names, sites, and relocating residents.

As I will demonstrate in subsequent sections, the difficulty of relocating residents would put the probusiness and pro-public-housing contingent of the growth coalition at odds. Under the control of Democratic leaders, urban renewal in Philadelphia was a complicated endeavor, seeking to accomplish two opposing goals—the redevelopment of Center City into the corporate nucleus of postwar Philadelphia and providing low-income and poor Philadelphians with adequate housing. Just as the growth coalition shaped the political landscape in the postwar period, so too would the coalition developed in opposition to the Crosstown Expressway.

From the Lombard to the Crosstown Expressway

The Clark and Dilworth Administrations (1950–1962)

Following the city's formal announcement of the redevelopment plans for the South-Central region, the area fell into a period of rapid decline. Such decline was not necessarily the product of any action by the city per se, such as eminent domain or zoning, but instead the result of anticipation—the anticipation of massive construction through South Street, the heart of the Black Seventh Ward, and demolition of existing buildings and structures in surrounding areas. The anticipated urban renewal plans for the South-Central area made those who lived and worked in the area fearful.

In response, residents flooded the City Planning Commission office with letters indicating their fears about the pending redevelopment. In these letters, many residents made known their willingness to sell their businesses and homes in order to maximize the return on their asset before the area was taken over by city-planning and highway officials. A letter from Seventh Ward resident Ned Hosier to the City Planning Commission perhaps best characterizes the concerns residents had about urban renewal and highway construction and how the anticipation of redevelopment left many residents and properties in limbo:

> I bought and moved, with my brother, into the property at 2416 Waverly Street, Philadelphia on July 29th, 1949. I understand that the City of Philadelphia plans to destroy the homes on the entire south side of the 2400 block on Waverly Street to make room for an apartment building. When I bought my property it was in quite bad shape. Since, I have…built a cinder-block wall around the courtyard and replaced the gate…I have had almost the entire first floor walls replastered and painted…had book shelves built on one side of the living-room wall, up to the ceiling…had a new floor laid, the walls completely replastered and painted…last week [I] had a complete new roof put on the building. Consequently, gentlemen, you can appreciate how much I regret to see the money spent, planning, patience and many long hours of work come down with my home in a heap of dust and debris. Is there nothing that I can do, as a taxpayer and citizen of Philadelphia, to avoid this? If not, can you at least inform me definitely when the 2400 block of Waverly Street will be razed? I do not want to invest another penny in a worthless cause. Therefore, I reiterate, will you kindly let me know if and when this uncalculated project will be inevitable?[26]

Hosier's predicament was not unique. Given the city's plans, spending money for property maintenance and day-to-day business operations seemed economically unwise for owners and proprietors as much of the area would be razed in order to construct the Crosstown Expressway. As a result, many homeowners, landlords, and proprietors abstained from maintaining their properties and running their businesses in the area. Here, then, the specter of urban renewal is perhaps just as significant as actual redevelopment, particularly as it relates to neighborhood change. In neighborhoods with politically and economically marginalized residents, policies of urban development generate fear and such fear creates subsequent abandonment and disinvestment as residents in politically disenfranchised areas anticipate little political recourse against sweeping local policies impacting their neighborhood.

Such actions exacerbated conditions for the area's black residents, most of whom were low-income renters, as the buildings they occupied continued to fall into disrepair. It was the same for business leaders and homeowners who remained loyal to the area, as relocation of residents would mean the loss of customers and a shift in the neighborhood from a primarily residential enclave to a business district buttressed by a six-lane highway. While some were more than willing to abandon the area, most of the area's black residents were either unable (due to economic constraints) or unwilling (due to the area's long history as a predominantly black enclave) to leave the neighborhood behind.

Additionally, the RA struggled to relocate residents. Although it was able to move some black residents to parts of Southwest, South, and North Philadelphia, with no significant increases in housing construction, relocation efforts were largely ineffective. Further, reports and studies on the efforts of the RA found that black residents who relocated, either voluntarily or with the assistance of the RA, tended to live in housing that was most often worse than that which they had occupied in the Seventh Ward. Those leaving voluntarily often moved in with relatives in black areas in North, South, and West Philadelphia, which in turn, increased the overcrowding in homes and neighborhoods in those black areas (see Figure 4.3). Relocation, then, emerged as the Achilles' heel of the growth coalition's plans to redevelop Philadelphia.[27]

Despite the robust black protests occurring throughout the city against discrimination, the consequences of urban renewal for the Black Seventh Ward was receiving less attention from more established black organizations. Although the issues of relocation and demolition were perhaps "black" issues, in the late 1940s through the early 1950s major black civil rights organizations in Philadelphia such as the NAACP and the Urban League were focusing their energies, activism, and resources on issues of educational and economic inequality. Although the civil rights leadership had successfully protested against the Philadelphia Transit Company's practice of "refus[ing] to hire blacks to positions of 'motorman' or conductor on the company's trolleys and subway cars," by 1950 such leadership was fraught with conflict.[28] The NAACP, in particular, was just recovering from a protracted period of internal conflict.

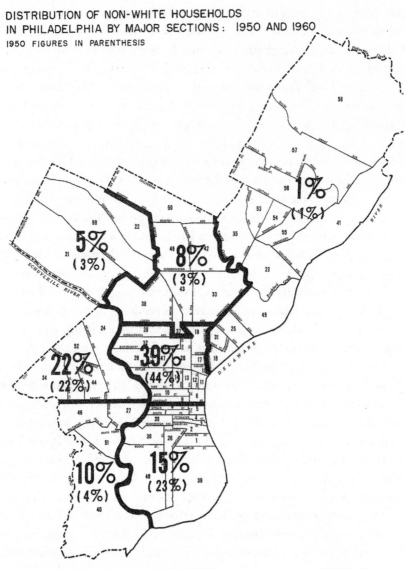

DISTRIBUTION OF NON-WHITE HOUSEHOLDS
IN PHILADELPHIA BY MAJOR SECTIONS : 1950 AND 1960
1950 FIGURES IN PARENTHESIS

PREPARED BY THE COMMISSION ON HUMAN RELATIONS
PHILADELPHIA, SEPTEMBER 1961
SOURCE : U.S. CENSUS

FIGURE 3

FIGURE 4.3 Distribution of nonwhite households by regional area within Philadelphia in 1960. Map indicates the secondary migration of black residents between North, South, and West Philadelphia. Note the decreases in South Philadelphia.

Source: Commission on Human Relations, "The Housing of Negro Philadelphians," City Archives.

This conflict "within the Philadelphia NAACP was ostensibly focused on whether civil rights activism would be helped or hurt by working in coalition with the Communist Party and its Popular Front allies."[29]

The development of the growth coalition, however, helped to allay such conflict as it had successfully unseated the Republican leadership that many civil rights leaders had held responsible for the persistence of local discriminatory policies and practices. Specifically, the civil rights "coalition viewed reformers' control of the charter commissions as providing a great opportunity to establish the principle that a basic function of city government was to protect its citizens from racial and religious discrimination." The growth coalition also involved black leadership in the development of the city charter, which lead to the inclusion of "human rights section with provisions that included bans on discrimination in the use of all city property, facilities, and services as well as in civil service employment, and a requirement that all city contracts over $2,000 include a nondiscrimination clause."[30]

When the Clark administration announced expressway plans in the Black Seventh Ward, disagreement and protest would initially only come from residents in the South-Central area. This lack of attention to the expressway construction through the Black Seventh Ward confirmed the initial sentiment that the gradual decline of the neighborhood rendered it an ideal site for urban renewal. With little direct protest regarding the Crosstown Expressway from Philadelphia's major civil rights organization, the city pressed on with its plans bringing the "urban bulldozer" to Black Seventh Warders' front door.

With the ineffectiveness of the RA's relocation efforts, a pending highway, and a neighborhood in a persistent state of decline, black residents, under the leadership of George Dukes and Alice Lipscomb (shown in Figure 4.4), developed community organizations to give themselves and the area's businesses a voice. With hopes of shifting the city's bias away from demolition and toward an approach that integrated community preservation, Dukes and Lipscomb became key critics of the administration and the larger growth coalition. With the promise of extensive highway construction and the city's apparent lack of interest in the area's residents and businesses, George Dukes and Alice Lipscomb like many of their black neighbors believed it was their responsibility to protect and save their neighborhood. Like George Dukes, Alice Lipscomb was a Black Seventh Warder, and had witnessed the changes to the neighborhood. Marked by a combination of tragedy and fondness, Lipscomb's biography highlights the type of background and events motivating Black Seventh Warders to be protective of their neighborhood.

FIGURE 4.4 Alice Lipscomb (*c.* 1980).
Source: http://theblackbottom.wordpress.com/communities/hawthorne/history/

　　Born in 1916, Lipscomb was the seventh of eleven children. A graduate of
South Philadelphia High School, in 1943 she married longshoremen John
Lipscomb, and they had one daughter, Deloris. A native of the Black Seventh
Ward, Lipscomb was called to her activism after the tragic death of her niece
in a tenement fire in the early 1950s. Occurring in the dead of winter, the fire
was all too reminiscent of that which killed the Spease family in 1936. Seeing
that flames were engulfing the Black Seventh Ward tenement, Lipscomb ran
inside where she found a young girl. The fire had caused a water pipe to burst
and soon the stairways were covered with a sheet of ice, making their escape
quite difficult. Just as Lipscomb went to cover the young girl with her coat,
she discovered that the child was her six-year-old niece.[31]

　　Gasping for air, Lipscomb headed out with her niece and firemen and
police officers tending to the fire rushed them to the hospital. Just as the doc-
tors pronounced her niece dead, Lipscomb saw her niece's eyes open, head
turn, and heard her call her name, "Aunt Alice." "The doctor was amazed. To
me it was an omen," Lipscomb told *Philadelphia Inquirer* reporters, adding:
"[T]here was something she wanted me to do, to make sure it doesn't happen
to another child." While for some Philadelphians the Black Seventh Ward was
"the city's worst slum," Lipscomb held mostly positive memories and feelings
about the neighborhood. Such fond memories of the neighborhood and her
family were profound motivation for Lipscomb's community involvement:

　　　　That's what got me so involved in the community....I grew up poor
　　　　but my mother taught us manners and respect. We were a good
　　　　Christian family and we were raised in a good atmosphere. We sat

down for breakfast, blessed our food, went to school together and did our chores. You don't see much of that anymore. It was just a loving family. Good buddies all of us. Girlfriends and boyfriends.[32]

Here, then, Lipscomb's biography is reflective of the ways in which working-class black Americans, like those in the South described by historian Robin D. G. Kelley, translate tragedies in and care for their neighborhoods into an activist stance antithetical to the approach of those who formally control local planning and development.[33] Her narrative reveals an infrapolitical perspective rooted in neighborhood preservation and encouraging residents to take ownership of the area of the city they call home. Where many saw a deteriorating community, Lipscomb, and residents like her, saw an opportunity to empower a community-based program of redevelopment.

By 1956, Dukes and Lipscomb had channeled their concerns, organizing and chairing respectively the Rittenhouse and Hawthorne community councils. While both organizations focused on compelling the city to preserve the communities in the South-Central area while also providing financial assistance to support revitalization, the Lipscomb-led Hawthorne Community Council was especially interested in bringing attention to the ineffectiveness and inaction of city officials with respect to efforts to provide adequate and affordable housing to the area's black residents.[34]

Gathering signatures, coordinating rallies, and inundating the City Planning Commission and the mayor's offices with letters, Dukes's and Lipscomb's efforts helped to delay the city's plans to build the Crosstown Expressway throughout Clark's tenure. By the conclusion of Clark's term in 1955, plans to build the Crosstown Expressway were halted and key leaders within the growth coalition sought to push harder to see the urban renewal plans for the area come to fruition. With promises that he would move urban renewal forward using federal funds, Democrat and founding member of the Young Turks Richardson Dilworth was elected to replace Clark as mayor of Philadelphia, assuming the role in January of 1956.

Holding true to his commitment to the Crosstown Expressway, throughout his first term Dilworth held informational meetings and hearings in the South-Central area to address and possibly allay the rising anti-urban renewal sentiment that had thus far thwarted the expressway's construction. These meetings also provided a venue to discuss the benefits of the soon-to-be-built Hawthorne Square homes, a high-rise public housing complex located within the South-Central redevelopment area. Located between South and Christian Streets, Hawthorne Square was positioned as the city's measure for addressing the difficulties of relocating the area's black residents. In addition, city officials argued that Hawthorne Square projects (later renamed Martin Luther King Jr. Plaza), demonstrated the city's commitment to the area's black residents by providing affordable housing for low-income black families. Though officials believed such a measure would provide reassurance to residents and owners in the area, it instead intensified fear and anger.

Between 1956 and 1960, the hundreds who appeared to voice opposition to the Crosstown Expressway left the various hearings convinced that the city did not intend to rebuild the area but was more interested in demolishing the Black Seventh Ward in order to grow Center City, and develop it into a primarily commercial and upper-middle-class white district.[35] The promise of Hawthorne Square, too, angered many black residents. As historian John Bauman notes, black leaders "denounced the Housing Authority's practice of cramming public housing in or near ghetto sites."[36] The issue of overcrowding notwithstanding, black discontent was also tied to how public housing manifested in the wake of the tenement collapse in 1936. In the years following the completion of the Richard Allen and James Weldon Johnson Homes, the provision of public housing projects no longer registered with black residents as a completely positive prospect. Indeed, black residents were likely to perceive public housing projects as a racially motivated and limited response to their persistent housing concerns.[37] Here, then, black residents were calling for a more holistic response that addressed the long-term significance of housing inequities, as by 1960 public housing projects in myriad cities across the United States were shown to demonstrate the housing inequalities between blacks and whites.

This pushback was also a consequence of the fair-housing campaign of the NAACP that began in 1958. Although not focused explicitly on the Crosstown Expressway or the Black Seventh Ward, by the late 1950s civil rights organizations such as the NAACP and Students Non-violent Coordinating Committee (SNCC) had broadened their focus to include fair housing. Endeavoring to create ties with community organizations disappointed with its inability to attend to many of the local issues plaguing black neighborhoods like housing, the NAACP coordinated a "one-day institute for organizations of the community at South Philadelphia High School on March 29, 1958." Describing the day-long event, historian Matthew Countryman observes: "In their promotional materials, conference organizers made it clear that the primary purpose of the meeting was for the NAACP's leadership to hear from representatives of the community organizations."[38]

Urging community organizations to send representatives, conference materials sought to motivate black Philadelphians to participate in a dynamic conversation: "[W]e'll Blueprint the Future for the Negro Citizen.... Where Do Philadelphia's Negroes Stand?... Let's find out!!!"[39] Such promotion compelled 150 representatives from eighty-six community organizations to participate in the day-long institute which was divided into four parts—each part thought to reflect the major issues facing blacks Philadelphians: the Education Problem, the Political Problem, the Housing Problem, and the Economic Problem. The conversation that day was lively and covered a variety of questions regarding how best to provide relief to urban blacks and strategizing how, for example, to "enlist the aid of local and state political machines to achieve the goal of first class citizenship." Indeed, this meeting, and the sentiments and solutions expressed, reflected the advice DuBois offered in *The Philadelphia Negro* to address the problems he observed in the Black Seventh Ward: "It is the duty of the Negro to raise himself by every effort to the standards of modern civilization and not to lower those standards in any degree."[40]

However in line with DuBois's commentary this event was, the outcome would only demonstrate the continued discord among black activists and leaders in Philadelphia, particularly regarding urban renewal. In the months following, NAACP leaders Harry Greene and Charles Shorter focused specifically on passing fair housing legislation to "end the problem of discrimination in housing." This focus, while on housing, was not targeted at the problems of housing or demolition caused by urban renewal. The focus, instead, was on the larger housing shortage.[41] Therefore the NAACP's fair housing campaign, like the plans of the growth coalition, had significant gaps with regard to redressing the issues emergent from urban renewal. Whereas issues of educational and economic inequality were situated by civil rights organizations such as the NAACP as what political scientist Cathy Cohen refers to as a "consensus issue," urban renewal represented a "cross-cutting" issue seen to impact a segment of the larger black population. Further, this lack of attention to and framing of urban renewal as a consensus issue highlighted a gap within local and black politics regarding the effects and problems of urban renewal.[42]

Having attended the various public hearings and meetings, by 1960 Black Seventh Warders sought to address this gap and bring attention to the city's urban renewal plans. Like housing advocates in Newark and Chicago, black Philadelphians were convinced that what the city was situating as urban renewal amounted to nothing more than "Negro removal." A study conducted by the HADV printed that same year indicated that, between 1955 and 1960, of the 7,000 families displaced by urban renewal efforts, eighty percent were black, and of those black families only one of every ten found dwellings that were satisfactory. Also in that same year Hawthorne Square was opened for occupancy, and despite its billing as a solution to the problems of relocation, the 576 units it contained provided only a cursory fix to the housing problems in the area.[43]

Despite the opening of Hawthorne Square, relocation for the area's black residents still proved difficult for the RA. The sentiment against the public housing project also provides an indication of the interdependency among black neighborhoods. Black residents had a long memory with regard to how the city had gone about addressing their housing needs by constructing public housing in the past. The advent of the Allen and Johnson homes revealed that such housing options were limited in their ability to provide housing to those in need, as the number of homes they provided were usually in the hundreds while thousands of black families were in need. Furthermore, such projects had also been divisive and created competition among disadvantaged black Philadelphians. In the wake of the tenement collapse, such competition inadvertently distracted black Philadelphians from compelling white officials to develop a more comprehensive housing approach that would facilitate the development of affordable public housing options within the black neighborhoods inundated with housing problems. With twenty years between the completion of the Allen and Johnson Homes and Hawthorne Square, black residents had time to witness the costs and benefits of public housing projects, drawing varied conclusions about the long-term safety and stability such housing provided.

However unsuccessful the RA was in its relocation efforts, construction for the Crosstown Expressway still loomed as a top priority for urban renewal in the South-Central area. In fact, the Crosstown Expressway was prominently featured as a part of the Philadelphia Comprehensive Plan adopted by city officials in 1960. Although the housing shortage continued to hamper the relocation efforts of the RA and the efforts of Dukes and Lipscomb delayed construction of the Crosstown Expressway, the growth coalition, with Dilworth at the helm, had success with the construction of the Delaware (I-95) and Schuylkill (I-76) Expressways. The Schuylkill Expressway, running east–west through the city along the Schuylkill River, was completed by 1959. Just as the construction of the Schuylkill Expressway concluded, the city began construction on the Delaware Expressway. Such construction connoted to those both in favor of and against the Crosstown Expressway that

construction was inevitable, because, from its inception, the expressway was
framed as a necessary link between I-95 and I-76. As a result, many Black
Seventh Warders were fearful of the looming plans to build the Crosstown
Expressway.[44]

Although construction for the Crosstown Expressway had yet to begin,
residents were right to be fearful. As scholar John H. Staples shows in his
study of urban renewal in twenty-two American cities, Philadelphia had a
relatively high completion rate for urban renewal projects (see Table 4.1).
At a completion rate of eighty-five percent by December 31, 1959,
Philadelphia was executing plans at lower costs and higher rates than cities like Chicago, Boston, Detroit and New York City, whose completion
rates were sixty-six percent, fifty-two percent, sixty-eight percent, and
fifty-two percent respectively. Even in Chester, Pennsylvania, a predominantly black suburb just a few miles southwest of Philadelphia, the rate of
completion was also high, 100 percent.[45] Given the figures for Philadelphia
specifically and Pennsylvania more generally, the concerns of Black
Seventh Warders were justified, as was their disbelief in the assurances of
public officials.

We can look again to sociologist Herbert Gans's research on Boston for
comparison. In his research, Gans found that residents of Boston's West End
neighborhood were complacent in the face of urban renewal:

> One of the original reasons for making a study was to discover
> how the West Enders as individuals and as a community were
> reacting to the eventual—and then imminent—destruction of
> their neighborhood. Had West Enders exhibited the expected
> stress, the book might have dealt with these phenomena in much
> greater detail. As it turned out, however...most West Enders did
> not react in this fashion, and continued to follow their normal
> routines.

Indeed, with a fifty-two percent completion rate, Boston had not been nearly
as successful in its execution of urban renewal projects, with nearly half of all
projects remaining incomplete; thus providing the impetus, or, at the very
least, a partial rationale for the complacency of residents Gans observed in his
study of the West End. This distinction in the completion rates of urban
renewal projects in different cities, then, points to why some residents, that is,
those in the Black Seventh Ward, chose to fight against urban renewal, and

Table 4.1 Urban renewal success and expense rates for
twenty-one US cities (*c.* 1959)

City	1960 population	Avg. cost of project (federal expenditures, $)	Percent completed December 31, 1959	Mean no. of months
New York City	7,782,000	4,693,000	52	158
Chicago	3,550,000	4,255,000	66	122
Philadelphia	2,003,000	2,016,000	85	92
Detroit	1,670,000	4,568,000	68	171
Baltimore	950,000	2,028,000	100	99
St. Louis	750,000	1,626,000	64	66
Boston	697,000	3,194,000	52	108
Cincinnati	503,000	4,275,000	69	132
Kansas City	476,000	1,128,000	92	78
Newark	405,000	2,673,000	93	84
Birmingham	341,000	2,091,000	41	111
Rochester	319,000	5,025,000	29	102
St. Paul	313,000	1,321,000	59	137
Norfolk	306,000	3,446,000	63	146
Syracuse	216,000	709,000	100	33
Providence	207,000	2,158,000	64	73
Nashville	171,000	4,643,000	51	171
Hartford	162,000	1,745,000	38	87
Little Rock	108,000	1,089,000	69	133
Harrisburg	80,000	4,688,000	40	108
Binghamton, NY	76,000	1,686,000	39	89
Chester, PA	64,000	515,000	100	62
Means		$2,706,000	65%	107mo.

Source: John H. Staples, "Urban Renewal: A Comparative Study of Twenty-Two Cities, 1950–1960," *Western Political Quarterly*, 23, no. 2 (1970): 294–304, at 297.

others, for example Italian Americans in Boston's West End, remained complacent or apathetic.[46]

Though Dilworth appeared to be ineffective in moving the Crosstown Expressway forward, the completion of the parent roads I-95 and I-76 signaled that construction of the Crosstown Expressway would soon begin. Despite the initial failures to complete the expressway, Lipscomb's recollection of a meeting in the late 1950s between Dilworth and members of the Hawthorne and Rittenhouse Square community groups demonstrates the city leadership's commitment to building the roadway:

We invited [Dilworth] and asked him what he was doing with the crosstown expressway. He said he wasn't doing anything. He said we'd have to pick ourselves up by the bootstraps. They told us they were going to build that expressway. We told them 'over our dead body.'[47]

When the city unveiled plans for Center City in 1963, the Crosstown Expressway was again prominently featured and characterized as "reinforcing the margins of Center City"; thus the Crosstown Expressway would provide a physical boundary between the redevelopment zones to the south and solidify the perimeters of the commercial and residential district comprising the revamped Center City area. In response, Dukes and Lipscomb worked in tandem to develop a new coalition that would represent the interests of both blacks and whites in the area.

With the completion of I-95 and I-76, developing an interracial alliance that attempted to holistically represent the area's stakeholders seemed the best and only way to "kill" the Crosstown Expressway. Further, the continued failure of the RA empowered and legitimized the claims of black residents of the racism embedded in the city's urban renewal policies and practices, as without an increase in the housing stock, the continued displacement of black residents appeared inhumane and racially motivated. With the goal of putting the Crosstown Expressway debate to rest, black residents under the leadership of Dukes and Lipscomb embarked on an unprecedented endeavor to align the interests of black and white residents in the area to push the city to throw out plans for the Crosstown Expressway and instead encourage a grassroots-based revitalization of the South-Central area.[48]

The Rise of the Crosstown Community

The Tate Administration (1962–1971)

In 1962, when Dilworth resigned from his post as mayor to enter Pennsylvania's gubernatorial race, the growth coalition supported Democrat and city council president James Tate was appointed as the interim mayor of Philadelphia. That same year Tate began his official campaign to become mayor and was elected in 1963, defeating district attorney and Republican Arlen Specter. Much like Tate's mayoral triumph, John F. Kennedy's presidential election brought renewed hope to the city's growth coalition as he too ran on promises of urban redevelopment. Upon his election Kennedy sought to make good on his campaign promise for massive urban renewal establishing the Department of Housing and Urban Development (HUD) and a "renewal pie" of $2 billion. In response, Tate sought to use the city's $120 million share of Kennedy's $2 billion renewal budget to aggressively pursue continued revitalization in Center City, resuscitating the highly contentious Crosstown Expressway. Additionally, Tate appointed Gustav Amsterdam, board member of the Old Philadelphia Development Corporation (OPDC) to head the failing RA. As a member of the OPDC, Amsterdam was an active voice in the city's corporate community, promoting its growth stance and call for a revitalized Center City and construction of the Crosstown Expressway.[49]

Given his position and place in the OPDC, Amsterdam was an ideal choice to revamp the RA as its failures continually hampered efforts to build the Crosstown Expressway. The continued failed relocation efforts of the RA had given legitimacy to black-led resistance against urban renewal in the area, which in turn, thwarted plans to build a series of highways throughout the city to create a new landscape for transportation within the city. Both Tate and Amsterdam were consistent in the belief that Center City was the "heart of a great metropolitan region," thus renewing the city's commitment to not only relocation of residents and businesses in the South-Central area but also to building the Crosstown Expressway.[50]

With Tate at the helm and Amsterdam heading the RA, urban bulldozers took to the South-Central area quickly. With the appearance of bulldozers, many business owners, landlords, and homeowners believed the end had finally come. Already suffering from the disinvestment occurring in anticipation of the city's renewal plans, the invigorated Tate-led redevelopment schemes proved to be overwhelming for many. Alongside the deterioration of the neighborhood, both from the razing of properties and also from abandonment, crime and poverty in the area thrived. Further the "threat (or more correctly the prospect)" of expressway construction "encouraged real-estate speculators to buy up properties which they allowed to stand vacant and to deteriorate" in order to sell these properties for high prices to local and federal organizations charged with facilitating urban renewal in the area.[51]

Within Tate's first term, both Dukes and Lipscomb actively went through the neighborhoods within the South-Central redevelopment area to encourage black and white residents and proprietors to fight against the city's plans for the area and to compel the city to redevelop the area in a manner that was more agreeable to those who lived and worked in it. Yet, just as Lipscomb and Dukes were looking to creating an interracial anti–Crosstown

Expressway coalition, rioting consumed the black section of North Philadelphia for three straight days in late August of 1964. The riot began just after two police officers, John Hoffer and Robert Wells, attempted to remove a drunken black couple from a stalled car stuck in the intersection of Columbia Avenue and 22nd Street.

At 9:35 p.m. on Friday, August 28, 1964, Hoffer, who was white, and Wells, who was black, found themselves in a violent confrontation with the couple, Odessa Bradford and James Mettles. When Hoffer and Wells tried to forcibly remove Bradford from the vehicle, Mettles attacked the white officer and a crowd began to emerge at the intersection. While Wells radioed for assistance, Mettles continued his attack and bystanders began throwing bottles and bricks at police cars and officers. The night's events would again escalate after a white police officer was accused of having beaten and shot to death a pregnant black woman. As a result of these events, by 11 p.m. that same night rioting commenced and consumed the area. From 23rd Street, "the crowd then moved down the Columbia Avenue retail strip toward Twenty-First Street, smashing windows and looting stores." From August 28 to 30, 1964, "black Philadelphians attacked the police and looted white-owned businesses throughout Philadelphia." During those three days, rioters specifically attacked white-owned businesses and white police officers, "sparing black-owned businesses." By late Sunday, August 30, 1964, 339 people had been wounded—including 239 black resident and 100 police officers—308 arrested, and two people had been killed.[52]

Such tension between black residents and police officers would become a sign of the times, as similar riots would take place throughout the mid-1960s in cities like Detroit, Newark, and Chicago during the "long hot summer" nights. As in black Philadelphia, a series of persistent issues gave rise to the riots in cities like Detroit, highlighting the tenuous race relations that provoked such rioting. Describing the socioeconomic and political climate of preceding the Detroit riots, historian Thomas Sugrue writes: "For those who cared to listen, there were rumblings of discontent in the late 1950s and early 1960s. The problems of limited housing, racial animosity, and reduced economic opportunity for a segment of the black population in Detroit led to embitterment." Such embitterment did more than just fester during this period in both Detroit and Philadelphia as this sentiment fostered violent outbreaks, often positioning urban black residents against the police force or local white businesses. As a result, city leaders and activists focused less attention on rallying around seemingly amorphous programs such as urban renewal, despite their substantial implications for race relations and the racial geography of the city.[53]

While all of the city's attention and most of its police force focused on quelling the violence in North Philadelphia, the plans for the Crosstown Expressway were still unfettered. The rioting, however, did demonstrate the power of racial narratives and issues in Philadelphia. Such a revelation would provide a salient way for Lipscomb and Dukes to frame the Crosstown Expressway. To engage those in the area, Dukes and Lipscomb relied on a series of critical arguments to frame the "costs" of the Crosstown Expressway.

First, they contended that the Crosstown Expressway would effectively function as "Philadelphia's Mason-Dixon Line," placing a physical barrier between the "white middle and upper class community" and the "poorer and greatly neglected Negro area." This framing of the Crosstown Expressway was particularly resonant with black residents throughout the South-Central area. Given the climate of the civil rights movement, race-based arguments were effective as they were in line with a general sentiment among black Americans broadly invested in changing racial policies across a range of social issues including public housing and urban renewal.[54]

Second, Dukes and Lipscomb held that the Crosstown Expressway would also subject those in the area to overwhelming levels of air pollution, characterizing the proposed highway as a "carbon monoxide curtain." Positing the environmental effects of highway construction appealed to residents across racial and class lines, as neither black nor white residents believed urban renewal should take precedence over the health of residents. Last, they argued that urban renewal, as city officials envisioned it, hampered the ability of residents and proprietors to form a more grassroots and community-based revitalization effort. Emphasizing the importance of the needs and ideas of residents, this argument prefigured provisions such as community block grants and the model cities programs offered under later federal moves. Indeed, such arguments empowered residents to remind local officials that those who lived and worked in the area, perhaps, knew best how to redevelop it and should thus play a critical role in any effort to revitalize residential areas.[55]

Taken together, these three major framing arguments resonated not just with the nearly 6,000 Black Seventh Warders, but also with black and white Philadelphians throughout the South-Central redevelopment area. Whereas earlier positions emphasized the protection of the predominantly black parts of the South-Central area and affordable and adequate housing, anti-Crosstown Expressway arguments proffered in the wake of Tate-led urban renewal tapped into the fears and anger of white residents in the area as well. Shifting away from rhetoric that relied heavily on race-based arguments against the Crosstown Expressway was perhaps fortuitous if not strategic, as between 1962 and 1964 Philadelphia's wards and legislative districts were reapportioned (see Figures 4.5, 4.6). Following landmark Supreme Court decisions between 1960 and 1964, namely *Baker v. Carr* and *Reynolds v. Sims*, Philadelphia, like many other cities across the United States, reapportioned its legislative districts and wards. Referred to as the "one man one vote" decisions, the Supreme Court decisions called for legislative districts to be equal in population. As a result, between 1961 and 1963 Philadelphia was reapportioned and the Black Seventh Ward was folded formally into the Thirtieth Ward, with the white area of the Seventh Ward being combined with the Eighth Ward; thus consolidating the Thirtieth Ward as a predominantly black working-class area and the Eighth Ward as a majority white upper-middle district.[56]

Just as many American cities were reconfiguring their legislative districts, the country was already witnessing the success of the Civil Rights Movement. Within a span of two years, President Lyndon B. Johnson signed into law a series of civil rights legislation seeking to end race-based discrimination in the United States: the Civil Rights Act of 1964 and the Voting Rights Act of 1965. While such legislation reflected key shifts in American race relations, at the municipal level civil rights activists continued to pursue local efforts against discrimination. Indeed during the same period, Philadelphia civil rights organizations such as the NAACP and the SNCC were in a battle over the direction of black politics and the Democratic alliance born from the efforts of the growth coalition.

Under the direction of Cecil B. Moore, Philadelphia's NAACP branch had spent much of its time from 1963 to 1965 protesting discrimination in construction contracts given by the city and the selective enrollment practices at Girard College, a local boarding school founded in 1848 by successful entrepreneur Stephen Girard. Meanwhile, the SNCC, which originally had been largely focused on the discrimination in the South, was seeking to expand its reach and develop coalitions with blacks in the North. The two organizations would come to a head by 1965, as their competing interests proffered differing visions for black politics moving forward.[57]

Whereas Moore would channel his popularity into a mayoral bid, SNCC leaders sought to disempower the Democratic coalition the organization viewed as taking for granted the black vote. Indeed, SNCC leaders and staff were quite critical of Moore's "Operation Girard" protest. Not only were

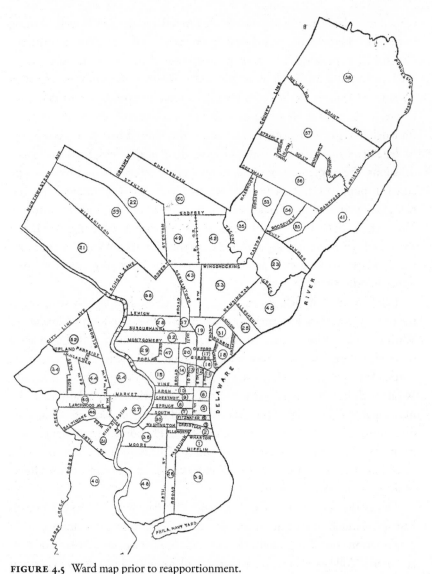

FIGURE 4.5 Ward map prior to reapportionment.
Source: *Evening Bulletin*, August 5, 1964. Temple University Libraries, SCRC, Philadelphia, PA.

Philadelphia SNCC members "very much opposed to" Operation Girard, but also characterized the protest as "just another effort...to get white folks to let us come into their" organizations. Seeking to achieve an independent black political bloc, SNCC leaders such as Charyn Sutton committed themselves to split the black "community [between] the Cecil people and the NAACP" and "the black nationalists." Thus in the wake of civil rights legislation,

Philadelphia's civil rights leadership was fraught with conflicting visions about black politics, and the issue of urban renewal continued to fall into the gulf separating these opposing perspectives, leaving residents like those in the Black Seventh Ward to determine their own means to deal with the Crosstown Expressway.[58]

In 1967, Dukes's and Lipscomb's efforts were strengthened after residents and proprietors received sudden notices by registered mail from state planning officials about the South-Central area: "You are hereby notified…that in order to make studies, surveys, sounding and/or appraisals…agents of the Department of Highways…will enter your property on or about 10 days after receipt of this notice.…We trust you will cooperate fully with them." Garnering white support along with the existing support they had as chairs of the predominantly black Rittenhouse and Hawthorne community councils, Lipscomb and Dukes began to develop new organizations indicative of the emergent interracial alliance set to protect what they termed the "Crosstown Community." Further, not only were their arguments persuasive but they also encompassed problems that united the diverse interests among those who lived and worked in the area.[59]

With the relocation efforts of the RA still a failing enterprise, even members of the growth coalition began to break ties. Most notably, Cushing Dolbeare, housing advocate and managing director of the HADV, criticized city planners for aggressively pursuing the Crosstown Expressway without an effective relocation program, commenting: "Where will people go in the meantime? Our conviction is when a public agency takes property and displaces people it has a moral obligation to relocate them." Registered mail, an emergent fracture in the growth coalition, and persuasive arguments of Dukes and Lipscomb forced city planning officials to reconfigure their proposal for the Crosstown Expressway.[60]

In response to claims about air pollution and the decimation of the Black Seventh Ward, city officials made plans to change the Crosstown Expressway from an above-ground highway to a depressed highway (see Figure 4.7). However, even the plan for a depressed highway meant altering the residential character of South Street and displacing residents in order to dig beneath existing structures to build the expressway. In addition, new plans for the Crosstown Expressway proposed that a depressed highway would solve pollution issues. New plans also slated the Crosstown Expressway to change from a six-lane to an eight-lane highway running "between South and Bainbridge sts., from 2nd to 22nd sts., and from there south to an interchange with the Schuylkill and Cobbs Creek Expressways" with a new estimated cost

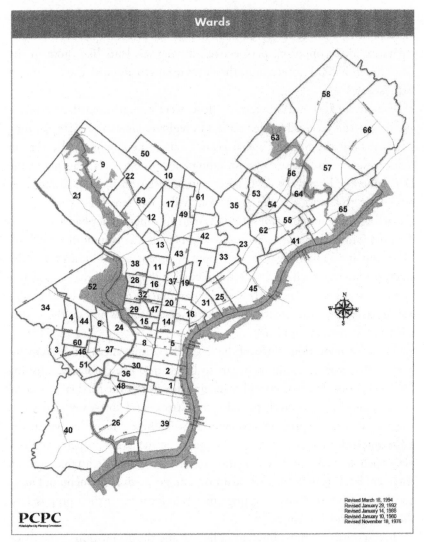

FIGURE 4.6 Ward map after reapportionment.

Source: Philadelphia City Planning Commission, City Archives.

of $320 million. The new plan for the expressway now impacted the adjacent Grays Ferry area, as it would be the southern area wherein the interchange between the highways would be located.[61]

When these plans became public in 1967, residents and proprietors were only more incensed by the continued unwillingness of the city planners to remove the Crosstown Expressway from city plans altogether. Stretching the Crosstown Expressway into the Grays Ferry area provided just the ammunition

Dukes and Lipscomb needed to strengthen their efforts and to establish a larger constituency against the expressway. That same year, Dukes along with 200 residents in the area filed a legal injunction in the Court of Common Pleas. Additionally, in April of 1967, Lipscomb and Dukes sponsored a heavily attended public meeting in conjunction with predominantly white residential group, the Society Hill Association, at McCall Elementary School located at 7th and Delancey Streets.[62]

At the meeting freshman state representative and white resident in the South-Central area Norman Berson, whom Dukes and Lipscomb invited to speak, characterized the Crosstown Expressway plans as "a grievous mistake" and "insidious," adding: "It is my judgment that the emphasis on highway construction in densely populated urban areas is a mistake." Speaking to the various residents who filled the seats of the elementary school's auditorium, Berson's words captured the sentiment of those who called the Seventh Ward, especially South Street, home. Continuing his critique, Berson foreshadowed a different vision for how the federal funds for urban renewal in the area should be used: "Our efforts should be turned toward a fast, rapid and cheap system of mass transit." Berson further informed the audience that "70 percent of the families living in the path of the road have incomes below the poverty level … [and] at the present time there is a drastic shortage of low-priced standard housing … conservatively estimated at 40,000 units." Highlighting the inability of the RA to relocate residents, Berson commented that the RA had been able to relocate only "one-third of its cases" and that the construction of the expressway would "increase … the caseload by 50 percent."[63]

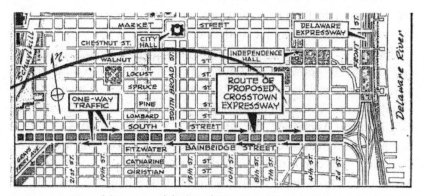

FIGURE 4.7 Map of the proposed depressed Crosstown Expressway.
Source: *Philadelphia Inquirer*, 1972. Temple University Libraries, SCRC, Philadelphia, PA.

In his comments, Berson echoed much of the sentiments of not only those who had long been in opposition to the Crosstown Expressway, but also urban scholars such as Jane Jacobs, who was a staunch critic of the national urban renewal movement in American cities. Indeed, Berson's comments drew inspiration from Jacobs's sentiments about expressway construction published in her 1961 book *The Death and Life of Great American Cities*:

> Erosion of cities by automobiles entails so familiar a series of events that these hardly need describing.... Because of vehicular congestion, a street is widened here, another is straightened there, a wide avenue is converted to one-way flow, staggered-signal systems are installed for faster movement, a bridge is double-decked as its capacity is reached, an expressway is cut through yonder, and finally whole webs of expressways. More and more land goes into parking, to accommodate the ever increasing numbers of vehicles while they are idle.[64]

While Jacobs's comments were not about Philadelphia per se, such commentary was, for Berson and for many of those at the meeting, an effective characterization of the type of urban renewal that Philadelphia's growth coalition promoted vis-à-vis the Crosstown Expressway. Residents (black and white) in attendance also expressed concerns about schooling. Many asked what "provisions would be made for children of displaced families" in terms of schooling, wondering where plans were for schooling relocated children and if children in the area would be forced into "other overcrowded slum schools."

Capitalizing on the growing anti-Crosstown Expressway sentiment, in that same month Dukes and Lipscomb organized a new organization, the Citizens Committee to Preserve and Develop the Crosstown Community (CCPDCC). Set up as an umbrella organization, encompassing and working on behalf of the various community councils affected by the Crosstown Expressway, the CCPDCC was representative of the newly emergent interracial coalition opposing the city's plans for the South-Central and Grays Ferry areas. Groups included in this coalition were: the Rittenhouse Community Council, Society Hill Residents Association, Hawthorne Community Council, Queen Village Neighborhood Association, Areas I and H of the Philadelphia Anti-Poverty Action Council, Armstrong Association (Urban League), Ministers of the Crosstown Expressway area, and the Schuylkill–Grays Ferry Residents Association. The coalition was unprecedented, including upper-middle and working-class whites from the Society Hill and Grays Ferry sections, along with black residents throughout the South Philadelphia.[65]

The summer of 1967 was a busy one for the newly formed CCPDCC, as members began an aggressive campaign to raise awareness and increase its membership (see Figure 4.8). Additionally, Dukes and Lipscomb set up head-quarters for CCPDCC at 2102 South Street, in the middle of the site upon which the Crosstown Expressway was to be built. From that row home on South Street, Dukes and Lipscomb began an aggressive writing campaign, wherein they developed mass memos that framed the organization's goals and function in an effort to mobilize a broader network of concerned citizens. In a memo to businesses in the area the CCPDCC, led by Dukes and Lipscomb, made clear its objections, purpose, and proposals:

> The purpose of the CCPDCC is to foster the development of the Crosstown Community. Continued planning and the construction of the proposed Crosstown Expressway as an open, depressed highway through this community is destructive of this development and, there-fore, unacceptable. The Committee specifically opposes: 1) the lack of any provision whatsoever to provide adequate reimbursement and rehousing for the estimated 6500 people who will be displaced by the Expressway. 2) The construction of an open, depressed highway through the center of this community, which, because of its coincidence with seg-regated housing patterns, will act as a barrier to interaction between people of diverse races. 3) The lack of any provision to ease the other harmful effects of the proposed Expressway, such as the dislocation of commercial centers. The Committee specifically proposes: 1) That the planning for the Expressway on the proposed route and other related activities, such as property assessment, be suspended. 2) That the involve-ment of the community is an overriding objective in any improvement effort in this area, and that residents, businessmen, civic groups, and agencies affected by this effort must participate actively and meaning-fully in the review of the State's proposals and in the development of policies and plans submitted to City Council. The CCPDCC offers the following three alternatives to the construction of the Expressway: 1) Unless the need for any Expressway can be demonstrated the planning and construction of it shall be stopped. 2) The route for the proposed Expressway shall be relocated. 3) The Expressway shall be built on the proposed route, only if the following requirements are met: a) Demonstrate the need for an Expressway placed specifically between South and Bainbridge Streets; b) Develop a comprehensive rehousing agenda, business relocation, and community development plan.

This memo, like many other notices and letters sent by members of the CCPDCC, emphasized a community-based approach to city planning and urban renewal and assailed city officials for their lack of interest in the wants and needs of those who lived and worked in redevelopment areas. Further, this memo reveals the ways in which the growth coalition's targeting of the area gave way to what scholar Benedict Anderson terms an "imagined community," a constituency whose membership or community boundaries are not physically determined but rather culturally and/or sociopolitically constructed. Much like the nation states that Anderson characterizes to elaborate on this concept, the CCPDCC amplified the mutual interests and stakes of those who lived and worked in area upon which the Crosstown Expressway would be built to establish a network of political constituents united by the cultural boundaries developed within the city's redevelopment framework.[66]

Further, the organization brought together the various political players in the area as well, hoping to generate pressure from within the local political network. Most notable in this regard was white politician and South-Central resident Norman Berson, whose voice and involvement added a level of political legitimacy to the CCPDCC. Mobilizing this new network of concerned citizens, Dukes and Lipscomb set to have a rally in November of 1967 just before Philadelphians headed to the polls for the mayoral election. Inviting mayoral candidates Arlen Specter, James Tate, Reverend Leon Smalls, and Cecil B. Moore, Dukes and Lipscomb hoped to leverage the voting bloc contained in their new coalition to compel candidates to promise to finally eliminate plans for the Crosstown Expressway. The CCPDCC also wanted candidates to address the actions of the state highway department, which had begun to appraise properties and place bids for homes, despite city officials' claims that designs for the Crosstown Expressway were not settled.[67]

Given the attention the CCPDCC had been able to draw to the Crosstown Expressway issue and the well-covered problems of relocation, Mayor Tate was quick to respond. On November 6, 1967, Tate sent a personal letter to Dukes to assure him and members of the CCPDCC that there was no connection between the actions of the state highway department and his administration. Tate's response suggested friction between state and local plans and actions and reassured Dukes that relocation and provisions for low-income housing were key pieces of the local Crosstown Expressway effort:

> The action of the State Highways Dept. to resume appraisals for the Crosstown Expressway is a purely unilateral action by the State without any approval whatsoever by my administration. The meeting next

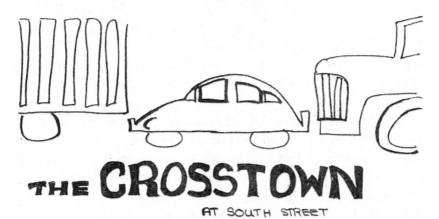

FROM THE WONDERFUL FOLKS WHO GAVE US THE SCHUYLKILL EXPRESSWAY...

THE CROSSTOWN

AT SOUTH STREET

STOP IT . . . CALL THE MAYOR (MU 6-9700)

Or write Hon. James H. J. Tate
City Hall
Philadelphia, Pa. 19107

FIGURE 4.8 Sample advertisement from CCPDCC's "Stop the Crosstown Campaign" (*c.* 1967).

Source: Philadelphia City Planning Commission Papers, City Archives.

Thursday was likewise called at the request of the Secretary of Highways and any implication that the City is planning at that meeting to move ahead on the present design of the State Highway Department for the Highway is completely erroneous. In fact the timing of these actions and the leaking of them to the press by the State Highway Dept. is an obvious attempt to embarrass the City Administration by implying that we are cooperating with actions which the State is taking wholly on its own. Furthermore, it is not true that the City has ever officially, or unofficially notified the State that the relocation problem in connection with the Crosstown Expressway has been solved. The City Administration's position remains unchanged. The proposed Crosstown Expressway should not proceed until we have developed plans and financing which will permit the Highway to be covered with structures which are residential, predominantly for low income housing.

With the Mayor's reassurance, CCPDCC chairman Dukes opted to rework the format of the rally. Rather than bring people into the area, Dukes gathered a group of "property owners, tenants and businessmen who reside or conduct business along the path of the proposed Crosstown Expressway" in a downtown plaza where planning meetings were being conducted. Announcing to planning officials his purpose, Dukes declared: "We have come to denounce the illegal tactics of the State Highway Department that has been appraising our properties without the consent and/or with the duplicity of the City of Philadelphia which is, in the words of Mayor Tate, still committed to working out the problems the Expressway will create."[68]

By election night, Mayor Tate contended that the Crosstown Expressway was "dead or dying a slow death" due to the inadequacy of relocation efforts and rallying cries of the CCPDCC. Following such statements, Tate was reelected and quickly set up a committee to study the area and generate proposals to solve the problems of the Crosstown Expressway. While the CCPDCC lauded Tate's shift on the Crosstown Expressway, state as well as some local officials were angered and assailed Tate in private meetings and in the press.

Tate, however, was not alone in his ambivalence about the Crosstown Expressway, as even founding members of the city's growth coalition were voicing opposition to the expressway being built in the area. Perhaps the most notable voice of dissent was that of the original advocate of the Crosstown Expressway, Robert B. Mitchell. As former head of the City Planning Commission, Mitchell was once a huge proponent of the expressway, but by December of 1967 he assured Tate that his reluctance was commendable:

> According to the newspapers you are having new difficulties about construction of the Crosstown Expressway. Having been one of those most responsible for its being on the map—or proposed—I now strongly recommend that it be abandoned or moved to another location and that its design be restudied.... Psychologically, the City cannot afford at this time one more symbol of separation between the black community and City Hall.[69]

Mitchell's letter was a timely reminder of the political ramifications of demolishing a black enclave for the purposes of urban renewal given the Civil Rights climate engulfing the nation generally and the city specifically.

Just as President Johnson signed into law the Civil Rights Act of 1968 (also known as the Fair Housing Act of 1968) to effectively end housing discrimination, Dukes and Lipscomb capitalized on Mitchell's position, building a larger coalition that included a citywide contingent of concerned parties. Although the Crosstown Expressway was now declared "dead or dying" by the mayor's office, the area continued to decline because the Crosstown Expressway was still contained in the city's comprehensive roadway plans. Lipscomb, in a letter to the City Planning Commission, reminded officials of the continued decline of the area due to specter of roadway construction, arguing that removing the Crosstown Expressway from city plans will "enable the rehabilitation [of the area] to go forward."[70]

Despite his claims about the state of the Crosstown Expressway, in 1969 Mayor Tate seemed to change his position, arguing that indecision around the expressway held up federal funds for general urban renewal in the area specifically and the city more generally. Although unclear about where he stood exactly, Tate's about-face on the issue was amplified when state highway officials authorized signage for the Crosstown Expressway on the Delaware Expressway (I-95). In response, CCPDCC members aggressively pursued a citywide coalition to finally end the specter of the Crosstown Expressway. Developing the Citywide Coalition to Oppose the Crosstown Expressway (CCOCE) that same year, Dukes and Lipscomb went to locations throughout the city to encourage Philadelphians to compel the city to abandon its road construction plans in the South-Central area. In this way, Dukes's and Lipscomb's actions reveal how community-based organizations can expand, rather than contract, even as structural conditions change seemingly in favor of the plans of those in power.

As a result of Dukes's and Lipscomb's efforts, by 1969 the citywide coalition had the support of various organizations and leaders, some of whom were integral members of the city's growth coalition, including the HADV, the Philadelphia Regional Chapter of the American Institute of Planners, the Council of South Philadelphia Ministers, the South Street Ministers, the Crosstown Development Corporation, and the Citizens of the Crosstown Corridor. Also in that same year the CCPDCC and CCOCE were invited to present their case before the Federal Highway Administration by transportation secretary John A. Volpe, recently appointed by President Richard M. Nixon. Impressed by the CCPDCC's and CCOCE's arguments and plans for the area, the federal government called for city officials to make a formal decision on the expressway, tying a significant portion of the city's federal funding for urban renewal to a decision on the Crosstown Expressway.[71]

By 1970, the mayor's Crosstown Study Committee had concluded its survey of the area and made clear that, given the scope of the construction of the expressway alongside the housing shortages and relocation issues, the Crosstown Expressway should either be relocated to another area or removed from city plans altogether. Further, the report also confirmed fears that construction of the expressway would have a disproportionate impact on low-income black residents in the area, revealing that black households accounted for more than seventy-five percent of total households in the South–Bainbridge Street corridor. Many corporate leaders, too, were in agreement, issuing a statement to Mayor Tate in the spring of 1970 that proclaimed that "the Greater Philadelphia Chamber of Commerce, feel[s] that the Crosstown Expressway should not be built as it is presently planned in the South–Bainbridge Street Corridor because it will compound traffic congestion, increase pollution, and create a human disaster." That same year the mayor's office issued a press release proclaiming that Mayor Tate "accepted the recommendation of the Mayor's Crosstown Study Committee to abandon the Crosstown Expressway, and called for the Department of Housing and Urban Development to permit the Redevelopment Authority to begin Neighborhood Development Program Activities in the South Central and Grays Ferry" areas.[72]

By framing the Crosstown Expressway as a citywide and multiclass issue, black residents were able to situate urban renewal as a consensus issue for all neighborhoods and residents impacted by the roadway. Furthermore, capitalizing on the appeal of such rhetoric, black and white residents mobilized to compel officials to remove expressway plans in the South-Central area. In this way, the political agency of urban black residents generated new tensions in the emergent growth machine and called into question the larger political structure controlling planning and resource allocation in the city. With continued secondary migration due to the specter of construction, the ties black Philadelphians shared with the Black Seventh Ward became significant, as they likely helped facilitate the creation of a cross-neighborhood effort to thwart plans to build the Crosstown Expressway and added to the continued pressure black Philadelphians placed upon white leadership during the civil rights movement in the city. Taken together, then, the mobilization efforts and rhetorical strategies employed by black residents and activists confronted structural processes embedded in urban renewal, seeking to make visible the marginalization of black residents emergent in the city's pursuit of redeveloping Philadelphia in the postwar era.

FIGURE 4.9 The signage for the proposed Crosstown Expressway being placed on Delaware Expressway (I-95).

Source: Evening Bulletin December 30, 1969. Temple University Libraries, SCRC, Philadelphia, PA.

The Crosstown Community's Last Stand

The Rizzo Administration (1971–1974)

On May 23, 1972, Alice Lipscomb and George Dukes were gathering residents and proprietors from the South-Central area once again to stage a protest against the Crosstown Expressway. However successful their efforts had been during the Tate administration, the CCPDCC again faced the threat of the expressway based on a proposal for the area developed by Democrat Frank Rizzo following his 1971 mayoral election victory. Proposed by Rizzo as the "Southbridge Plan," urban renewal in the area now included the Crosstown Expressway along with other provisions such as a parking garage and high-rise/low-rise apartment building construction alongside the roadway. Still slated to run along South Street and to connect the Delaware and Schuylkill Expressways (see Figure 4.9), the Southbridge Plan also called for the expressway to serve as a transfer road with the proposed Cobbs Creek Expressway (located in the city's Southwest area). Announcing such plans in late 1971, Rizzo used much of the same rhetoric of previous mayoral administrations, emphasizing the importance of the roadway for reducing congestion in Center City and connecting the Delaware and Schuylkill Expressways. Different, however, from previous iterations of the Crosstown Expressway, was Rizzo's conception of expressway construction occurring at the same time as extensive residential construction. Dubbed the "megacity" plan, the Rizzo-led city planning model proposed to develop a mixed-income residential community alongside the expressway.[73]

In response the CCPDCC and CCOCE developed their own plans. Referring to the proposal as the "Hawthorne Plan," members of the CCPDCC and CCOCE proposed redevelopment in the area with a focus on rehabilitating and renovating existing residential structures. The proposition of renovation and rehabilitation was a significant difference from existing city planning models, as the Hawthorne Plan incorporated such measures to prevent and reduce displacement.

Rehabilitation was a key aspect of this plan, and stood in stark contrast to previous and existing plans for the Crosstown Expressway that privileged demolition and relocation. Included in this plan was making use of abandoned buildings, such as old school buildings, to accommodate the needs of poor and working-class residents in the area. Meeting at the Bellevue-Stratford Hotel, Lipscomb and Dukes finalized what they believed was a community-based proposal for redevelopment in the area. In addition to support from the area's residents and proprietors, the Hawthorne Plan had also received the approval of the City Planning Commission, the state government, and the Department of Housing and Urban Development (HUD), following Tate's formal disavowal of the Crosstown Expressway plans. Following a final discussion of the Hawthorne Plan, the CCPDCC and CCOCE left the Center City hotel and headed to City Hall to confront Rizzo. When the group arrived, Lipscomb immediately confronted Rizzo: "stop this expressway and start the Hawthorne Plan."[74]

With the Hawthorne Plan in hand, Lipscomb highlighted that continued discussion about the expressway only caused continued decline in the area, and that plans developed by the community should instead be used. Lipscomb further highlighted that the HUD had also approved nearly two million dollars for the Hawthorne Plan. Somewhat taken aback by Lipscomb's sudden appearance at City Hall, Rizzo was reluctant to speak. Lipscomb, however, was not. She criticized the mayor's plans, challenging him to kill the Southbridge plan on the spot, which Rizzo suggested could be done only after he had talked it over "with all of the people." While efforts to directly confront Rizzo were not immediately successful, they had brought attention to the issue once more and facilitated new alliances, most notably that with HADV affiliate and head of the Philadelphia Council for Community Advancement W. Wilson Goode.

Born in 1938 in a one-room house in the rural southern town Seaboard, North Carolina, Goode "was the next to the youngest" of seven children. From an early age he had been influenced by his mother's generosity to a local homeless man, with whom his mother would share the family's already limited food supply. Witnessing his mother's generosity would motivate Goode to "summon within himself a desire to help others," especially after settling in Philadelphia and observing the city's acute housing problems. Urged by his sister to join her in Philadelphia, Goode and the rest of his family arrived in the Paschall neighborhood in Southwest Philadelphia in 1954. Goode's calling to Philadelphia mirrored that of many southern black migrants who moved North. The mechanization of the tobacco industry, fear of "an abusive father's release from prison," and the call of kin had all formed a combination of push and pull factors prompting the Goode family to move to Philadelphia. Although the Goode family "thought that [they] were moving to the promised land," they soon discovered the subtle yet impactful nature of discrimination in the urban North. However, within fifteen years of his arrival, Goode was running the Philadelphia Council for Community Advancement, "tak[ing] vacant land and building housing for low-income families," and receiving attention at the state and national levels for his efforts. Having become an emergent leader in housing and redevelopment in Philadelphia, Goode's support would provide a necessary boost to the CCPDCC and CCOCE.[75]

Goode's support of the CCPDCC and CCOCE was significant as it further legitimized the Hawthorne Plan and helped mitigate some of the division among residents around Rizzo's Southbridge Plan. Due to the provision of mixed-income housing alongside the expressway, there were those who began to believe that the Southbridge Plan was the best way to revive the area. Opponents of the plan highlighted the emergent revitalization of the lower end of South Street by private businesses and investors following Tate's press release, as well as the importance of a community-based approach to redevelopment in the area and across Philadelphia. Such differing positions led to violent outbursts at various public gatherings on the matter throughout much of 1972.[76]

Given the growing bitterness and friction among supporters and opponents of the Southbridge Plan, Goode's housing expertise helped sway the debate. Goode was less than confident in the city's ability to generate enough housing to minimize the effects of displacement. Expressing his sentiments at one of Rizzo's public hearings on the matter, Goode exclaimed:

> So Southbridge, as it has been proposed, is absurd. What will we get if the Crosstown Expressway is accepted today? At best, a $200 million underground road, and an expansion of Society Hill with homes only the wealthy can afford. More likely, after displacing thousands of families, wreaking havoc with surrounding neighborhoods, destroying an irretrievable historic section, polluting the air, and congesting traffic, we will have expanses of vacant land slowly developed as capital and labor become available. What will be built will be determined by what is most profitable for developers, not the paper idea before us.

Providing opponents with further legitimacy, Goode's statements resonated with many in the area and led some to write letters to the mayor.

The letters inundated Rizzo's office, as residents reminded Rizzo and city planning officials of the cause of the area's decline, often writing: "A twenty-year threat of demolition is enough to cause any area to decay." By 1973, Goode's critique of the Southbridge Plan, along with the continued efforts of the CCPDCC garnered the support of Pennsylvania governor Milton J. Shapp and Edward W. Furia, regional director of the United States Environmental Protection Agency. However resistant Rizzo was to "burying" the Southbridge Plan, with the lack of state and federal support he was compelled to give in to the demands of the CCPDCC.

Subsequently, by 1974 the Delaware Valley Regional and City Planning Commissions dropped the plans for the Crosstown Expressway. In that same year federal legislation dictated that funds formerly slated for the expressway be used to develop mass transit. Such funds, then, were used by the Southeastern Pennsylvania Transportation Authority (SEPTA) to pay for 120 subway cars on Philadelphia's Broad Street line, 100 commuter rail cars, 110 trolleys, and 190 buses for regional and local routes. With the redirection of funds to enhance regional and local mass transit, plans for the Cobbs Creek Expressway were also dropped; thus ending the nearly twenty-five-year debate over the Crosstown Expressway.[77]

By defeating the Crosstown Expressway, black and white residents in the South-Central area altered plans for revitalizing Philadelphia. While managing to protect those residents who were predominantly poor and working-class blacks from the displacement prompted by expressway construction, such activism had anticipated and unanticipated consequences.

On the one hand, black-led activism forced city planners to acknowledge the voices and desires of urban black residents who were otherwise disenfranchised from the local political structure. Such acknowledgment, on the other hand, did not correspond with increased resources in the area as the specter of the Crosstown Expressway prompted those with means to withdraw and withhold their investments until after the city finalized a decision on the highway.

Admittedly, this failed urban development project was tied to federal and state funds that were lost once local officials and planners laid the Crosstown Expressway to rest. Here, then, saving the neighborhoods of black and white residents in the South-Central area was coupled with the loss of funds that could have been used to address some of the serious housing issues in the area. The failed urban project left an indelible mark on the city, forcing city planners to rethink and rework city highway plans, cancel the construction of complementary roads in other areas of the city (e.g., the Cobbs Creek Expressway), and redirect slated funds for the roadway to support public transportation, while also fostering lasting friction among proponents of the growth coalition.

An Expressway Paved with Good Intentions

As with most stories of urban renewal in the postwar period, the story of the Crosstown Expressway is a complicated one—replete with successes, failures, plans, name changes, and myriad disagreements. Yet despite this complicated narrative, the story of this failed urban project provides a clear opportunity to view the ways in which structure, politics, agency, and activism collide. Specifically, there are three interrelated lessons that we can extract from the story of the Crosstown Expressway.

The first lesson is that black and white residents were not passive to urban renewal. As the chapter demonstrates, the political agency of residents, particularly black residents, confronted the structure of postwar city planning and urban renewal. Occurring in the midst of the larger civil rights movement, the activism against the Crosstown Expressway exposed the fragility of the growth alliance and the failings of Philadelphia's newly empowered Democratic coalition. In order for urban renewal to succeed, several things needed to happen sequentially—site selection, relocation, demolition, and construction. That is, urban renewal was a structural umbrella for a series of state-sanctioned policies and actions that all needed to be fulfilled in order to accomplish planning goals. By protesting the Crosstown Expressway, residents made visible the gaps in Philadelphia's urban renewal program, wherein families and businesses in the Black Seventh Ward and neighboring communities were implicitly being asked to disproportionately carry the burdens of redevelopment.

Confronting city officials (perhaps already weakened by the protests against Woolworth, the Philadelphia School District, and Girard College), the anti–Crosstown Expressway coalition helped to forge a new interracial constituency that questioned whether redeveloping the city and protecting residents and neighborhoods were mutually exclusive. In his documenting of Philadelphia's civil rights movement and the myriad sit-ins and protests against race-based discrimination, historian Matthew Countryman asserts "activists in Philadelphia increasingly turned away from state action and biracial coalition politics and toward traditions of black collection action and self-help to achieve substantive advancements in black employment, education, and housing."[78] However, as the Crosstown Expressway debate demonstrates, not all black activism during this period bypassed biracial coalition politics. Due to its shrinking size (relative to emergent black neighborhoods in North and West Philadelphia), those in the Black Seventh Ward, perhaps out of necessity, utilized a biracial coalition to bring attention to the consequences of urban renewal. Whereas issues of educational and economic inequality were situated by civil rights organizations such as the NAACP as what political scientists refer to as "consensus issues," urban renewal represented a "cross-cutting" issue, seen to impact a smaller segment of the larger black population. Given the marginalization of the Crosstown Expressway as pivotal issue for *all* black Philadelphians, a biracial alliance was not only ideal but necessary as well.[79]

The second major takeaway is that there are unanticipated consequences to sanctioned federal interventions like urban renewal even if such projects prove unsuccessful. Here, the political agency of black residents helps to contextualize the costs and benefits of urban renewal. When introducing the initial plans at Gimbels department store in 1947, city officials and planners seemed to have made all considerations before promoting the Crosstown Expressway. However, as black residents began to protest and frame the roadway's effects as racial, environmental, and far-reaching, the Crosstown Expressway began to appear as a symbol of an uncaring and hegemonic state. That is, renewing Philadelphia appeared less concerned with the livelihood of citizens and their housing needs, and instead as a tool of the rich, white, and powerful who had only economic motivations and concerns when making the plans for the roadway. In this case, efforts to redevelop the city hinged on shifting the population of the seemingly vulnerable and impoverished Black Seventh Ward to other parts of the city.

The city's redevelopment plans led to the decline of area businesses and homes, which, in turn, accelerated the secondary migration of blacks and whites out of the area. This secondary migration led to an increased black presence in neighboring wards, particularly those north and south of the Seventh Ward. As a result, overcrowding, poverty, and congestion increased not only in the Black Seventh Ward, but throughout black sections of city. Although such out-migration decreased resources within the Black Seventh Ward, the in-migration of those same resources (human, economic, and other) provided vital assets to emergent black neighborhoods throughout Philadelphia.

Additionally, the activism of black residents forced the city leadership out of complacency regarding the housing shortage. Given the consistent rhetoric of black residents and leaders around the failed relocation efforts of the Redevelopment Authority, black-led activism forced city planners to address the housing shortage and more profoundly consider the human impact of their growth machinations. The CCPDCC, led by Dukes and Lipscomb, forced city planners to consider the human costs of urban renewal and to take seriously the ideas, feelings, and livelihoods of the marginalized black population throughout the South-Central area; thus facilitating critical fissures within the growth coalition that controlled city planning.

In addition to the relocation (or not) of Black Seventh Warders influencing the landscape of the city, the specter of the Crosstown Expressway also impacted the larger racial geography of the city as well. The third lesson emergent from the story of the Crosstown Expressway is protests and activism against urban renewal were facilitated by how growth coalitions partitioned the city in order to pursue urban renewal projects. As sociologist Jeffrey Alexander reminds us, "those whom civil society has repressed in the name of a restrictive and particularistic conception of civil competence, it can also save. More precisely, it can offer resources so that they can save themselves."[80] In this case, urban renewal, by virtue of its vastness and the need for massive demolition in order to be successfully executed, provided black activists with a key resource with which to unite and protest—the Crosstown Expressway, a roadway that clearly crossed racial and neighborhood lines.

As was the case in cities across the United States, in the postwar period urban planners in conjunction with growth coalitions often assigned arbitrary regional designations in order to pursue redevelopment and urban renewal; hence the emergence of the South-Central and Crosstown zones. While such designations were meant to provide perimeters around redevelopment zones and/or socioeconomic boundaries within the city, this case reveals the critical ways that black residents mobilized around such designations in order to empower those impacted by urban renewal. As a result, those within the growth coalition were forced to rethink their positions, and such reconsideration redefined the membership and interests of that coalition as the city pursued the Crosstown Expressway.

Although the designation of the area as South-Central or Crosstown was developed by city planners to clarify redevelopment areas and specify how and where funds should be used, black residents and leaders retooled this framework and amplified such distinctions to generate a multiclass and interracial alliance that shifted the city's priorities and fostered friction within the growth coalition. Black and white activism against the Crosstown Expressway made urban renewal efforts difficult not only in the South-Central area, but also in other areas across the city, such as the Grays Ferry and Southwest sections (as they were the sites of proposed connected highways). Black-led resistance to urban renewal, then, shaped the larger city and patterns of redevelopment.

Plagued by overcrowding, poverty, poor relocation efforts, and the specter of expressway construction, black Philadelphians challenged the city and federal government to rethink urban planning and redevelopment. Such a challenge gave way to a community-based approach to urban redevelopment and to an unprecedented interracial alliance; thus an examination of this critical juncture reveals that changes in and across neighborhoods were the product of a series of interdependent relationships: between the urban renewal in one black area and that of another; between the out-migration of social problems and resources from one black neighborhood and the growth and increased density of another black neighborhood; between the relocation of black residents in one black neighborhood and the construction of public-housing in another black neighborhood.

To be sure, the story here animates a period and type of political mobilization we find happening in other parts of urban America as well. Indeed, numerous biracial coalitions formed across the United States during urban renewal, particularly related to urban transport. For instance, in Washington DC a biracial coalition was able to stop the development of a highway system, the Inner Loop, which had similar implications for the livelihood of the historic black neighborhood U-Street/Shaw. As Steven Gregory demonstrates in his examination of the Black Corona neighborhood in Queens, a biracial coalition was critical to preventing the construction of an elevated rail system providing access to LaGuardia airport that would have passed through that neighborhood.[81]

Anti-Crosstown protests managed to create a climate of failure around white leadership's ability to reshape the city, facilitating the rise to prominence of local black political interests in the post–civil rights era. The protests of black and white residents in the South-Central area led to repeated failed attempts to follow through on growth coalition urban renewal plans, and signaled a shift in the political climate of the city, wherein the voices of black residents, leaders, and activists were influential and facilitated interracial strategies and activism emergent in post–civil rights Philadelphia. The activism around the Crosstown Expressway forged new alliances and shifted the city's racial geography in ways that would prove significant as black Philadelphians pursued political office during and following the successes of the civil rights movement. In fact, many who were active participants in the Crosstown Expressway battle became key local political leaders in the years that followed, most notably W. Wilson Goode. In light of such shifting sociopolitical conditions, next I consider the sociopolitical history of the Black Seventh Ward in the context of increasing black political representation, particularly in local political office.

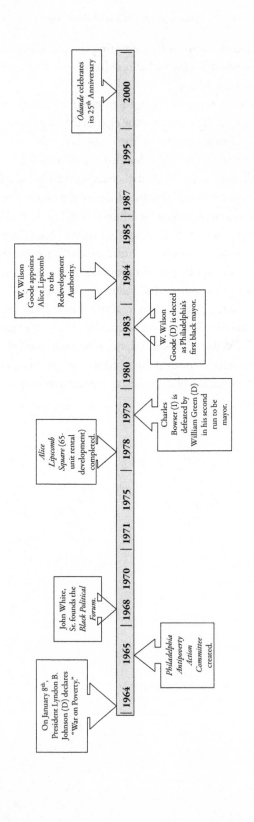

On January 8th, President Lyndon B. Johnson (D) declares "War on Poverty."

Philadelphia Antipoverty Action Committee created.

John White, Sr. founds the *Black Political Forum*.

Alice Lipscomb Square (65-unit rental development) completed.

Charles Bowser (I) is defeated by William Green (D) in his second run to be mayor.

W. Wilson Goode (D) is elected as Philadelphia's first black mayor.

W. Wilson Goode appoints Alice Lipscomb to the Redevelopment Authority.

Odunde celebrates its 25th Anniversary

1964 | 1965 | 1968 | 1970 | 1971 | 1975 | 1978 | 1979 | 1980 | 1983 | 1984 | 1985 | 1987 | 1995 | 2000

5

Philadelphia's Black Belt

"PHILADELPHIA IS A city of neighborhoods. We cherish our communities and our community leaders," remarked recently reelected Mayor W. Wilson Goode at an award ceremony held at City Hall to honor Alice Lipscomb in January of 1989. As the city's first black mayor and longtime friend of Lipscomb, Goode spoke glowingly:

> Alice Lipscomb has spent the last 34 years of her life helping to forge a better community in the Hawthorne area....Not far from Independence Hall, Alice Lipscomb fought her own battle of independence in the 1950s. She fought for tenants' rights and formed the Hawthorne Community Council as a response to the Code Enforcement Program and the relocation of families who had to leave due to urban revitalization during that time.

Referring to Lipscomb's prominent role in defeating the Crosstown Expressway, Goode reminded those in attendance of both her historical importance as a black activist and leader and her contemporary role as a member of the Redevelopment Authority (RA). Having appointed Lipscomb to the RA following his election in 1983, Goode had come to rely on Lipscomb's leadership as a central feature of his administration's efforts to revitalize black neighborhoods across Philadelphia.[1] This ceremony held for Lipscomb was indicative of the political efforts of black Philadelphians in the years following the Civil Rights Act of 1964. Once disenfranchised from the local political scene, Goode and Lipscomb stood together that night as symbols of the successful electoral strategies enacted by black residents, leaders, and activists in post–civil rights Philadelphia.

Indeed, this scene from Goode's time as Philadelphia's mayor was a far cry from the state of black politics in Philadelphia described by W. E. B. DuBois in *The Philadelphia Negro*, where he found that "about 5500 Negroes were eligible to vote in the city of Philadelphia, in 1870," and the "Negro [vote was] a tool of the Republicans." However different the sociopolitical context was from DuBois's era, there are some similar dynamics that appear, though not exactly in the manner DuBois depicted. DuBois's characterization of the black vote is especially useful and insightful:

> The experiment of Negro suffrage in Philadelphia has developed three classes of Negro voters: a large majority of voters who vote blindly at the dictates of the party and, while not open to direct bribery, accept the indirect emoluments of office or influence in return for party loyalty; a considerable group, centering in the slum districts, which casts a corrupt purchasable vote for the highest bidder; lastly a very small group of independent voters who seek to use their vote to better present conditions of municipal life.[2]

While black electoral politics may not be easily divided into DuBois's three subsets during the post–civil rights period, his characterization does signal an underlying heterogeneity among black voters that cannot be overstated. During DuBois's time in Philadelphia the notion of a black mayor was perhaps unimaginable, and thus he did not fully account for the intraracial dynamics that encapsulate post–civil rights black politics. As a result, DuBois would have focused less on how his three voting distinctions work within the context of black political leadership and the rise to power of a black mayor, Philadelphia's Wilson Goode. This chapter brings together DuBois's depiction of the dynamics of black voting as it interacts with black electoral and civil rights gains.

Goode's electoral victory signaled another, and perhaps final, transition for the Black Seventh Ward, from a physical site of black residences to one of cultural and historical memory. While physical black neighborhoods matter for urban landscapes, so too do memories of former black enclaves. However, efforts to preserve such black urban legacies often require particular political, cultural, and social conditions. In the case of Philadelphia, such conditions emerged from the efforts of black residents, leaders, and activists to take hold of key political and appointed positions within city government, which in turn led to Goode's election as the city's first black mayor. The rise to prominence of both Goode and Lipscomb as witnessed in the award ceremony was no accident, but the product of the work of what I refer to as Philadelphia's "black growth coalition."

Informed by discussion of postwar growth machines and coalitions by John Mollenkopf, John Logan, and Harvey Molotch, here I use the concept of a black growth coalition to account for the shift in political power and control over resource allocation in post–civil rights Philadelphia. While Logan and Molotch's framework illustrates the ways in which class, politics, inequality, and capitalism converge in urban America, critiques of this perspective have suggested that within this framework little attention has been given to the impact of racial domination. To address this gap, scholars such as Joe Feagin have offered what has been referred to as the "new urban paradigm."[3] Using this paradigm, Feagin and others have suggested that the political and economic practices of white officials and elites have marginalized and disenfranchised urban minorities and the neighborhoods they occupy. However, despite the emphasis on racial domination, such a perspective largely privileges the actions and attitudes of whites, paying significantly less attention to the agency of urban minorities and the affect of such agency on patterns of urban change.[4]

To understand the intraracial and interneighborhood dynamics of black Philadelphians over time, I build from the conception of the city as a growth machine developed by growth coalitions. Whereas researchers have emphasized the competition and coalitions among white elites and stakeholders, I focus instead on black residents, groups, institutions, leaders, and activists. Along similar lines, scholars such as political scientist Adolph Reed offer the notion of "black urban regimes"—"black-led and black-dominated administrations backed by solid council majorities." Though Reed includes Philadelphia among the "thirteen U.S. cities with populations over 100,000," wherein such regimes control municipal affairs, as I will show in this chapter the notion of a "regime" assumes an organized purpose and consensus among urban black Americans, which was not always present in Philadelphia's black leadership.[5] Though on its face the network of black leadership emergent in post–civil rights Philadelphia would later dominate key electoral offices (before, during, and after Goode's victory), such leadership mirrored more of a "coalition"—the loose but substantial coordination between black leaders across black neighborhoods to wrest municipal powers from white leaders.

Similar to what the postwar growth coalition sought to accomplish for corporate leaders and white Democrats, the black growth coalition worked to increase the political power and representation of black interests and access to resources for black Philadelphians. Though the postwar growth coalition relied on a shift in the city's power base from Republican to Democratic—drawing a broad base of blacks across neighborhoods—the emergent black growth coalition depended upon shifting power from a predominantly white electoral base to a black electorate. The various efforts of distinct black neighborhood councils, sociopolitical organizations, activists, and leaders shifted the city's political landscape and racial geography in ways that profoundly shaped Philadelphia and the Black Seventh Ward; such efforts in post–civil rights Philadelphia serve as the focus of this chapter.

In the years following the demise of the Crosstown Expressway, the once vibrant Black Seventh Ward had become the site of gentrification. From 1975 to 2000 the area went through significant changes, with the east side of South Street (located below Broad Street) emerging as a distinctly artsy and commercial area, while the west side of South Street (above Broad Street) became a combination of high-end condominiums and businesses. Despite the black secondary migration out of the area, black Philadelphians sought not only to maintain a presence in the area, particularly along western South Street, but also to preserve the historical legacy of the area as the former center of urban black life.

As a result, two different yet equally important efforts took place on opposite sides of South Street. On South Street (to the east), Lipscomb and the Hawthorne Community Council redeveloped the predominantly black Hawthorne neighborhood into a vibrant enclave, renovating old structures once used in the heyday of the Black Seventh Ward. Bounded by South Street, Broad Street, Washington Avenue, and 11th Street, the Hawthorne neighborhood was perhaps the lasting physical vestige of the Black Seventh Ward. At the same time, on South Street (to the west), under the leadership of longtime black residents Lois Fernandez and Ruth Arthur, a new cultural tradition, Odunde, was established to preserve the area's urban black legacy, gesturing to black memories of days when South Street was the "blackest" street in Philadelphia. Pronounced "Oh-Doon-Day," the festival emerged from its humble beginnings in 1975 into a cultural occasion attracting blacks from across the United States to celebrate their culture and history in a day-long event located upon the site of the Black Seventh Ward.

In this chapter, I examine the changes in the Black Seventh Ward through the lens of the Hawthorne neighborhood and Odunde. I begin by providing background for black political development in post–civil rights Philadelphia; the increasing political power of black Philadelphians provides the historical backdrop for substantive changes in the area formerly constituting the Black Seventh Ward, and it facilitated what I contend was a project of urban black memory. Indeed, black Philadelphians' fond memories of the Black Seventh Ward, particularly South Street, encouraged significant developments helping to preserve the black character of the area (even if black residents were not physically living there). Both the Hawthorne neighborhood and Odunde illustrate the important work that urban black Americans do to reify and sustain black space within the city, despite continued displacement brought on by processes such as gentrification and urban renewal. In this way, this chapter uses the political agency of black Philadelphians in the post–civil rights context as a window into the patterns of sociopolitical change in the city in the last decades of the twentieth century, thus demonstrating the continued roles of black Philadelphians as citymakers and as shapers of the Black Seventh Ward in the decades following the defeat of the Crosstown Expressway.

From Middlemen to Mainmen: Black Politics in Post–Civil Rights Philadelphia

In the decades preceding Goode's election, black Philadelphians were engaged in a persistent battle with the local government. Protests against the Crosstown Expressway dovetailed with activism of black residents in other areas of the city. Just as Lipscomb and Dukes were rallying residents in the South-Central area against the city's urban renewal plans, black leaders and residents in North and West Philadelphia organized around a series of issues including police brutality, housing discrimination, educational inequity, and labor discrimination (to name a few).

Much like the Crosstown Expressway protest led by Lipscomb and Dukes, black-led protests in other areas of the city assailed local officials for their lack of attention to the various issues plaguing black Philadelphians. As historian Matthew J. Countryman observes in *Up South: Civil Rights and Black Power in Philadelphia*, the period preceding Goode's election was highly contentious, particularly in the black sections of North Philadelphia, commonly referred to as "the Jungle." Indeed, organizations such as the Philadelphia branch of the National Association for the Advancement of Colored People (NAACP), the 400 ministers, Philadelphia's Welfare Rights Organization, and the Congress of Racial Equality (CORE) led successful campaigns against discrimination in the city. For example, throughout the 1960s Cecil B. Moore led the Philadelphia NAACP in waging a successful battle against the long-standing educational practices of Girard College, which allowed only poor white orphaned males to attend the school. Located in the heart of black North Philadelphia, the efforts of the Moore-led NAACP forced the school's administration to admit black children to the boarding school, thus opening up more educational opportunities for the city's black students and ending the Girard College's century-long race-based exclusionary practices. At the same time, the 400 ministers, a civil rights organization that comprised 400 of the most influential black ministers in the city, led a highly effective selective patronage campaign against Tastykake, a Philadelphia-based baked-goods corporation. Referred to as the "Don't Buy Where You Can't Work" campaign, the 400 ministers successfully led black stores and consumers in a boycott against Tastykake, forcing the corporation to reform its employment practices and increase the number of its black employees.[6]

Missing, however, from Countryman's analysis, and provided here, is the historical and contemporary relationship between Black Seventh Warders and larger black sentiment and activism in Philadelphia. Just as protests against Girard College and Tatsykake in North Philadelphia facilitated critical racial shifts in local politics and policy, so too did protests against urban renewal such as that evidenced in the Crosstown Expressway. Situated within Center City, Black Seventh Warders criticized white officials on a different and equally important front. Like education and employment, processes of urban redevelopment, such as urban renewal, significantly impact the social realities of black residents. Therefore, the activism of black and white residents against the Crosstown Expressway was constitutive of the larger shift in the local political structure.

While each of these black protests was by no means based on a single issue, it is clear that like the black-led activism against the Crosstown Expressway, that against Girard College and Tastykake relied on the ability of black leaders to function as what sociologist Mary Pattillo terms "middlemen/middlewomen"—black power-brokers "spanning the space between established centers of white economic and political power and the needs of a down but not out black neighborhood."[7] However, as both the black population and the political power of the local Democratic coalition increased, black Philadelphians, like their counterparts in Cleveland, Gary (Indiana), Detroit, New York, and Atlanta, sought to gain formal political power through successes in electoral politics. Many scholars have highlighted this goal as the move from "protest to politics." Constituting a "new black politics" this shift characterizes black political efforts across the United States following the civil rights movement, representing the critical turn from organized protests to pursuits in electoral representation.

As I will show in subsequent sections, the quest to move from middlemen to *mainmen* was a contentious project both within and outside of the black electorate. To be clear, as Pattillo rightly acknowledges, given the larger marginalization of urban blacks, black politicians despite political office are perhaps always middlemen. However, what I am emphasizing with the distinction between middlemen and mainmen is the critical shift in the way urban blacks framed their political aspirations in the post–civil rights era, seeking offices that in previous periods were virtually unattainable and off-limits. Although the mayor of a city is arguably a prototypical middleman, given the fact that urban residents live locally, this political office is often perceived as the source of political power and control over resource allocation; hence the national significance and coverage of black mayors in the post–civil rights era.

The shift in focus on electoral representation suggested to white power-brokers that Philadelphia's black electorate was not a rank-and-file bloc within local politics but instead a political constituency insisting on expanding political power alongside its increasing growth in physical size and presence across the city. Further, as scholars such as Katherine Tate contend, the pursuit of electoral politics functioned as a major focus for urban blacks across backgrounds and political dispositions.[8] I extend such claims, by revealing how this focus helped forge a black growth coalition alongside the white-led postwar growth coalition.

However successful and important black electoral efforts were, they did not necessarily create or sustain cohesion among black Philadelphians. Ambivalence and anger about white Democratic leadership within black Philadelphia characterized black politics in the wake of successful black-led protests. In the era preceding Goode's election, advancing black political interests was difficult, often leading to conflicts among black political organizations and with the larger Democratic coalition. Intraracial conflicts notwithstanding, attempts to advance black interests in Philadelphia created the political terrain that allowed for the election of the city's first black mayor and the consolidation of black areas constitutive of those interests within the city, which I refer to as Philadelphia's "Black Belt" (see Figure 5.1). Much like the black enclaves of Chicago, famously examined in St. Clair Drake and Horace Cayton's *Black Metropolis*, the black presence in the city grew dramatically throughout the waves of the Great Migration and spread across the city's southern, western, and northern areas.

With increased attention to race relations and racism, Philadelphia's Black Belt became a major political force in the post–civil rights era, often single-handedly determining the fate of local political candidates. Although the Black Seventh Ward continued to decline, the shift in local political power facilitated the efforts of black residents to preserve and sustain black memories and a smaller black enclave in the Lombard/South Street area.[9]

While a full discussion of the myriad political endeavors of black Philadelphians in the years preceding Goode's election is beyond the scope of this chapter, a brief discussion of the city's antipoverty efforts and major black

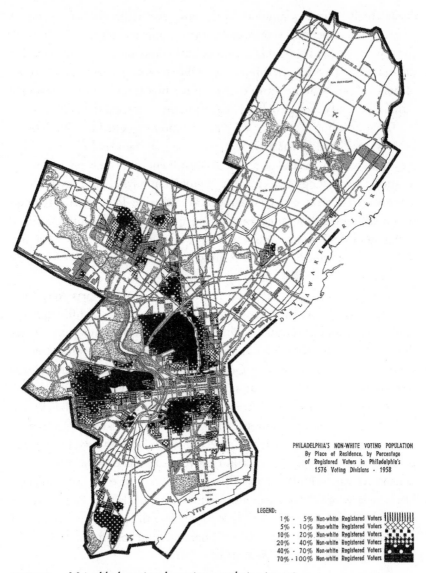

PHILADELPHIA'S NON-WHITE VOTING POPULATION
By Place of Residence, by Percentage
of Registered Voters in Philadelphia's
1576 Voting Divisions · 1958

LEGEND:
1% · 5% Non-white Registered Voters
5% · 10% Non-white Registered Voters
10% · 20% Non-white Registered Voters
20% · 40% Non-white Registered Voters
40% · 70% Non-white Registered Voters
70% · 100% Non-white Registered Voters

FIGURE 5.1 Major black sections by voting population in 1958.
Source: Philadelphia City Planning Commission (1958), City Archives.

electoral victories perhaps best illustrates the climate within which changes in
the Black Seventh Ward occurred in the decades following the Crosstown
Expressway protests. For this discussion, I focus specifically on the social
history of the Philadelphia Antipoverty Action Committee (PAAC), and
specific black electoral victories preceding Goode's mayoral bid. Emergent

from the civil rights legislation led by President Lyndon B. Johnson, Philadelphia's poverty programs set the stage for the shifting focus in black activism from protest to politics. Lessons from the PAAC prompted black leaders and activists to develop electoral strategies that helped forge Philadelphia's black growth coalition and ultimately led to Goode's historic election.[10]

The Philadelphia Antipoverty Action Committee

On January 8, 1964, President Lyndon B. Johnson declared a "war on poverty" during his State of the Union address. Seeking to address the so-called "culture of poverty," or the assumed cycle of pathology by which many, especially minorities, remained impoverished, Johnson proposed legislation that would confront the problems of America's poor. By August of 1964, Congress passed Johnson's War on Poverty program under the Economic Opportunity Act of 1964. To oversee the national antipoverty efforts, the Office of Economic Opportunity (OEO) was established. Proposed as a "hand up, not a handout," this legislation sought to bring an end to persistent poverty by investing in social-service programs that would allow the poor to develop skills enabling them to be self-sufficient and hirable. Central to the Johnson administration's War on Poverty was the focus on community involvement in the development of local efforts to mitigate poverty. This federal policy provided for the Community Action Program, developed to provide block grants to local antipoverty agencies under the theory that residents and organizations would know best how to address localized poverty and its myriad effects. In order to receive these grants, the federal government required that there be "maximum feasible participation of the poor" in the implementation and design of local antipoverty efforts.[11]

Given the provision of federal funding to address growing poverty, Mayor James Tate was quick to establish the Philadelphia Antipoverty Action Committee. Formally announcing its organization, on February 10, 1965, Tate declared that the PAAC would comprise a board of five mayoral appointees, representatives from fifteen civic groups including local chapters of the NAACP and CORE, the Chamber of Commerce, and the Catholic archdiocese, as well as twelve members from the city's "poverty community." Tate also announced that the representatives of the poor would be appointed following an election to be held on May 26, 1965. For that election, residents from the city's twelve poverty districts would elect a twelve-member Community Action Council (CAC) to organize antipoverty activities in neighborhoods throughout each of those districts. As a final step, each CAC would then select one representative to sit on the citywide PAAC.[12]

In its first meeting, held in March of 1965, the PAAC (without the representatives of the poor) agreed to have an executive director appointed by the mayor who would oversee the city's antipoverty program, with the provision that a six-person subcommittee drawn from the PAAC would recommend nominees. The selection process would prove difficult however. Given the focus on poverty and the provision for federal assistance, many black leaders wanted a place on the PAAC, particularly in the role as executive director. The battle between the NAACP's Cecil B. Moore and the Tate-supported black leader Samuel Evans was most notable.

Although neither Moore nor Evans seemed to want the job, each did want to select the person who would serve as executive director. For Moore, Isaiah Crippins, legal counsel for Philadelphia's NAACP, was the best choice. However Evans, who had worked with and supported Moore and the NAACP in the past, suggested Charles Bowser assume the role of executive director. Though Bowser, a black attorney, had done work for both the NAACP and the Police Advisory Board, Moore believed he was not the best candidate for the job. In Moore's estimation, Bowser was a good lawyer but was "not identified with the masses" of poor black Philadelphians. Hoping to rally interested parties behind his candidate, Moore proclaimed: "Crippins comes from the poor, works with the poor, and understands the problems of the poor." Adding to his proclamation, Moore threatened resignation from the PAAC if Crippins was not appointed as executive director. Though Moore's stance was strong, he was later undercut by Evans and Crippins in a deal made with Mayor Tate in which Evans's candidate, Bowser, would be executive director, and Crippins, Moore's candidate, would serve as legal counsel. With both Bowser and Crippins in agreement, Moore's resistance was thwarted and Bowser was appointed executive director.[13]

As executive director of the PAAC, Charles Bowser was the highest ranking and highest paid ($17,000 annual salary) black official in the Tate administration. In his first major task as executive director, Bowser oversaw the initial election for the CACs. While turnout was modest (with the highest percentages coming from black sections in North Philadelphia), the election was a success in that all slated positions were filled. The election also proved significant for women across the city, particularly black women, as women were elected to seventy-three percent of CAC seats. As Tate required, following the election, representatives from CACs were then appointed to the PAAC as representatives of the poor. Due to the high proportion of women elected to CACs, eight of the twelve representatives appointed to the PAAC were women. Among those black women elected to a CAC were Clara Baldwin, director and founder of the Baldwin Settlement House in North Philadelphia, and Abigail Pankey, president of West Philadelphia's Mantua Housing Committee. With the CACs and PAAC in place, the OEO director Sargent Shriver approved the city for $5.9 million to be used to support Philadelphia's antipoverty programs. While a source of success, the federal funding given to the PAAC soon devolved into a source of contention.[14]

Though Bowser was executive director, his close relationship with Evans remained, and the two worked in tandem to use the federal funding for the program to advance black interests in the city. Bowser was not alone in his alliance with Evans, as Evans had worked closely with Tate in the appointment of mayoral appointees to the PAAC. With black men and women accounting for the majority of seats in both the PAAC and the CACs, and a budget of nearly $6 million, Evans and Bowser transformed the PAAC into a black political patronage organization, divvying out funds based upon personal and political goals and hopes for black Philadelphians.

Reflecting on his time and approach as executive director, Bowser would later comment that during his time on the PAAC: "We didn't want to give them jobs and give them food and give them houses.... We wanted to teach them how to operate so they could get it for themselves." In part, Bowser's comments reveal that his approach was one that favored a sort of rugged individualism, empowering poor black Philadelphians to provide for themselves. His comments also reveal that under his leadership issues such as providing public and affordable housing were not necessarily high priorities, despite the continuing housing woes for many black Philadelphians. This stance, however, conflicted with the goals of CAC representatives and neighborhood councils headed by black women, such as the Hawthorne Community Council in South Philadelphia and Baldwin Settlement House in North Philadelphia, led by Alice Lipscomb and Clara Baldwin respectively. The differing focus of the PAAC led by Bowser and Evans and neighborhood-based councils and CACs highlighted the heterogeneity of purpose and interests among black leaders, and foreshadowed the competition between and among black political interests groups as black Philadelphians sought electoral power.[15]

By March of 1966, only three of the thirty-five proposals from CACs had been approved, and soon dissension erupted within the PAAC. Many PAAC representatives charged that Evans, with Bowser's consent, had used the organization and the emphasis on poverty to legitimize his selective approach to doling out funds. CORE representative to the PAAC David Fineman, for example, charged: "The community action councils have been ready, willing, and able to do their part in mounting a War on Poverty in Philadelphia.... However, they have been forced into the status of penniless orphans by the established welfare agencies." Discontent was not uniform, as those black representatives on the PAAC who benefited from Bowser and Evans's approach provided quiet consent.

For instance, the established black organization Opportunities Industrialization Centers (OIC) benefited greatly under the Bowser and Evans regime. Organized by black minister and leader Leon Sullivan, the OIC had been established in 1964 on the heels of the "Don't Buy Where You Can't Work" campaign to provide black workers with programs that would help them develop and enhance job skills, allowing them to take advantage of job opportunities emergent from the campaigns to negotiate the end of black selective patronage in the 1960s. Through the Bowser-led PAAC, Sullivan's OIC received nearly $2 million, while CACs, the local organizations for which the funding was slated, received fairly little. Though the PAAC was originally conceptualized as a mediator between the federal government and local community efforts against poverty, under Evans's and Bowser's leadership the PAAC was more likely to support established social welfare agencies. In the case of white service groups, PAAC funding was used to try to compel organizations such as the Board of Education and the Catholic archdiocese to provide equal access for black Philadelphians to their social services.[16]

The climate of intraracial divisions within the PAAC, are emblematic of larger dynamics involved in post–civil rights consensus-building among urban black Americans. With black leaders and activists attempting to mitigate the effects of systematic racism, debates around resource allocation were contentious and often revealed distinctive interests groups among urban blacks. Indeed, from its inception the PAAC seemed to create a climate of distrust and competition among black-led organizations such as CORE, NAACP, and OIC. Interested in maximizing their positions as middlemen, PAAC board members sought to allocate federal funds and the relative political power attached to such funds in ways that would revitalize urban black life, allaying issues of poverty, crime, and housing.

Leveraging federal funding, ignoring the proposals of CACs, and the continued discontent of Moore and members of the CORE and the NAACP, led to an active campaign by black leaders and residents (with the assistance of the OEO) to remove Bowser from his position as executive director in order to decrease Evans's influence. Such efforts would prove futile. The OEO withheld future funding until Evans's and Bowser's power on the PAAC was reduced. However, even after Crippins and Bowser both resigned, Evans retained control over the board. Indeed, only the demise of the national War on Poverty effort ended Evans's reign. By the winter of 1968 the War on Poverty was on a path of decline as congressional cuts dramatically reduced the PAAC's funding. As a result, the PAAC's board was forced to reduce its budget, and with the demise of the CACs the end of the PAAC soon followed.[17]

However admirable Bowser's and Evans's intentions had been, as a result of their selective funding scheme the various CACs were virtually destroyed, with many of the staff dejected and absent. Such an occurrence is reminiscent of what political scientist Cathy J. Cohen refers to as "secondary marginalization"—when efforts by black leaders, organizations, or individuals to articulate a supposed consensus issue of the black masses results in the disenfranchisement of the interests or efforts of segments of the larger black population, usually women and sexual minorities.[18] In this case, the efforts of the CACs to combat poverty in districts throughout the city were never given a real chance to thrive. With black women at the helm of many of these CACs, Bowser and Evans, whether directly or indirectly, further marginalized these organizations and their black female leadership by selectively funding established social-service agencies in the city. Hoping to use the PAAC as a tool to leverage new possibilities and opportunities for black Philadelphians, Evans and Bowser privileged some black organizations such as the OIC over others, creating a hierarchy of interests and groups within black Philadelphia.

The PAAC proved to be an ephemeral enterprise; its short-lived history however revealed the potential for black people to achieve significant political power in post–civil rights Philadelphia. Having witnessed the turnout of black voters in what amounted to a primarily black election in order to create the various CACs, many black leaders sought to mobilize the emergent black electorate to win public office and elect the city's first black mayor. Perhaps one of the major lessons derived from the PAAC episode is that it demonstrated that under the current Democratic coalition, black political power remained limited and contingent upon the willingness of white officials to create and place black people in positions of authority. Additionally, the PAAC experience further illustrated that state and local officials seemed willing and able to address the social realities of black Philadelphians only under political conditions that allowed the white Democratic regime to receive more federal funding. Though the PAAC was a new organization, it operated similarly to the various defunct offices, councils, and organizations created by white officials (Republican and Democratic) over the years to address the social realities of poor and working-class blacks—a short-lived black-led bureaucracy limited in power and scope by the white power-bloc controlling City Hall.

In the years following the demise of the PAAC, a variety of black leaders, activists and groups, at times working in tandem, sought to place black interests at the forefront of Philadelphia policy-making and politics. Comprising what I refer to as the *black growth coalition*, the efforts of these individuals and groups shifted the city's power base from the white male dominated Democratic leadership (often centered in upper- and middle-class white areas of the city), to black areas and constituencies in South, West, and North Philadelphia. Here, then, black Philadelphians aspired to push against the political ceiling that historically allowed for black politicians to serve only as middlemen at best. In this way, black Philadelphians embarked on a historic journey to take the levers of power out of the hands of the predominantly white Democratic regime, operating from emergent black political bases that together comprised Philadelphia's Black Belt. While similar to white-dominated growth coalitions emergent in the postwar era in its focus on increasing the city's size and power, the black growth coalition that I detail in the following section sought to shift black Philadelphia from a *separate city* into an incorporated electorate with significant political control of the total city.[19] Together these three major black regional areas within the city represented both a physical belt around City Hall, the formal epicenter of political power in Philadelphia, and the various black political interests producing the black leadership that would control the city from the highest office in post–civil rights Philadelphia.

Electoral Politics and the Rise of the Black Mayor in Philadelphia

In the spring of 1970, black Philadelphians awaited the arrival of Richard Hatcher. Chosen in a historic election as the first black mayor of Gary, Indiana, Hatcher came to Philadelphia to encourage, inform, and empower black Philadelphians to achieve a similar victory and elect a black mayor of their own. Prepared to deliver a message drawing from the experiences of blacks in Gary (and elsewhere), Hatcher was slated as the keynote speaker for the annual conference organized by the recently formed Black Political Forum (BPF). The BPF was founded in 1968 by West Philadelphia black activist and leader John White Sr., who also served as the organization's first president. Set to oust what he deemed the "plantation politics" of the Democratic City Committee (DCC), the White-led BPF was founded as a coalition of black activists, leaders, and Democrats disillusioned with the status quo.[20]

In many ways the BPF, from its inception, was determined to diminish the power of the DCC, as it was the party's highest governing body deciding the party's candidates at all levels of government. Indeed, in 1970 most all of the party's ward leaders were white. Further, the BPF members, referring to themselves as Black Independent Democrats, contended that candidates selected by the DCC were chosen based upon allegiance to the Democratic machine and its white leadership and not on their records of service to black Philadelphians. In other words, BPF members suggested that black representatives at the time were merely symbolic figures with little political power and equally little investment in pursuing the interests of black Philadelphians. What BPF members were identifying as problematic in Philadelphia's political structure was a feature found in local politics in many cities. Indeed, scholars such as Dianne Pinderhughes, Carol M. Swain, and Mack Jones have identified similar conditions in Midwestern and Southern cities, and they characterize such black leadership as *symbolic representation*, connoting the gap between the descriptive representation (place-holders) and substantive representation (policy-makers) of urban blacks in American cities.[21]

While from the beginning BPF members were determined to lead black Philadelphians to elect the city's first black mayor, the path to such an electoral triumph was by no means clear. Additionally, many black Philadelphians believed that the likelihood of a black person being elected to be mayor of Philadelphia was improbable given the city's persistent antagonistic racial climate. Hatcher's presence at the conference, then, provided a strategic opportunity to invest black Philadelphians in the BPF's fundamental goal, electing black representatives into the highest political offices possible.

To bring attention to the event and to encourage black Philadelphians to invest in the conference and its goals, BPF organizers also honored nine black working-class neighborhood activists from across the city, including: Mary Rouse (leader of the Council of Organizations on Philadelphia Accountability and Responsibility), Roxanne Jones (leader of Philadelphia Welfare Rights Organization), Black Power activists David Richardson and "Freedom" George Brower, Rose Wylie (leader of the Residents Advisory Board), and Alice Walker (a parent organizer from Philadelphia's Tutorial Project's education self-help centers). Making such links with black organizations throughout the city, the BPF sought to forge an interneighborhood and multiclass alliance of black Philadelphians in order to end the Democratic machine's control over resource allocation and policy specifically, and Philadelphia's black electorate more generally. Announcing the BPF as an emerging player in Philadelphia's political scene, its founders arranged to have two of the leading Democratic candidates in Pennsylvania's gubernatorial race, state auditor Robert Casey and Philadelphia businessman Milton Shapp, make statements preceding the keynote address from Hatcher.[22]

Hatcher had been invited by the BPF on the heels of his historic election, and his arrival was a highly publicized event. He did not disappoint BPF organizers, as he spoke powerfully using the experience of blacks in Gary to urge the more than 1,000 black Philadelphians in attendance to avoid "suicidal notions of armed revolution or [the] creation of separate black communities." Further he implored black Philadelphians to "get [their] hands on the levers that control power" and to organize in "political unity," as only an unified approach would pave the way to blacks winning "control of many of the nation's cities." Hatcher's words echoed much of what members of the BPF had hoped to convey to black Philadelphians. White, too, took time at the event to urge the audience to "let the politicians know that we demand representation," adding: "Right now, the leaders do not consult the people in the community on anything. They just vote the party line." As a result of such political complacency, White charged, "the people are [left] out" of the political process.[23]

BPF members moved quickly to action following the conference, beginning a grassroots effort to empower Philadelphia's black electorate. Using a storefront in West Philadelphia as its base, BPF members held seminars and strategy sessions, and trained poll watchers, potential candidates, street campaigners, and canvassers from black neighborhoods throughout the city. Those leading the effort included BPF founder John White Sr., West Philadelphia activist and attorney Hardy Williams, Wilson Goode, and Deputy Superintendent of Schools Bernard Watson. Attending training and strategy sessions held by the BPF were a number of future elected officials representing a new cohort of black political leadership in Philadelphia, namely Reverend William H. Gray III, David Richardson, Roxanne Jones, Chaka Fattah, Marian Tasco, John F. White Jr., and Shirley Hamilton (who would later serve as Mayor Goode's chief of staff).[24]

Endeavoring to shift political power in Philadelphia in favor of black residents, BPF leaders rallied behind Hardy Williams as the first electoral hopeful, setting the stage for a historic election in the black areas of West Philadelphia.

Having experienced a continued influx of black residents (due in large part to within-city migration), West Philadelphia's 191st District, encompassing the Third and Sixtieth wards, had become predominantly black by 1970. Williams, with Goode and Paul Vance as campaign managers, spent the summer in a door-to-door canvassing campaign that ultimately thwarted the DCC hold on the district. Defeating Paul Lawson, the DCC-supported black candidate and incumbent, Williams's primary victory that summer was unprecedented, as an outside candidate in a Democratic primary had never before defeated a DCC nominee for local office. That fall, Williams defeated his Republican opponent and was elected to the Pennsylvania House of Representatives. Williams's election was significant in that it revealed that at the neighborhood and district level, black activists could defeat the DCC and replace existing political representation with a new cohort of black political leaders. Indeed, the *Philadelphia Tribune* heralded Williams's election as "one of the most stunning upsets in Philadelphia political history."[25]

The BPF was not alone in its efforts as several distinct black organizations worked successfully to elect their own homegrown black leaders to political office. For example, BPF-trained David Richardson transformed his grassroots organization the Young Afros, located in the northwestern Germantown neighborhood, into a black political machine, which in turn facilitated his election to the State House of Representatives alongside Williams in 1972. Other BPF-affiliated black leaders also ran successful campaigns. Among those elected to public office were Lucien Blackwell, West Philadelphia labor leader, elected to the city council in 1975, and Chaka Fattah, elected to the State House of Representatives in 1982. In North Philadelphia, Milton Street, president of the Black Street Vendors Association and brother of future mayor John Street, also led a successful campaign and was also elected to Pennsylvania's House of Representatives. Leading what he dubbed a "poor people's crusade against racial repression in Philadelphia," Street's efforts also facilitated his younger brother, John, being elected to represent North Philadelphia in the city council. The work of black Philadelphians in the crosstown communities of South Philadelphia also led to the election of white allies as well, namely Norman Berson, who served as the area's Democratic representative in the State House of Representatives.[26]

Although such electoral accomplishments were a source of inspiration for some black Philadelphians, they were a source of ambivalence for others. While many black Philadelphians supported the efforts of black political organizations such as the BPF, Young Afros, and the Black Street Vendors Association, a great deal feared that by contesting existing black leadership

and the Democratic coalition, such efforts to counter the status quo would
further marginalize black interests and leadership. This became especially
resonant in the wake of Williams's 1971 bid to become mayor, in which the
Democratic vote was split, to the benefit of Frank Rizzo.

As police commissioner, Rizzo had become notorious in black neighborhoods across the city. He was a racially motivated leader who now, in the
estimation of Republican city councilman Thacher Longstreth, campaigned
on the message of "stop[ping] the black people, who represent the crime in
the streets and the problems in the school system and whatever else is bad
about Philadelphia." While Williams suggested later that his presence in the
race was meant to empower black voters and produce a significant turnout for
the Democrats, his presence in the race split the vote. In the end, Rizzo
defeated William Green, the Americans for Democratic Action (ADA) nominee, by a margin of 48,000 votes, with Williams placing third with 50,000
votes (twelve percent of the total). Though Williams's mayoral bid facilitated
Rizzo's rise to mayor, the symbolic virtues of his efforts lay the foundation for
two black mayoral hopefuls, Charles Bowser, former executive director of the
PAAC, and BPF activist W. Wilson Goode. Whatever reluctance existed
among black Philadelphians dissipated over the course of the eight-year mayoral reign of Frank Rizzo.[27]

Perhaps providing the ideal political conditions for the rise of a black
mayor in Philadelphia, Rizzo's tenure was one marred by continued violence
between the Philadelphia Police Department and black residents throughout
the city that many believed was promoted by the Rizzo administration.
Staging a third-party campaign, Bowser formed the Philadelphia Party. Joined
by a contingent of black political activists from across the city including
Goode, John White Sr., and William Meek, Bowser mounted a mayoral
campaign over a five-year period. In the 1975 mayoral race, his first attempt,
Bowser received nearly 150,000 votes (100,000 more than the Williams
campaign in 1971). Though a noteworthy effort, Bowser's first attempt
received a mixed reception from black voters. Harkening back to Williams's
mayoral bid, some black leaders and activists suggested that Bowser's
Philadelphia Party could have better used its constituency to negotiate with
Rizzo and generate black political power within his administration. The
thinking here was that leveraging the black vote to enter into a power-sharing
situation with the Rizzo administration was the best solution. However, when
Rizzo attempted to amend the city charter in order to run for a third term,
Bowser and his Philadelphia Party used the issue to bring attention to his
cause. Successfully leading the "Vote No to Charter Change" campaign,

Bowser was able to channel anti-Rizzo sentiment and develop a broad coalition of blacks and whites.[28]

Using such political synergy, Bowser mounted his second mayoral bid in 1979. Incorporating the broader base for his Philadelphia Party, Bowser's strategy was to garner a unified black vote with the hope that the presence of a white liberal and white conservative candidate would split the white-majority vote. Despite his best efforts, when two of the three white candidates withdrew from the race and endorsed Democratic nominee William Green, Bowser lost the election by nine percentage points. Having received the majority of the black vote, Bowser's loss enraged his supporters. To defuse such anger, Green and Bowser reached a power-sharing deal of sorts, wherein Green appointed Goode as the city's first black managing director (the second highest position in city government) following his mayoral inauguration in 1980; thus the stage was set for Goode's subsequent election as the city's first black mayor in 1983.[29]

Such negotiations were prominent in urban areas with significant black populations in the post–civil rights era. Also prominent was the intraracial debate around pursuing political office in opposition to the dominant Democratic coalition. Given the interest Democrats had in federal assistance and social welfare programs, urban black leaders and activists often feared that in their quest for political office, the larger voting bloc would be split and in turn lead to the election of Republican officials, who tended to be fiscally and socially conservative.

During Green's tenure, black leaders in the city council shifted local policies on city contracts in efforts to increase black employment and entrepreneurship. In 1982 the city council established the Minority Business Enterprise Council to oversee an ordinance it created that required twenty-five percent of the work provided under city contracts be given to contractors who employed subcontracting firms operated and owned by minorities and women.[30] Here, black councilmen in Philadelphia, like black officials in other cities across the United States, used their increased political power to focus on increasing black employment. As Rufus P. Browning, Dale Rogers Marshall, and David H. Tabb show in their study of ten California cities, like Philadelphia during the same period, the increasing political power of blacks and Hispanics correlated with increases in city hiring and contracts given to minorities. Other research, too, has affirmed this as a national trend, indicating the general positive relationship between the increased presence of black officeholders and black employment within city government.[31]

Whatever power-sharing arrangement had been made in the wake of Bowser's defeat did not necessarily ease Green's experience with black leaders and activists. For example, in 1983 black members of the city council critiqued the Green administration's continued focus on the downtown area in urban redevelopment plans. When Green's annual budget was presented before the city council in 1983, the three most prominent black councilmen—Joseph Coleman (president of the city council), John Street, and Lucien Blackwell—joined together and attacked what they determined to be a downtown bias reflected in the mayor's budget. With a budget that included provisions for a downtown convention center and waterfront redevelopment, John Street contended: "I don't call that a program that reflects any interest in the residents of the city," further adding: "We pay and we pay and we pay, and all we see is fancy buildings going up in the center of town."[32]

The work of black city councilmen during Green's tenure demonstrates the ways in which black elected officials joined together to push white leadership to focus on the interests of black residents. To be sure, Street's "we" likely referred to black Philadelphians, particularly in West and North Philadelphia, whom many black leaders believed had yet to benefit from urban redevelopment. Implicit within the black councilman's critique was the call for a shift in resource allocation to focus on black neighborhoods. Unlike white leaders, black leaders in the post–civil rights era had a decidedly neighborhood-based approach to city redevelopment, one in which black neighborhoods were placed as focal points for revitalizing the city. Whereas the white postwar growth coalition situated a revitalized Center City as the foundation for redeveloping Philadelphia, black elected officials argued that black neighborhoods in the city were a better tool to gauge revitalization in Philadelphia. Black officials, then, operated with the notion that a redeveloped Philadelphia was interdependent with redeveloped black neighborhoods throughout the city, as black neighborhoods, in their estimation, were the true reflections of the effects of urban decay and disinvestment that revitalization was meant to redress.

Benefiting from the large bloc of black voters empowered in Bowser's mayoral bid, Goode staged an effective campaign throughout 1983. Unlike in previous efforts, black leaders across the city lined up behind Goode, actively winning over voters one neighborhood at a time. In addition to his support from leaders such as the Street brothers, David Richardson, Lucien Blackwell, and Charles Bowser, the work of Alice Lipscomb, housing activist and South-Central area resident, proved significant as well. Whereas leaders such as the Streets and Richardson relied on predominantly black constituencies,

Lipscomb's interracial alliance constituting the Crosstown Community forged in the years of protests against urban renewal (discussed in chapter 4) brought significant white support as well.

Furthermore, business leaders from the city's growth machine, such as Provident and PSFS Banks, the CEOs of Smith and Kline, and Arco Chemical Company, rallied their support behind Goode. In the end, Goode won the general election by 123,000 votes, defeating Frank Rizzo by sixteen percentage points (fifty-eight to forty-two percent). The impact of the black vote in favor of Goode was reflective of the demographic shifts in Philadelphia's larger population. Between 1960 and 1980 Philadelphia's total population declined from 2.1 million to 1.7 million, with white flight greatly contributing to these population decreases. As scholar J. Phillip Thompson III points out, this out-migration of white residents was occurring across cities that would later elect black mayors: "Between 1950 and 1960, 1.2 million whites left Chicago, Philadelphia, and Newark, New Jersey, and 301,000 blacks moved in. In New York City, between 1950 and 1965, one million whites left and a nearly equal number of blacks and Puerto Ricans entered." From 1960 to 1977 "more than 200,000 whites but only 20,000 blacks are estimated to have left the city of Philadelphia." Drawn to the suburban communities like Burlington, New Jersey (formerly Levittown), and those in Bucks County, Pennsylvania, whites left Philadelphia as manufacturing and development took shape. According to recent research by Mathew Creighton and Michael Katz, from 1970 to 1990 the share of Philadelphia's larger metropolitan population in suburban job centers, such as those in Bucks and Burlington counties, increased from 12.4 percent to 13.7 percent, while the city's core declined from 37.5 to 29.9 percent.[33]

Despite decreases in Philadelphia's white population, due largely to white flight to suburban destinations, Wilson's victory still required a largely biracial coalition and voter turnout. Much like his counterpart in Los Angeles, Tom Bradley, Wilson also had to leverage the white vote in order to win. We can look to J. Phillip Thompson III's research on black mayors for comparison with Los Angeles, for example:

> When Tom Bradley, one of the most moderate black mayors, was elected [in 1972] in the first wave [of black mayors] as mayor of Los Angeles, blacks…were a small minority of the population. Although Bradley was not a civil rights mayor, he had built a strong biracial coalition emphasizing racial moderation, and the politically influential Jewish community provided substantial support.[34]

Wilsons's election, then, is reflective of the importance of and need for biracial coalitions in places with white majorities, like Los Angeles and Philadelphia, in order to successfully elect a black mayor. In other cities like Detroit, however, as Thompson argues, "many mayors were accused of maintaining the bitter racial atmosphere that surrounded their elections as a way to rally black voters to their side in reelection campaigns." Indeed, black candidates like Coleman Young, the Detroit's first black mayor, were often accused of "maintaining the bitter racial atmosphere that surrounded their elections as a way to rally black voters to their side." Such reliance on racial antagonism and bitterness is reminiscent of the tactics of the black urban regimes of Detroit and Washington DC, while in places with white majorities, like Philadelphia and Los Angeles, we find the development of a coalition that centered black interests with white allies.

This use of a biracial alliance as a means of growing and developing the city, especially the black areas, we find evident the night of Goode's election. Speaking to a packed audience in the Convention Hall, Goode called for Philadelphians black and white to help him grow Philadelphia:

> I want to build a better Philadelphia. Will you help me? I want to put the unemployed people back to work. Will you help me? I want to wipe out corruption in this city. Will you help me? I want to give children a chance to be all they can be. Will you help me? I want to change educational priorities. Will you help me? I want to change the landscape of our neighborhoods. Will you help me? I want to build a trash-to-steam plant and do what is needed to improve the quality of life in this city. Will you help me?

Philadelphians in attendance stood and in a powerful wave responded back "Yes! Yes! Yes! I will help you." In this way, Goode's comments reflect the important balancing act undergirding the development of a black growth coalition, wherein black leaders had to walk a fine line between empowering black residents to take the reigns of politics and change in the city, all the while not pointing to white residents and leaders as responsible.[35]

Essentially, the black growth coalition forged in post–civil rights Philadelphia, shifted political control from predominantly white Democratic leadership and, in turn, transformed blacks areas in North, South, and West Philadelphia into black political power bases. Such a shift helped to bring black interests and politicians to the forefront of city politics, and facilitated efforts of black residents remaining in and around South Street to pursue redevelopment strategies and preserve the memory of the Black Seventh

Ward. Already in a state of flux in the wake of the Crosstown Expressway debacle, the Black Seventh Ward shrunk dramatically in physical size, virtually reduced to the boundaries of the Hawthorne neighborhood, an area avidly protected by the Hawthorne Community Council, led by Alice Lipscomb. Due in large part to Lipscomb's alliance with Goode, forged during the years of protest against the Crosstown Expressway, the smaller though still profoundly black Hawthorne neighborhood thrived. Although gentrification and secondary migration plagued South Street, the new era in black politics also facilitated the creation of new black cultural enterprises, namely Odunde, aimed at unifying black residents all the while preserving black collective memories of the Black Seventh Ward.

Above Broad Street, below Broad Street: South Street, The Hawthorne Community Council and Odunde

"I believe South Street will remain the Mason-Dixon line for years to come," Dr. I. Henry Grant told *Philadelphia Tribune* reporters in the May of 1979. Grant, who first arrived on South Street in 1937, had over the last forty years watched racial change occur along South Street, with his dental practice declining as black residents continued to move out of the area. Reflecting on the changes in the area, Grant added: "South street was lively, businesses were everywhere. You could get anything you wanted on South Street. You were not afraid to walk on South Street.... What hurt the area was the crosstown expressway plans." While Grant was sad to see his dental practice (located at 1506 South Street) decline, he remained hopeful that South Street would again emerge as a prominent social center in Philadelphia.[36]

Grant was not alone in his observations of South Street, as Alice Lipscomb also noted similar changes:

> Its not like it used to be... I remember when [South Street] was a real shopping strip. People came from all over the city.... Long time ago in the 1100 block there was Dave's restaurant, and I remember the Standard Theater where they used to stage shows. That goes back a long way. I remember it as a place where all the Blacks did their shopping. It was an avenue for Blacks. It was a good time. There used to be butcher shops, shoe shops, clothing shops.

Lipscomb's reflections harken back to the Black Seventh Ward in the days and years before urban renewal and the Crosstown Expressway. Though

Lipscomb's efforts to thwart the Crosstown Expressway were successful, in her campaign she hoped like Grant that the area would maintain a substantial black presence: "When we fought successfully to stop the construction of the Crosstown Highway through South and Bainbridge streets, we thought we'd see a comeback." Yet, there was a comeback in the area, as in the years following the Crosstown Expressway debate whites were coming back. Commenting on the return of whites to the area, Lipscomb offered: "I call them the hippie crowd." Such "hippies," were in effect the whites who had begun residing along South Street in the late 1970s gentrifying the area throughout the rest of the twentieth century.

Grant and Lipscomb's observations were consistent with much of the change in the Black Seventh Ward in post–civil rights Philadelphia, particularly in the years following the Crosstown Expressway debate. Grant's comments capture the larger transition of the Black Seventh Ward from the physical site of black residences to one of collective black memory. In the wake of the failed Crosstown Expressway, the black residential area once located in and around South Street contracted, so that virtually all that remained was the Hawthorne neighborhood, an area bordered by Washington Avenue and South Street (from north to south) and Broad and 11th Streets (from east to west). In the last two decades of the twentieth century, black residents forged new boundaries and traditions upon the "graveyard" of the Black Seventh Ward.

During the late twentieth century, the Black Seventh Ward remained alive, though under different conditions and within and among a new generation of black residents. Much like New York City's Harlem, Chicago's Bronzeville, and Pittsburgh's Hill District, the Black Seventh Ward retained a significant place in the collective memories of black residents. In the years following Goode's historic election, such powerful black memories of the area compelled black Philadelphians to protect those residents who remained, and preserve the black presence on South Street through cultural means. In what follows, I examine two major efforts to preserve the black presence in the Lombard/South Street area in the wake of Goode's electoral victory: the redevelopment and preservation of the Hawthorne neighborhood, and the establishment of the cultural festival Odunde.

A Vestige of the Black Seventh Ward: Alice Lipscomb and the Hawthorne Neighborhood

While the city had made promises throughout the 1960s and 1970s to provide affordable housing for displaced black residents living in the Lombard/South Street area, by the late 1970s those promises remained unfulfilled.

Additionally, by the mid-1970s the interracial alliance among black and white residents deployed to thwart expressway construction was fractured. With highway construction no longer looming, neighborhood organizations such as the Hawthorne Community Council (HCC) and the Society Hill Civic Association began to pursue different neighborhood-based revitalization efforts. While the predominantly white upper-middle-class Society Hill neighborhood managed to generate outside investment to begin to revitalize east South Street (located from Front to Broad Streets) black residents remaining in the area continued to live in dilapidated housing. Much like New York's Harlem, east South Street was undergoing a gradual process of gentrification, wherein a legion of white bohemians and businessmen who lived in the area drew in outside corporate interests.[37]

While the interracial alliance may have fractured, the demise of the Crosstown Expressway did provide some promise for the area's black residents with regard to housing. Alice Lipscomb had continued to pursue the Hawthorne Plan even after the coalition of neighborhood organizations against the Crosstown Expressway had dissipated. Though Lipscomb's Hawthorne Plan had received much praise from local and federal officials, city leaders were reluctant to provide adequate funding for the plan, still focusing most of their attention on Center City, particularly along Market Street, the area's major street. With the specter of highway construction removed, the HCC had been able to gather the support of private lenders in the business community, namely the Provident Savings Association. Additionally, the plan had received an allotment from the United States Department of Housing and Urban Development (HUD). With such funds, the HCC facilitated the development and construction of a sixty-five-unit rental development, which was later named after Lipscomb in 1978.

Important to such redevelopment plans was the preservation of existing structures in the neighborhood. Indeed, from its inception the Hawthorne Plan sought to forge a revitalized black neighborhood while also preserving existing structures that were imbued with black cultural and political memories. Whereas white-led progrowth policies in the postwar era equated redevelopment with razing existing residences and buildings, thereby completely remaking the built environment, the HCC model, like neighborhood-based approaches, imagined revitalization as a combination of preservation and rehabilitation. In Lipscomb's estimation, the housing needs of black residents did not necessarily require the destruction of existing residences, but instead renovation and remodeling that would generate a better quality of life and provide a modern flair to the neighborhood, fusing together new structures with historic ones. In particular, the black legacy of the area was integral, and perhaps made the Hawthorne Plan appealing to black residents and white investors. Given the focus on restoration and rehabilitation such plans were without the contentious virtues of previous redevelopment plans for the area, as displacement was not a necessary part of the process of redevelopment the HCC and Lipscomb advocated.[38]

However successful the HCC had been, displacement of black residents continued through the 1970s into the early 1980s. While the HCC had not been able to prevent the larger displacement of Black Seventh Warders, building Alice Lipscomb Square provided symbolic support in addition to the actual homes it provided. The presence of Alice Lipscomb Square helped to consolidate the neighborhood and prevented continued displacement of black residents from that neighborhood, establishing it as a significant black enclave in the South-Central area. The Hawthorne neighborhood served as the predominant black neighborhood near the area that once constituted the historic Black Seventh Ward—perhaps its last vestige.

The construction of Alice Lipscomb Square notwithstanding, the HCC's efforts continued to be hampered by the larger fear of displacement throughout the South-Central area due to the continued work of the Redevelopment Authority in the area. While the HCC had managed to redevelop parts of the Hawthorne area, black residents continued to live throughout the Lombard/South Street area. The specter of displacement, much like expressway construction, was frustrating for black residents, as the work of the HCC had managed in many ways to change the qualitative attributes of the neighborhood. Although such developments should have prompted city planners to realize that poor and working-class black residents were capable of planning and supervising redevelopment in the city's black neighborhoods, the proximity of the area to Center City meant the area was in a constant state of anticipation—awaiting the continued displacement of black residents and continued increase of white businesses and residents in the area. Lipscomb, however, like black activists and leaders throughout the city, worked to shift the political power in the city in favor of the black residents, with a focus on shifting the politics of the RA. Though her calls for moving away from razing black residences remained unaddressed, the shifting political climate which placed the interests of black residents at the fore provided the terrain that would allow the small yet significant black Hawthorne neighborhood to thrive.[39]

Upon Goode's election, Lipscomb and the HCC finally received the break they needed. Having maintained her connection with Goode throughout the

1970s, Lipscomb continued to press issues of housing as a significant black issue. In particular, she wanted to ensure that rehabilitation of existing housing and the construction of affordable housing would preserve the dying black neighborhoods in and around the once black South Street area. On Monday, January 9, 1984, just a few days after his inauguration as the Philadelphia' first black mayor, Goode appointed Lipscomb to the five-member board of the RA.[40] Such an appointment was significant as the RA was responsible for the relocation and redevelopment of sites once selected. Indeed, during the Crosstown Expressway conflict, the RA was often the source of contention, as it was often responsible for displacing residents most of whom the agency was unable to relocate. Here, then, Lipscomb's appointment represented a shift in the Philadelphia's political landscape, wherein under Goode's leadership major roles in city government were being given to black leaders and activists whose tireless work throughout the 1960s and 1970s facilitated Goode's triumph.

Although the Hawthorne neighborhood was predominantly black, black populations in North and West Philadelphia had begun to outpace it beginning in the 1960s. Lipscomb's efforts, though, were supported by black leaders throughout Philadelphia, including Lucien Blackwell in West Philadelphia and John Street in North Philadelphia. Lipscomb took her job seriously and went to work immediately to broker relationships with the business community in order to generate the capital necessary to fund her Hawthorne Plan. Within three months of her appointment, Lipscomb managed to invest several financial and community organizations in her efforts, namely the Atlantic Financial Federal corporation, the Philadelphia Council for Community Advancement, and the HUD.

In July of 1984, just seven months into her appointment, Lipscomb and the Hawthorne Community Council had facilitated the construction of a fifty-seven-unit townhouse development. A series of homes adorned with tiny flower gardens, red brick walls, and terraces stood in place of the dilapidated housing that had once been primary housing for black residents. Located at 12th and Bainbridge Streets, the Hawthorne Townhouses were praised as a grassroots redevelopment effort. "We started years ago, when there were programs coming in the area that weren't going to benefit us," Lipscomb told reporters at the grand opening of the units. Business leaders were on hand as well and gladly complimented the HCC's efforts. Melvin H. Porter, a mortgage consultant for Atlantic Financial Federal, noted that the housing development was successful in two major ways: "The Hawthorne Community Council has really produced something for their neighborhood ... and for the

individual recipients, the housing provides something they're not supposed
to have in today's economy—a house at moderate cost." Built at a cost of
nearly $80,000 each, the town homes stood as a symbol of the perseverance
of black residents in the Hawthorne area. Additionally, the HCC rehabili-
tated nineteen homes in the neighborhood. In response to such successful
redevelopment efforts Lipscomb spoke plainly: "Neighborhoods don't have
to be the way they are...they don't have to be run down...you can save your
neighborhood. You can do for yourself and you can remain in your own
community. It just takes real commitment." Lipscomb added: "It's been hard
work, but we're proud of our neighborhood.... This is no longer the worst
slum in the city." Lipscomb's words bespoke the spirit of hope that the HCC's
efforts had conjured for black residents throughout the city.[41]

The following year, 1985, the HCC received a $350,000 loan from the city
to rehabilitate the Hawthorne Elementary School, which had closed just six
years earlier. This project was perhaps the capstone on redevelopment in the
area, as the elementary school was of particular importance for the neighborhood's residents. As Lipscomb straightforwardly intimated: "We named the
area for Hawthorne after the school." Built in 1907, the school was closed due
to low enrollment in 1979. Derived from a two million dollar grant given to
the city by the HUD, the funds were slated to transform the old school
building into a series of affordable housing units for black elderly residents.
"It's a big school—85,000 square feet—and it was well built.... It was a wonderful old school, and we couldn't see its being used for anything other than
for the community," Lipscomb commented as she discussed plans for redeveloping the old school building. Located on 12th Street between Bainbridge
and Fitzwater Streets, Hawthorne Elementary School was slated to contain
forty-seven studio apartments and eight one-bedroom apartments. Lipscomb
also assured residents that people in the Hawthorne neighborhood would be
given priority. With a total cost of $2.1 million, the renovation of the school
was a costly endeavor. To meet its total costs, the HCC received a series of
loans from several organizations and lenders including: $550,000 loan from
the Philadelphia Housing Development Corporation, $745,000 investment
from the Sun Company, $595,000 loan from Cigna Corporation, and
$200,000 from the Enterprise Foundation of Baltimore.[42]

On Tuesday, June 2, 1987, Marie Smith (age 76) stood in front of the
Hawthorne Elementary School. Smith beamed with pride and anticipation as
she held onto her aluminum cane. Having attended the school as a young
child in the 1920s, Smith remembered the days when Black Seventh Warders
headed to the school for their daily instruction. "We used to have a good time

here.... I don't remember too many of the teachers. The only one I remember was Mrs. Knice. She was nice, considering teachers in those days, but she was strict. She kept everyone in line." As fond as Smith's memories of the school were, she was there to await the beginning of the building's new chapter as Hawthorne Villa, a rent-subsidized apartment unit for black senior citizens.

Soon after Smith's arrival, Goode and Lipscomb stood in front of the building to officially welcome Hawthorne's black elderly to the new and improved school building. As prospective residents walked inside, they were amazed. Though renovated to become a living space, the redevelopers had managed to preserve pieces of the old school wherever possible. Long and wide hallways, hardwood polished floors, and even some of the black chalkboards remained, all of which comprised the charm of the building. With the building serving as a new home for former students, such touches provided added comfort as it reminded many of days long passed. Such had been the case for Robert Smith (age 63) and his niece Lisa Singleton (age 35) as they moved Smith's belongings into his new studio apartment. Singleton was especially sentimental: "I went to kindergarden right across the hall here.... Right there, Room 214. Miss Burton was the teacher. And Miss Ash was right down the hall in Room 208.... It sure does bring back memories." The apartments, like all the other townhomes built under the HCC's leadership, were quickly occupied.[43]

The success of the HCC is indicative of the larger shifts in political power in the days and years following the demise of the Crosstown Expressway. The work of the HCC and Lipscomb thrived under the political and social conditions that gave rise to Goode's historic election. Important here, though, is the way in which the organization worked to preserve the neighborhood, embellishing previous structures important to black residents, as evidenced in the renovation of the Hawthorne Elementary School. Lipscomb's model for redevelopment sought to empower residents to take the reins on the revitalization of their neighborhoods and demonstrated that old memories can be preserved alongside new developments. As a vestige of the Black Seventh Ward, the Hawthorne neighborhood constituted new boundaries for where and how black residents moved in and around the South Street area.

Whereas in previous periods much of South and Lombard Street was significantly black, displacement and urban renewal contracted such residential boundaries. However small the Hawthorne neighborhood was, the housing successes of the HCC and Lipscomb were huge. Bringing together corporate and housing leaders, Lipscomb shifted the RA into an agency better facilitating the redevelopment of black residential areas. Throughout her appointment,

Lipscomb changed the RA from an agent of displacement into a broker of new black residential possibilities. Yet, as Lipscomb and the Hawthorne Community Council were making changes below Broad Street, a different, but equally important effort would change South Street above Broad Street, Odunde.

Odunde: Black Festivals and Black Memories

During a trip to the town of Oshogbo, Nigeria, in January 1972, Lois Fernandez, a black Philadelphia native, partook in a Yoruba tradition that would change her life and the cultural fabric of South Street. Fernandez headed to Nigeria in search of inspiration following the demise of her business, the Uhuru Hut, an Afrocentric boutique she co-owned with fellow black South Street area resident Ruth Arthur. Adorned in African garb and with an afro, Fernandez arrived in Nigeria and was immediately enraptured by the religion of Nigeria's Yoruba people, Ifa. In a religious structure akin to Catholicism, Ifa believers worship one god and approximately 401 *orishas*, or saints. Of particular importance for Fernandez, was Oshun, the orisha of the river and goddess of love. The town of Oshogbo was the home of the shrine of Oshun. In a religious custom, Fernandez participated in a processional to a river in Nigeria where she was taught how to make offerings to Oshun by placing flowers and fruit into the river. While the entire trip was of significance for Fernandez, the custom of offering gifts in honor of Oshun would shape her efforts to create a new tradition for black Philadelphians upon her return.[44]

After returning that year, Fernandez and her former business partner, Ruth Arthur, planned from their row homes a cultural festival that would employ all that she had learned in Nigeria, with the hope of inspiring black Philadelphians to embrace their history and culture. Soon after developing their plans, Fernandez and Arthur were given a small grant of one hundred dollars from local black businessmen and began to consider possible locations. The choice of where to stage their new black cultural festival was by no means difficult for Fernandez and Arthur, as the duo believed South Street was the ideal spot. Reflecting on the choice in location Fernandez offered: "South Street is the home of our ancestors."

The combination of localized memories of the Black Seventh Ward and religious memories of Oshun provide a particularly potent fusion of black history and culture, or memory capital. Making use of Yoruba religion and black Philadelphia history, Odunde founders localized black collective memories of migration into and within Philadelphia, employing religion as a way to meld together the experiences of black Americans. Such a process is reflective of scholar Maurice Halbwachs's discussion of collective memory and its deployment. In particular, Halbwachs's discussion of the function of religious memory, such as that of Oshun, bespeaks the memory project encapsulated in Odunde: "[religious memories] reproduce in more or less symbolic forms the history of migrations and fusions of races and tribes, great events, wars, establishments, discoveries, and reforms that we can find at the origin of the societies that practice them."[45] In this way, Odunde founders, from the inception of the festival, incorporated such understandings of memory to develop a black festival informed by Philadelphia's black past as well as that of the larger African diaspora.

In April of 1975, the duo welcomed Philadelphians to the inaugural fest, dubbed the Oshun Festival. Located at the intersection of 23rd and South Streets, the first festival welcomed a few hundred black residents interested in novel enterprise. Occurring from noon until 10 p.m., the festival opened with a march to the nearby Schuylkill River, located just a few blocks west at the South Street Bridge. As they walked toward the Schuylkill, participants carried oranges, cantaloupes, bananas, and apples that they would later throw into the river in worship and recognition of Oshun.

The following year, the duo renamed the festival Odunde, which means "Happy New Year," in the West African Yoruba language. By 1979, Odunde had grown in popularity and its boundaries were extended to accommodate the large, predominantly black crowd of participants, now occurring between 22nd and 23rd Streets and Grays Ferry Avenue and South Street. Odunde was moved to the second Sunday in June, and also included a series of performances by local and national acts. Throughout the early 1980s, Odunde continued to expand and Fernandez and Arthur could not have been happier. Ronald Gaines (age 30), who worked as a security guard at the festival in 1984 echoed the sentiments of the droves of black Philadelphians in attendance. Although black residents were no longer physically present along much of South Street, Gaines asserted that Odunde reminded black Philadelphians that: "The vitality is here; it's not something that is dead and gone." Indeed, out-of-towners such as Aliya Glover from Brooklyn, reflected Gaines's sentiment: "There's an excitement here, a high-pitched excitement that you don't see at the black cultural festivals in New York and Washington."

The festival became a place for black residents across neighborhoods to meet one another as well. Exemplifying such virtues of the day-long fest, Robin Drummond (age 23), South Philadelphia resident and long-time participant, commented: "The thing I like most is that every year I meet different people from all over the city." Black leaders were also avid participants and supporters as well. Each year David Richardson, Hardy Williams, and Goode were fixtures at the festival, with the mayor assuring organizers and participants of continued support throughout his tenure.[46]

In 1985, on its tenth anniversary, Odunde and its founders received a proclamation from Mayor Goode, establishing the day-long festival as an official Philadelphia tradition. Here, then, like the Hawthorne neighborhood, Goode's role as mayor and support provided an important legitimacy to the efforts to preserve the black legacy on and around South Street. Further, the fusion of pan-Africanism and Philadelphia black history transformed South Street into the origin of black life in Philadelphia, generating a continued anticipation around the celebration of black history, struggle, and survival. Whereas the preservation of the built environment was significant to redevelopment in the Hawthorne neighborhood below Broad Street, Odunde sought to remind black Philadelphians of the cultural history embedded in a built environment that had been razed and destroyed by the urban bulldozers above Broad Street. By 1991, the Odunde festival included performers from black areas across the African diaspora, including the National Dance Company of Barbados, the Kankouran West African Dance Company from Senegal, the international all-female vocal group Sweet Honey in the Rock, South African trumpeter Hugh Masakela, the Arthur Hall African American Dance Ensemble from Baltimore, Maryland, the Drum Spirit of America, and the South Philadelphia Drill Team.

Moreover, the emphasis on self-pride and pan-Africanism appealed to urban blacks inside and outside of Philadelphia, inspiring blacks to return to or visit Philadelphia. For example, Billy Paul—R & B artist and Philadelphia native, most famous for his songs "Me and Mrs. Jones," "Ebony Woman," and "Only the Strong Survive," came back to Philadelphia to serenade his hometown with the tunes that made him famous—remarked on the cultural importance of Odunde and the area for him: "Odunde and South Street and Philadelphia will always be dear to me. Wherever I go, I take Philadelphia and South Street with me." Adding to Paul's sentiments during the festival in 1988, state representative David Richardson reminded the predominantly black crowd, "Here is a man who has never forgotten South Street, or South Philadelphia. [Billy Paul] returns at a time when some people don't think that we belong here anymore." Richardson's comments bespeak the ways in which black residents actively sought to reclaim South Street, both physically—as the festival encompassed nearly eight blocks on and around South Street—and emotionally, by centering South Street as a significant site in urban black collective memory, despite the change of the neighborhood into a predominantly white upper-middle-class area.[47]

Richardson's commentary was perhaps timely, as by 1993 Odunde had become a source of conflict. With 25,000 in attendance, Odunde had grown tremendously and encompassed nearly ten blocks on and around South Street. Many white residents along west South Street had become weary of the day-long fest, which they saw as inviting undesirables into the otherwise safe neighborhood. Black Philadelphians and Odunde participants were outraged, suggesting unfair treatment of Odunde in light of other predominantly white festivals. The Mummers Parade, was, perhaps the most significant reference for those who supported Odunde. The Mummers Parade had a long history in the city, born from the white ethnic neighborhoods once also located within the Seventh Ward. Occurring on New Year's Day, the Mummers Parade is a day-long procession wherein white Philadelphians, predominantly of Irish descent, don costumes and operate floats along Broad Street in celebration of their culture, their roots in Philadelphia, and the New Year. One black resident and long-time Odunde participant characterized the call to move Odunde to another location as a reflection of continuing racism in the city:

> Whites have moved into a Black neighborhood and do not want the continuation of a Black Tradition. Look at what they've done with other cultural phenomena.... They haven't moved the Mummers, and people complain about the drinking every year.... Odunde is something that was born in the community. The Mummers came out of the community and people complain and that hasn't been moved.... This is a case of gentrification.

Odunde founder Fernandez added: "There is no reason under the sun for us to move; it is not even a consideration for us. We are spiritually tied to South Street.... We are the last vestiges of African-Americans on South street. Systematically, we are being removed." Fernandez further suggested: "This is our neighborhood and this is our celebration. Odunde is part of a continuum of African American celebrations and gatherings on South Street."

Through Odunde, black residents reappropriated South Street. Such (re) appropriation served as a means to signify South Street as constitutive of an important black cultural space, one which black residents owned even if they were no longer able to live in the area. As the arguments indicate, black residents called on the black legacy of the area and the roots of the festival in black efforts to sustain and create a place in the city to remember Philadelphia's black cultural past while also celebrating the black present and future.[48]

White residents in the area were not all moved by such arguments. While some white residents contended that they had no problem with the festival and in fact participated in it, Mary Carpenter's comments were representative of the tone of dissent:

> They urinate on the front pavement. They'll sit on my steps with their fruit and their garbage. It's just not fair...I'm Irish and we have our parade and the Irish get rowdy. I'm not saying we don't. But we have it on the Parkway where it's not a residential area....They should have never got a permit to begin with.

Carpenter's comments capture some of the tension surrounding Odunde, as it was a black celebration occurring in an increasingly white neighborhood disconnected from the area's black cultural and political past. White new-comers along South Street had not necessarily been drawn to the area because of the area's cultural or historical legacy, like the gentrifiers sociologist Japonica Brown-Saracino examines in her discussion of gentrification in Chicago. Rather than preserving the cultural legacy of the area, like Brown-Saracino's "social preservationists," white residents gentrifying South Street were drawn to the area because of the proximal relationship the neighborhood shared with Center City.[49]

Given the climate of increased black political power however, black leaders across the city rushed to the aid of the festival. Whereas in previous periods the city leadership would have often worked quickly to meet the demands of upper-middle-class white residents, such as those living in west South Street, in the era of increased black political leadership, the opposite occurred. With John Street now serving as city council president, the proposition of moving Odunde was contentious. Both Hardy Williams and David Richardson, who had become avid participants, called for a quick end to the dissension, request-ing black and white leaders across the city to aid the festival. Following a door-to-door effort to question South Street residents about whether or not they wanted Odunde moved, city officials concluded that not only was there more support than not for the festival, but also that the cultural importance of Odunde to the city outweighed the complaints.

Perhaps the biggest shift in response to the complaints of white residents was a change in how long the festival lasted. In response to the complaints,

Odunde was shortened by two hours (noon to 8 p.m.). When Fernandez was informed of the news that Odunde would continue to take place on South Street, she was elated and thanked all of those who supported the festival both politically and monetarily:

> I've said it before and I'll say it again, that our people will speak when confronted with a crisis.... They came through again. Kernie Anderson (WDAS general manager) donated $1,250 toward the city fee. We got $100 from Children's Safe House; Ayide (an African-American banquet hall facility in West Philadelphia) gave us $200 and people like Lana Felton Ghee and others came through, The African American Chamber of Commerce also promised us funds. And people like Hardy Williams and State Reps. David Richardson and Dwight Evans have also stepped forward to give us a hand. We can't forget City Council President John Street who stood behind us in keeping Odunde on South Street.

The Odunde festival since that moment has continued to be a staple in Philadelphia. Preserving the cultural significance of South Street among black Philadelphians, Odunde has managed to sustain black collective memories of the Black Seventh Ward, centering South Street as the origin of Philadelphia's black diaspora. Such cultural and political efforts have resonated beyond the boundaries of Philadelphia and Odunde has drawn crowds of more than 30,000 throughout the 1990s. On its twenty-fifth anniversary, Odunde was more vibrant and colorful than ever before.[50] Without question, the work of Fernandez and Arthur benefited from the shifting political climate and the continued work of black leaders to maintain the social history of black Philadelphians even as the built environment and larger black population continued to change. Odunde, much like the Hawthorne neighborhood, is emblematic of the work of black residents to fashion and forge new black spaces within the climate of urban renewal and gentrification.

Brown Faces in High Places

The social history of Philadelphia and the South Street area in the post–civil rights context reveals that processes of change and development of black and white neighborhoods have an interdependent relationship with the political gains of neighborhood-based black activists and leaders. In the wake of the Civil Rights Act of 1964, black residents used the resources of black neighborhoods, particularly human resources, to establish a new social and political terrain that helped to preserve and support black memories and residences along and near South Street.

Shifting local political power from predominantly white areas of the city to the Black Belt, black residents, leaders, and activists shaped patterns of urban change. Under the leadership of folks like John Street, Wilson Goode, and Hardy Williams, black Philadelphians placed the social realities and issues of black residents at the forefront of local politics and policy. Establishing a coalition of their own, black Philadelphians strategically endeavored to lay claim to and take power over the city, resource allocation, and agencies controlling the viability of urban black neighborhoods. The social history of black Philadelphians as I have presented it here signals the importance of black agency for patterns of urban and political change in the post–civil rights era. To be sure, black Philadelphians were not unique, as during the same period urban black and Latino/Latina residents throughout the United States were emerging as the major power bloc in local politics.

Such a shift in the local political terrain allowed projects of redevelopment, such as the Hawthorne neighborhood, and black collective memory ventures, such as Odunde, to not only thrive but also reshape the city's landscape. Here, then, the work of black Philadelphians is emblematic of how black political power sustained urban black legacies and helped consolidate the political, cultural, and social boundaries of urban black neighborhoods. Endeavoring to take ownership over Philadelphia and its development, the social history of black Philadelphians during the last two decades of the twentieth century demonstrates the important ways in which the interdependency among black neighborhoods fosters an environment wherein black leaders, activists, and residents can reshape and have actively reshaped urban America.

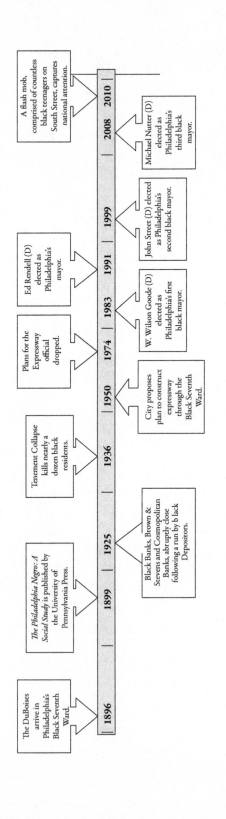

The DuBoises arrive in Philadelphia's Black Seventh Ward.

The Philadelphia Negro: A Social Study is published by the University of Pennsylvania Press.

Tenement Collapse kills nearly a dozen black residents.

Plans for the Expressway official dropped.

Ed Rendell (D) elected as Philadelphia's mayor.

A flash mob, comprised of countless black teenagers on South Street, captures national attention.

1896   1899   1925   1936   1950   1974   1983   1991   1999   2008   2010

Black Banks, Brown & Stevens and Cosmopolitan Banks, abruptly close following a run by black Depositors.

City proposes plan to construct expressway through the Black Seventh Ward.

W. Wilson Goode (D) elected as Philadelphia's first black mayor.

John Street (D) elected as Philadelphia's second black mayor.

Michael Nutter (D) elected as Philadelphia's third black mayor.

6

Flash (Mobs) Forward

ON MARCH 20, 2010, retired nurse Debi English, watching nearly 2000 black teenagers take over the South Street area, cried, "What's going on, Philadelphia?" From the windows of her twenty-fourth floor apartment, English watched the chaos, violence, and fear that gripped South Street for several hours on that late Saturday evening. Though English would watch the events unfold from her 15th Street high-rise apartment, others would unexpectedly find themselves in the eye of what would later be described in national media outlets as a violent "flash mob."

Just as English was asking if her eyes were deceiving her, black teenagers from across the city were receiving messages via text, Twitter, Facebook, and MySpace encouraging them to come to South Street. "Come to South Street. South Street is poppin'," read many of the messages to Philadelphia's black youth. Others received phone calls, as one black teen told reporters: "Some people call. . . . They tell you to come down, so you come down." Before long, the message had been received by thousands of black youths in the city who, in turn, filled Center City streets, especially the commercial areas of South Street east of Broad Street. Soon after the flash mob began, the smell of pepper spray used by Philadelphia Police to quell the mob replaced the night's air, and the glass of broken car and store windows, overturned trashcans, and bruised and injured pedestrians were scattered throughout South Street.

No one is exactly sure when the mobs began that night, but by 9:30 p.m. most businesses had closed their doors leaving those outside to fend for themselves, while those customers trapped inside witnessed a whirlwind of violence, crime, panic, and chaos. Barbara Bender, manager and waitress at a popular eatery, South Street Souvlaki, watched alongside her customers with fear and confusion. Though South Street Souvlaki is usually open until 11 p.m. on an average Saturday night, thirty minutes after the flash mob began Bender abruptly closed the eatery and maintained that those inside should remain until the police calmed the situation or the teenagers fled—whichever came first.

Having worked at the restaurant for many years, Bender was not unfamiliar with the intense energy of a Saturday night on Philadelphia's South Street and the accompanying hoopla. The night of March 20, in Bender's view, was altogether different. Commenting on the turmoil she witnessed, Bender did not mince words: "This is the worst I've ever seen it.... It's scary." Noting the economic consequences of the mob, Bender added: "It's a bunch of young kids that are creating havoc, and it's killing our business." Just a few yards away John DiSalvo, a cook at Joey's Stone Fired Pizza, locked the doors and windows, keeping customers inside for at least two hours. Echoing Bender's assessment, DiSalvo added: "It was scary.... It was not like there was one or two kids out there and you could defend yourself. There were hundreds." English, Bender, and DiSalvo were not alone in their fears, as from store and car windows many watched the flash mob grow and progress, overwhelming various bystanders as it moved up and down South Street.

A scene from a local eatery, Bliss restaurant, located on the edge of the South Street area at 220 N. Broad Street, perhaps best elucidates the sudden and violent nature of the incidents that collectively formed the flash mob. An auto-repair worker would later tell a reporter from the *Philadelphia Inquirer* of his sudden encounter while eating dinner at Bliss with his wife and another married couple. At around 11:30 p.m. on March 20, his dinner was suddenly interrupted when the other gentleman at his table was hit on the head at least three times by "a totally normal looking" black teenager. After a short and unsuccessful chase, his friend returned to the table having been unable to catch his assailant, only to be taunted by a subsequent group of black teenagers: "What's the matter, white boy, you scared?" As their voices faded into the distance he could hear the group of teenagers observing that in their estimation "all the white people [were] scared."

Reports also suggested that such scenes of violence did not always result in a white victim. Angel Flores, a Philadelphia assistant district attorney, would later add that many black Philadelphians were victims of the violence of the flash mob as well: "You didn't feel any safer if you were African American and saw these kids coming." Flores noted that an elderly black man had been assaulted during the flash mob: "They knocked down a 70-year-old African American gentleman," adding: "Then they ran over him."

By midnight the police had managed to curb the violence, prompting many of the flash mob participants to evacuate quickly. Of the several thousand thought to be involved in the chaotic scene, several hundred were detained, and several dozen were prosecuted. Most all of those prosecuted (usually in the forum of family court) were black teenagers currently enrolled in Philadelphia's public high schools. As the Philadelphia courts, police, mayor, citizens, and businesses began the work of trying to prevent such events from occurring again while also figuring out potential causes, a black teenager, participating in an unpublicized gathering to bring attention to needs of Philadelphia's youth also on the evening of March 20, offered a straightforward take on the violent episode. In the days following the flash mob, when asked by reporters for his thoughts on the flash mob, Khalif Dobson, an eighteen-year-old senior at West Philadelphia High School, drew from an oft-cited quote of Dr. Martin Luther King Jr. the reminder: "People should remember...the riot is the language of the unheard."[1]

The flash mob on South Street in late March was the latest in a string of recent defiant gatherings of black youth in Philadelphia; others had occurred on December 18, 2009, February 16 and March 3 of 2010. Violence and panic aside, the flash mob's participants and origin were a sign of the times, high technology and media colliding with the increasing discontent of a large segment of Philadelphia's population—black youth. These black youths or "citizen outsiders,"[2] a term political scientist Cathy J. Cohen uses in her recent book *Democracy Remixed*, disrupted the social environment of South Street and foreshadowed the flash mobs that were soon to come in Milwaukee and Chicago. Though we cannot know whether or not the flash mobs represented an effort to reclaim this area of the city as a black space (as the intentions of the teenagers appeared varied at the very least), the flash mobs provide a window into the continued presence and impact of the political agency of urban blacks and highlight many of the arguments I have put forth in this book.

The flash mob bespeaks the dramatic shift that occurred in the South Street area and Philadelphia over the twentieth century. Nearly a hundred years earlier, South Street would have been a likely place of residence to an average black teenager in Philadelphia. Today, however, we find the same area home to predominantly white businesses and residences that looked to the police to protect them from the flash mob of young black outsiders. Without question, the electronic and phone messages mobilized black youth in the city to gather in Center City along South Street and perhaps participate in the flash mob, suddenly and dramatically shifting the racial geography of the social environment of Center City and South Street. Like Black Seventh Warders before them, the exertion of political agency *en masse* by black youths in late March further demonstrates that urban black Americans play a clear role in shaping the city, intentionally or unintentionally. The flash mob in late March, as a historical episode, animates the continued struggles and tenuous relations within and across race in urban America. Indeed, like the black depositors of Brown & Stevens Bank, victims of the tenement collapse in 1936, activists like Crystal Bird Fauset, Alice Lipscomb, and George Dukes, the black youth of the flash mobs were and are *citymakers*—compelling city leaders and officials to change, make changes, or determine where change is needed. In what follows, I amplify the major arguments of the book and use events following the March 20, 2010 flash mob to provide some general take-aways and explore how this book fits into existing debates and scholarship on urban America.

Political Agency and Urban Change

In the days following the late-night flash mob on South Street in March 2010, the black Democratic mayor, Michael Nutter, took swift action. Besides relying heavily on an increased police presence on South Street, Nutter also incorporated performance into his response to the flash mob. Taking his family on a Saturday night stroll through South Street a week after the flash mob, Nutter sought to demonstrate the continued safety of South Street for consumers and passersby—*if it is safe for the mayor and his family, then it is safe for everyone.* "I'm really sorry," "How you doing?," Nutter asked as he encountered those who fell victim to the fear and damage spurred on by the flash mob.

Waving at pedestrians and greeting proprietors as he strolled a seven-block stretch of South Street, Nutter explained to reporters: "We think it's impor-tant, given some of the things that happened in the city...to demonstrate our love and commitment for Philadelphia." Speaking to reporters along the way, Nutter admonished those involved in the flash mob: "If you want to come out and have a good time, you should do that, whether you're a teenager or think of yourself as a teenager.... But we will not tolerate nonsense." Closing out his effort to recoup the image of safety and stability on South Street lost in the wake of the flash mob, Nutter ended his visit and the subsequent press conference by leading the gathering crowd in a chant: "This is my Philadelphia, and I love where I live!"[3] Here, then, we find the black mayor of Philadelphia, using a combination of rhetoric and performance to combat the framing and mobilization of black youths the night of the flash mob.

Nutter's South Street stroll illustrates a major argument in the book: Agency contextualizes and makes visible structural conditions. Framing the issues emergent from the flash mob, Nutter juxtaposes those whom he deems victims and those whom he believed to be culpable by amplifying the boundaries between young and old and those who "love" Philadelphia and those who don't. Using South Street as a microcosm of Philadelphia, he deploys his status as a "black Philadelphian" to provide a coherent critique of the flash mob and those who participated. This stroll indicates that despite racial and economic changes in Philadelphia, South Street continues to be a location upon which the city mediates and confronts itself. Despite the predominantly white racial geography of contemporary South Street, positive relations between black and white Philadelphians remain key to the maintenance of civility in cities like Philadelphia.

Nutter's frustrations, while rooted in a twenty-first-century flash mob, are not dissimilar from those being navigated, dismissed, and worked out in the Black Seventh Ward during the twentieth century. Like Nutter, Black Seventh Warders also found that South Street was a battleground of sorts. Whether it was the fight to reform poor housing, produce economic self-sufficiency, or defeat urban renewal, the Black Seventh Ward is a tremendous historical container for the battle between structure and agency that ensued in urban America over the course of the twentieth century.

Structure versus Agency

Although the notion that human agency matters and influences structural change is a seemingly straightforward and fairly agreeable point, as sociologist William H. Sewell Jr. notes: "structures tend to appear in social scientific discourse as impervious to human agency, to exist apart from, but nevertheless to determine the essential shape of, the strivings and motivated transactions that constitute the experienced surface of social life."[4] Here, then, Sewell observes that the centrality of and emphasis on structure in social scientific scholarship has overshadowed the important influence of human agency on such structure. Indeed, existing examinations and discussions of American cities often reflect the tension between agency and structure Sewell depicts, especially as it pertains to the relative influence of black political agency.

Throughout this book I have relied on the four-pronged conception of political agency to examine the Black Seventh Ward and change over time: framing, voting, mobilization, and migration. My emphasis on black debates and discourse regarding a series of issues including economic detours (chapter 2), public housing (chapter 3), and urban renewal (chapter 4) affirms the continued importance of what sociologists Jeffrey Alexander, Mustafa Emirbayer, and Anne Mische have referred to as "interpretation," or the ability of agents to use, manipulate, and construct narratives about the social world.[5] My attention to mobilization and migration, in particular, builds from social-movement scholarship, wherein the focus is on the ability to move and deploy personal and communal resources en masse often to enact or respond to structural change or opportunity.[6] As the social and political history of the Black Seventh Ward reveals, it is through the interaction between human agency and structure that patterns of institutional and community change emerge.

As this book also demonstrates, the actions and attitudes of urban black residents also confront structure. As sociologist Mario Small reminds us in his recent study of childcare centers, and Robin D. G. Kelley shows in his portrayal of southern working class blacks, the agency of urban minorities also contextualizes structure and structural changes. In this way, this book demonstrates the implicit and explicit contours of a multivocal black politics and people. As I show throughout the book, the combined efforts of black residents generate a synergy that facilitated or frustrated new structural opportunities.[7]

Furthermore, such efforts or political agency also make the state and structure, in the words of political scientist James C. Scott, *legible*, helping to delimit the various power relations and dynamics embedded therein.[8] Indeed, structure can be hard to see analytically and empirically. In my view, agency represents the practical knowledge of which Scott speaks; and, political agency provides a fruitful way to gauge the interface between individual agents and state-sanctioned actions, procedures, and policies. Here, then, agency is not situated as more important than or superior to structure. Rather, agency is situated as an empirical and analytic lens to gauge the range of attitudes and actions of black residents as they came up against structural changes over time.

Black Political Agency and Urban America

My reliance on the notion of political agency is also meant to shift our general gaze. When we begin to imagine the urban black populace, as heterogeneous and sometimes discordant, and all the while agentic, we can begin to determine the true relationship that urban minorities share with the city. Like many urban black neighborhoods, the Black Seventh Ward contained a vibrant mix of indigenous blacks, southern black migrants, well-to-do blacks, poor blacks, black Republicans, black Democrats, black artists, black musicians, black businessmen, black banks, black hospitals, black schools, and black theaters; and such heterogeneity often collided with and was reduced by structural changes in cities over time. As DuBois suggested in *The*

Philadelphia Negro, the importance of such heterogeneity cannot be over-stated: "[A]nd there is no surer way of misunderstanding the Negro or being misunderstood by him than by ignoring manifest differences of condition and power in the 40,000 black people of Philadelphia."[9]

Discussions of the agency of urban black Americans in the existing schol-arship focus primarily on the myriad subcultures emergent in disadvantaged urban black neighborhoods. In such research, urban black agency is generally characterized through the lens of subcultural practices that often rail against normative behavioral practices and beliefs. For example, scholars have posited varying concepts such as "street versus decent,"[10] "ghetto-related behaviors,"[11] "collective efficacy,"[12] and "under the table" employment practices,[13] to charac-terize the agency of urban minorities. While such concepts reveal important information regarding the neighborhood-level behaviors urban minorities employ to make sense of and negotiate structural, economic, and social issues in American cities, little attention is given to the interaction between these urban minorities' expressions of agency and larger processes of change thought to give rise to such attitudes and practices.[14]

As a result, recent debates and scholarship have privileged the role of the actions and attitudes of predominantly white power structures and residents, and situated urban black agency as reactive and not *proactive*. This focus is at least partially the by-product of the many cases in which whites represent the majority of the population of a given city and often disproportionately occupy key urban political and corporate positions. However, as some American cities have increasingly become majority–minority and others, such as Philadelphia, consistently contain a black population totaling nearly fifty percent, the need for a more comprehensive understanding of the signifi-cance of the agency of urban minorities cannot be overstated. Due to various changes including white flight, suburbanization, and deindustrialization, urban minorities are and have been inheriting America's cities.[15]

Bringing to the fore an analysis of the residential decisions of black Philadelphians, this book further elucidates the role of individual-level actions in the socioeconomic and political prosperity of urban black neighborhoods. While some researchers have highlighted the role of internal divisions within the larger black population, their work has focused on national origin and/or social class as the key internal divisions.[16] This book, instead, calls attention to other divisions, particularly those around culture and region (e.g., southern vs. northern and rural vs. urban), which in turn augment the larger discussion and theorization of the role of individual-level actions in the creation, main-tenance, and collapse of black neighborhoods. Focusing on the key events shaping black Philadelphia generally and the Black Seventh Ward more specifically, this book illuminates how the Black Seventh Ward emerged as a heterogeneous black neighborhood and later into a predominantly upper-middle-class residential and commercial district.

Other research, too, has taken a similar approach, yielding important information about the social realities of urban blacks. An array of scholars across a variety of fields including, Mitchell Duneier, Sudhir Venkatesh, Stephen Gregory, and Adolph Reed have shown in their analyses of urban America the influence of the actions of black residents, stakeholders, brokers or "middlemen," elites, and gentrifiers on patterns of neighborhood change.[17] Employing a similar black-centered approach, this book pinpoints the larger significance of urban black agency for conceptions of urban development and neighborhood change. The existing literature has been organized in part around the implicit assumption that urban and neighborhood changes have an interdependent relationship with the within-city migration of urban black residents (especially working-class, poor, and near-poor urban blacks).

Where other researchers have attributed white movement out of cities, or "white flight," to patterns of neighborhood and urban change,[18] I underscore the significance of the within-city migration of black residents, or what might be imagined as *secondary migration*, to explain processes of urban development. Secondary migration, as I illustrate throughout the book, accounts for the significance of within-city migration of black residents over time. Notions of secondary migration are present in existing literature, particularly as it concerns the impact of middle-class blacks leaving urban enclaves for the social, cultural, and economic trappings of suburban life.

For example, white flight, as discussed by numerous urban scholars like historians Amanda Seligman and Kevin Michael Kruse, involves the movement of resources out of urban neighborhoods. Secondary migration, as occurred in and around South Street throughout the twentieth century, is similar, in that black resources (human, sociopolitical, and cultural) are relocated. Distinguishing secondary migration, however, is the fact that it involves patterns of migration of black residents and business to other black enclaves in the city, and thus results in the consolidation of emergent and existing black urban neighborhoods. I employed this concept of secondary migration to account for both the voluntary and the coerced migration of black residents and black indigenous institutions. Secondary migration also speaks to an ongoing debate among urban sociologists, particularly with regard to the existence of middle-class blacks after deindustrialization. Whereas scholars

such as William Julius Wilson have emphasized the occurrence and significance of the out-migration of blacks from urban areas, secondary migration
challenges the assumption of out-migration, or leaving the city, as a primary
lens to understand how urban black people responded to structural changes
such as de-industrialization.[19]

In this book, I have emphasized the importance of within-city, or *secondary*,
migration as an influential response of urban black residents during periods
of substantial structural change over the course of the twentieth century.
Following Wilson's argument that the black middle class had disappeared
both physically and economically from black neighborhoods in the inner city,
scholars such as Mary Pattillo have shown that "the black middle class has not
abandoned the black poor, either ideologically or geographically."[20] The concept of secondary migration, as I employ it here, however, provides some
middle ground, as it accounts for the black out-migration Wilson characterizes, while also affirming the continued presence of black businesses and
middle-class residents within urban black areas identified by Pattillo. Further,
and perhaps most importantly, the concept of secondary migration helps to
recover the agency of black residents lost in conventional wisdom within the
context of processes of urban change such as gentrification and urban renewal.
To be clear, while processes such as urban renewal and gentrification forced
many blacks out of urban areas, those displaced residents still operated with
some agency (though limited), often choosing a residential path predicated
on within-city migration, resulting in many urban black residents finding
residence in black areas, such as North and West Philadelphia.

The movement of black residents has been seen as significant in existing
urban research, but much of this discussion has focused on either the flow of
southern migrants into northern cities from 1900 to 1960 (the Great
Migration) or the relationship between such movement and white flight.
Black residents were and are not always encroaching on established white
neighborhoods, but often moving into and out of established and emergent
black neighborhoods across a given city. Often prompted by perceived social
advances such as the construction of public and affordable housing, secondary
migration, as I show in the case of Philadelphia, has had a lasting impact on
urban development and the racial geography of the city.

In the chapters dealing with black economic development (chapter 2),
public housing (chapter 3), and urban renewal (chapter 4), I illustrate that
black residents have had continued secondary migration within the network of black neighborhoods in an effort to thrive and survive in
Philadelphia. Detailing such movement through the lens of the Black

Seventh Ward over time, I demonstrate that urban development and neigh-borhood change have been impacted by a persistent practice of within-city migration by black residents over the course of the twentieth century. This shifts the focus on secondary migration in existing research and scholarly endeavors from a debate about whether or not the urban black middle class and urban white residents have disappeared and/or migrated into suburban areas toward the important ways in which black within-city movement has impacted urban and neighborhood change over time. I argue that urban black neighborhoods, like the Black Seventh Ward, are the site and reflec-tion of critical events and debates shaping local black political agendas, the racial geography of the city, and larger processes of urban change (e.g., gen-trification, white flight, and urban renewal). Encompassing varying por-tions of the cultural, economic, social, and human resources of the larger local black population, urban black neighborhoods are indeed the source and site of competition and an important window into change in American cities.[21]

The Truly Disadvantaged as Citymakers

The second major thread in the book relates to a reorientation in the broader conception of urban black Americans as mere casualties of structural changes in American cities. This book demonstrates that the "truly disadvantaged" might also be seen as *citymakers*. These two conceptions of urban black Americans are not mutually exclusive but constitutive of the precarious posi-tion of being both black and urban.

Again, we can look to the response of Mayor Nutter to the South Street flash mob to animate this discussion. By August of 2011, the city was still attempting to make sense of why the flash mobs occurred. In the wake of flash mobs during the summer of 2011 in Chicago and Milwaukee, Mayor Nutter continued his quest to highlight and diminish such behavior. Taking to the pulpit at Mount Carmel Baptist Church in West Philadelphia, Nutter leveled a sharp critique on Philadelphia black youths involved in the flash mobs: "You've damaged yourself, you've damaged your peers and, quite honestly, you've damaged your own race. You've damaged your own race." Nutter, continuing his critique, added: "If you want...anybody else to respect you and not be afraid when they see you walking down the street, then leave the innocent people who are walking down the street minding their own damn business. Leave them alone."[22]

Here in the midst of his critique of those black youths participating in the flash mob, Nutter's comments reflect a larger tension in the view of urban black Americans. While such individuals comprise a larger constituency that is often undereducated, socially isolated, and underemployed, through their actions and attitudes they also influence the organization of the city. In the case of the flash mobs, black youth reminded those in power that the combination of discourse and mobilization of urban black residents can have a lasting imprint on the structure of urban policing, consumption, and the maintenance of what sociologist Elijah Anderson refers to as the "cosmopolitan canopy"—the areas of a city which promote and contain the social interaction and participation of its diverse citizenry.

To understand the intraracial and interneighborhood dynamics of black Philadelphians over time, I drew specifically from the work of scholars such as John Logan, Harvey Molotch, and John Mollenkopf, who characterize postwar urban America as a growth machine developed by progrowth coalitions. Whereas researchers have emphasized the competition and coalitions among white elites and stakeholders, I focus instead on black residents, groups, institutions, leaders, and activists. In order to understand how black interests emerge, compete, and compel local and state officials to act, I offer the Black Seventh Ward as an ideal case. Throughout the twentieth century, the Black Seventh Ward underwent substantial structural, cultural, and political changes that impacted the racial geography of Philadelphia. As I reveal throughout this book, black residents and leaders repeatedly made decisions that influenced and reacted to these changes.

For example, I show that prior to the civil rights movement, black Philadelphia existed as what scholars Christopher Silver and John V. Moeser refer to as a "separate city"—a "self-contained, racially-identifiable community separated from the larger white city."[23] Despite such separation, however, competing interests among black Philadelphians impacted patterns of within-city black migration and urban development. While political disenfranchisement may have limited the impact of black agency, choices black residents made regarding public space such as parks/playgrounds and housing helped to create and consolidate emergent black areas in other parts of the city (often prompting white residents to leave such areas). As I demonstrate in my discussion of urban renewal in the Black Seventh Ward (chapter 4) black-led protests hampered progrowth coalition efforts to expand Philadelphia's expressway system, which, in turn, created lasting friction among corporate and political allies endeavoring to redevelop the city and altered the built environment.

As Philadelphia entered the post–civil rights era, the quest for political enfranchisement gave rise to what I referred to as the "black growth coalition" (chapter 5). Though similar to the "urban black regime" in Atlanta that Adolph Reed describes in his recent book *Stirrings in the Jug*, the black growth coalition I discuss demonstrates that often what is seen as "collective action" by many is really a container for a combination of smaller-scale and more directed actions of several black constituencies across a city. Yet, much like its white counterpart emergent in the postwar period, the black growth coalition impacted patterns of neighborhood change and urban development in the post–civil rights era. Similar to what the postwar progrowth coalition sought to accomplish for corporate leaders and white democrats, the black growth coalition worked to increase the political power and representation of black interests and access to resources for black Philadelphians.

Whereas the postwar growth machine relied on a shift in the city's power base from a Republican to a Democratic regime, the emergent black growth coalition depended on transposing power from a predominantly white electoral base to a black electorate. Throughout each of the chapters, I reveal that the combined efforts of distinct black neighborhood councils and sociopolitical organizations, along with the residential choices of black Philadelphians, shifted the city's political landscape and racial geography in ways that profoundly shaped Philadelphia and the Black Seventh Ward throughout the twentieth century. In this way, we see a more dynamic city; one in which black Americans are both disproportionately disadvantaged by structural changes in the city, while also actively constructing approaches to challenge, navigate, and/or reconcile such changes.

How *The Philadelphia Negro* Changed Urban America

The third major thesis of this book is a straightforward one: The actions and attitudes of urban black Americans matter, particularly as they pertain to patterns of neighborhood and urban change over time. Indeed this argument takes cues from sociologist Mary Pattillo's characterization of what constitutes the "black community," wherein she asserts that in the process of urban black residents creating, debating, and maintaining supposed black interests and a black political agenda "the black community is forged."[24] Extending this claim, this book offers evidence that suggests that the process of forging a "black community" impacts the structure of the city and urban change, and provides an important, though underutilized, window into the structural changes in urban America. In this way, the creation of a black community is a reflection of urban black residents confronting and being confronted by patterns of structural change in an effort to make urban life feasible and equitable.

Employing the notion of political agency, I have addressed a significant gap in our understanding of how and why cities change and neighborhoods decline and/or persist. As I discussed early on, the actions and behaviors of black residents have received significant scholarly and popular attention. Here, I am recalling the research depicting the collective efficacy of urban black residents,[25] research that identifies the ways in which blacks deploy extended kin networks and fictive kin to mediate poverty and rear children,[26] research on racial residential segregation,[27] and research illustrating the arsenal of cultural narratives, or the cultural heterogeneity, urban blacks deploy to make sense of social issues.[28] Such research and discussions, however, tend to be limited to a focus on vulnerability or debates around the supposed pathology of urban black residents and the neighborhoods they occupy. Furthermore, such conceptual frameworks generally operate with an implicit assumption of black neighborhoods as distinctive and separate.

This book, I hope, illustrates that black neighborhoods are linked both empirically and theoretically. As scholars such as Michelle Boyd, Derek Hyra, and Kesha Moore have shown in their examinations of (respectively) New York, Chicago, and Philadelphia, black intraracial debates have important consequences for urban America.[29] The Black Seventh Ward provides an important historical case that demonstrates that contemporary black neighborhoods share important ties with those black neighborhoods that may have faded from public memory and contemporary maps of urban America. Given the persistence of the marginalization of black people generally, and urban black residents specifically, the case of the Black Seventh Ward as presented here and in *The Philadelphia Negro* reminds us of the persistent ties among urban black neighborhoods over time.

Like Los Angeles's Watts, New York City's Harlem, Washington DC's U-Street/Shaw neighborhood, Chicago's Bronzeville, Pittsburgh's Hill District, and New Orleans's Treme and Congo Square, the social history of the Black Seventh Ward is emblematic of the ways in which the secondary migration of black residents over time has given rise to new black enclaves, new black politics, new black cities, new black cultures, and new black leaders. My goal is that *Black Citymakers* begins a new focus on and understanding of urban black neighborhoods and communities. On a broader level, my hope is that the conception of political agency I offer and elaborate upon throughout sheds light on the larger importance of the ways in which urban minorities in a variety of contexts provide a collective synergy that facilitates and frustrates large-scale changes in cities such as Philadelphia.

Much of the history I examine in this book is not distinct from but rather similar to the contemporary realities of urban black residents. However, it is important to note that my discussion does not necessarily capture other critical urban battles during the twentieth century, such as disputes over labor and education. The lack of prominence of such debates is not to suggest that these matters were not also pressing for black Philadelphians. Rather, the critical junctures, or choice points, I employ to understand the Black Seventh Ward highlighted other areas of inequality.

Quests for affordable housing, political and economic enfranchisement and advancement, and protests against dominant white leadership persist. Countless ethnographic and historical portrayals of urban blacks continue to underscore not new problems but the persistence of inequality and the effect such racial and economic inequalities have on black and white residents.[30] Reminiscent of what sociologist Chris Rhomberg, in his sociohistorical discussion of Oakland, California, refers to as "reiterated problem-solving,"[31] my research suggests that contemporary problems are rooted in a past distinctively informed by urban racial relations and intraracial dynamics. The social history I provide here is clear and further evidence of the fact that urban black residents are contemporarily addressing not new but recurring issues endemic to the problems of urbanism confronted by indigenous and southern blacks in Philadelphia throughout the twentieth century.

Discovering some of the same phenomena that I have detailed throughout, W. E. B. DuBois offered this in his concluding chapter of *The Philadelphia Negro*:

Two sorts of answers return to the bewildered American who asks seriously: What is the Negro problem? The one is straightforward and clear: it is simply this, or simply that, and one simple remedy long enough applied will in time cause it to disappear. The other answer is apt to be hopelessly involved and complex—to indicate no simple panacea, and to end in a somewhat hopeless—There it is; what can we do? Both of these sorts of answers have something of truth in them: the Negro problem looked at in one way is but the old world questions of ignorance, poverty, crime, and the dislike of the stranger. On the other hand it is a mistake to think that attacking each of these questions single-handed without reference to the others will settle the matter: a combination of social problems is far more than a matter of mere addition—the combination itself is a problem.[32]

DuBois's admonishment underscores the link between our imagination of urban black neighborhoods and their residents, and the impact that framework has on how we study and analyze such neighborhoods, people, and the social issues plaguing them. Essentially, what DuBois is highlighting is that urban black neighborhoods and residents provide a window into the complex intersections of inequality emergent in urban America. In his view, if we merely look to urban black neighborhoods as an opportunity to expose social problems then we miss that these neighborhoods also reveal how such problems converge and get understood, manipulated, and communicated by urban residents.

Expanding this point, I will highlight what I see as some of the major implications of my discussion of the Black Seventh Ward. At the descriptive level this book, like those of a variety of urban historians such as Matthew Countryman, reveals that black residents were not passive witnesses of urban change by illustrating the significance of black political agency along similar lines as their urban white counterparts, vividly captured by historians such as Thomas Sugrue and John F. Bauman.[33] However, an important distinction between this book and existing debates and scholarship is that my research also suggests that urban and neighborhood changes such as housing reform, urban renewal, and urban growth were shaped by events in urban black enclaves and debates among urban black residents. Indeed, the sociopolitical history of the Black Seventh Ward reveals that black residents actively shaped narratives about urban changes and how local and federal officials should address issues associated with urban living.

My research also reveals that we must pay more attention to the interaction between black political agency and urban change and policy. While it is true that processes such as deindustrialization, federal intervention into local development, and white flight impacted urban America, this book demonstrates that an understanding of the full impact of such change remains incomplete without the inclusion of the types of black political agency I suggest here. Without question, the movement and politics of urban black residents have shaped American cities like Philadelphia. With respect to the prescriptive implications, the approach I suggest and elaborate upon here requires that we reconsider how we think about urban black neighborhoods and the agency of urban black residents. Certainly this book emphasizes a point that many urban residents contend with daily, both then and now: that is, that most all American cities have a racial geography informed by a racial past.

What is made clear in *Black Citymakers* also resonates in DuBois's *The Philadelphia Negro*; an examination of urban racial communities is key to understanding the city, as such communities are sociologically, politically, and historically rich reflections of why and how cities and their neighborhoods persist and change. Urban black neighborhoods and their residents are not just impacted by external forces of change, but are also forces of urban change better known as *citymakers*.

Betwixt and Between the Past and Present: The Case for Historical Ethnography

> Both history and ethnography are concerned with societies *other* than the one in which we live.... All that the historian or ethnographer can do, and all that we can expect of them, is to enlarge a specific experience to the dimensions of a more general one.
>
> CLAUDE LEVI-STRAUSS[1]

> [My] research became an *historical ethnography*: an attempt to elicit structure and culture from the documents created prior to an event in order to understand how people in another time and place made sense of things.... My purpose was to connect the past and present in a causal explanation.
>
> DIANE VAUGHAN[2]

What is an historical ethnography? This question haunted me as I explored the *life-world*[3] of the Black Seventh Ward during the twentieth century—the sociopolitical story and the peoples comprising the historic Philadelphia neighborhood immortalized by W. E. B. DuBois in *The Philadelphia Negro*. To be sure, this question is not unique to my research, or me, as it has plagued any sociologist braving the underexplored practice and terrains known as historical ethnography.

After nearly seven years of studying the Black Seventh Ward, I have come to much the same conclusion and explanation as that offered by Vaughan (in her historical ethnographic examination of NASA and the Challenger launch decision)[4], and I sometimes restate her words verbatim. Whether in defense or in anticipation of questions about what exactly constitutes historical ethnography, Vaughan's depiction of the function of historical ethnography addresses a gap and debate among and against ethnographers—the issue of causality and measurement. Extending Vaughan's claims, in this brief essay I outline the process through which I conducted my research so as to delimit the virtues of historical ethnography and its promise for developing causal inferences and social theories.

Whereas contemporary ethnography can and does become a historical record after publication or at the end of the research, historical ethnographers contend with the idea that history has *already* happened in the research process.[5] Indeed, history is critical to general causal theory as ethnography is critical to general urban theories. However, overlap between the two, particularly within sociology, remains underused at the very least and unclear at best.

Through the lens of my own research and existing ethnographic research and debates, I argue that historical ethnography, through temporally situated narrative construction and archival triangulation, exploits an important interdisciplinary methodological pathway betwixt and between history, anthropology, and sociology, and deductive and inductive ethnography. In my view, historical ethnography helps to elucidate notions of causality emergent from the communities, people, and organizations often made invisible in the general thrust of the historical record. In this way, the historical ethnographer is able to build causal inferences that lead to infrahistorical general social theories.

My discussion of historical ethnography draws inspiration from the notion of *liminality*[6]—the location of being betwixt and between phenomena, people, places, and philosophies. Using the concept of liminality, I seek to demonstrate the "returns to ethnography" emergent from historical ethnography's seeming "middleness"—a qualitative methodological sensibility necessarily concerned with time, place, and causal inference.[7] Focusing on the liminality of historical ethnography as an ethnographic method, I contrast this research method with its more "presentist" counterpart, contemporary ethnography. Surely, most all ethnographers occupy liminal spaces. That is, ethnographers are always engaging the betwixt and between, as (1) we can never know fully the interiority of another person, and (2) we are often confronted with moments where people provide narratives from the past—their own past, a general past, an imagined past, and so on—that must also be adjudicated. The liminality presented by historical ethnography, however, varies in important ways from its contemporary counterpart. Betwixt and between a variety of social phenomena, including past and present, deductive and inductive, structure and agency, historical ethnography holds real promise for sociologists seeking to combine culture, narrative, individual agents, and change into a coherent social theory.

Informed by extant discussions and debates (largely among urban ethnographers), I sought to explore the sociopolitical history of DuBois's Black Seventh Ward. However, before I could proceed I had to confront the fact that there was "no there there." In other words, how could I study a neighborhood and the community therein if they were no longer available? During the research process, I found this question extended to key areas of the ethnographic process: (1) Access, (2) Representation, and (3) Causality. Essentially, in the process of conducting this historical ethnography I found this method offered some new pathways for ethnographers while also representing a type of participant observation that fruitfully entangles and engages a series of disciplines and approaches. In this way, conducting my historical ethnography led to critical methodological takeaways of interest to most all ethnographers.

Ethnography Is ... Ethnography Is Not

There are many debates that animate the method of ethnography. To illustrate these debates and the critical methodological takeaways thereof, I focus my discussion largely on extant urban ethnography. This discussion of urban ethnographic methods is critical because resolutions made (or not made) directly link to how information is gathered, how sites and subjects are selected, and most importantly how we empirically ground our urban sociological imagination and make causal inferences using such data. More specifically, this brief discussion highlights the major axes of interest, debate, and innovation as pertain to ethnographic methods and theorization.

The field of urban sociology is not just a site of theory, but also a continual conversation and debate around issues of methodology, particularly as it pertains to the practice of ethnography.[8] Possibly because of its emergence alongside that of the Chicago school,[9] urban ethnography has been the means to build causal stories and social theories upon an empirical realism grounded in the observations and descriptions of the everyday.[10] To be sure, urban sociologists do not own the practice of ethnography.

However, in an effort to theorize the complexities of general themes and social problems such as urban/neighborhood change, communal cohesion, and disorganization, urban sociologists have relied heavily on ethnographic sensibilities, often suggesting new pathways for participant-observers. In this way, research and methodological statements by urban ethnographers illustrate many of the general disputes and suggestions regarding ethnography in broad terms, particularly as they pertain to issues of access, representation, and building casual inferences using ethnographic data. Indeed, as sociologist Gerald Suttles asserts: "urban ethnography is one of the ways in which the abstract conceptual content of sociology has kept in touch with the available world of empirical observation."[11]

Reviewing ethnographic methods, Suttles argues that there have been two overarching methodological approaches, which he refers to as "normative" or "situational." While an ethnography employing a normative approach provides an account of the social world by focusing on the distance between deviance and normativity, those using a situational approach look to contextualize the social world of those deemed deviant, aberrant, or disadvantaged.[12] To take more specific examples to highlight the distinction Suttles is making, a useful juxtaposition is that between Harvey

Zorbaugh's *The Gold Coast and the Slum* and Sudhir Venkatesh's *Off the Books*.[13] Whereas Zorbaugh's analysis demonstrates the lack of morality and deviance that abounded in the center of a postwar Chicago neighborhood (i.e., family life of the working class, black family structure), Venkatesh's description of the black South-side Chicago neighborhood Marquis Park contextualizes residents' decision making within the confines of the social situations in which they find themselves (i.e., gang violence, drug dealing, entrepreneurial debates). By highlighting periods of high productivity in the field of urban ethnography, Suttles argues that an abundance of situational accounts have been accompanied by "an effort to go beyond the static, normative account so available in sociological theory."[14]

As concrete examples, Suttles uses Ulf Hannerz's *Soulside* and his own work *The Social Order of the Slum*.[15] In both of these texts Suttles believes there is an explicit and implicit tension in the narrative, wherein there is an attempt to not describe observed behaviors as deviant, while also trying to demonstrate the situational nature of the decisions made by those they studied. For Suttles, although the myriad nuances revealed by situational approaches are critical in advancing the practice of ethnography and knowledge in the field, many researchers seem reluctant to fully let go of a normative approach. As a result, the work produced is full of the tensions and baggage normative accounts bring when studying those who are outside the mainstream. Suttles suggests that we produce work that sees the field site less as "objects for detailed dissection solely 'in their own terms' than occasions on which to examine how their members fashion and refashion cultural meanings that reach them from a great distance."[16]

Key debates have also focused on the politics of representation and interpretation, as evidenced in the debate spurred following Loïc Wacquant critique of several urban ethnographers.[17] Focusing on Katherine Newman's *No Shame in My Game*, Elijah Anderson's *Code of the Streets*, and Mitchell Duneier's *Sidewalk*[18], Wacquant asserted that Newman "glamorizes the skills and deeds of her low-wage workers," Anderson "dichotomizes ghetto residents into good and bad, 'decent' and 'street' and makes himself the spokesman and advocate of the former," and that Duneier "sanitizes the actions and neighborhood impact of sidewalk bookselling by systematically downplaying or suppressing information that would taint the saintly image of the vendors."[19] To be sure, much of Wacquant's critique harkens to Stephen Steinberg's concept of the "ethnographic fallacy"—a by-product of the ethnographer taking the behaviors and justifications of those in the field at face value.[20] While differing in their approach to Wacquant's critique, Anderson, Newman and Duneier retorted Wacquant underscoring the importance of inductive ethnographic approaches. Indeed, each retort outlined the significance in an ethnographic practice that allows for and draws from concepts and frameworks that bubble-up from the field.

While Suttles and Wacquant are concerned with the connection between urban ethnographic method and how ethnographers illustrate and characterize their field sites, Claude Fischer concerns himself with the issue of selection.[21] Critiquing the larger field for the practice of selecting and studying single communities, Fischer argues that what we know of the rural and urban is limited, particularly the similarities and differences between them.

Urban ethnographic method, for Fischer, has relied on implicit comparisons such that "the bulk of urban research…provide[s] points of comparison, but no actual comparisons of different communities."[22] Here, then, Fischer is highlighting a methodological deficit and is calling for an urban ethnographic method that does not take for granted an assumed "rural" and/or "urban" but instead is explicitly comparative. According to Fischer, within the practice of urban ethnography specifically, and urban sociology more generally "there is a lack of focus" and that the "central issue has been lost."[23]

To solve this dilemma, Fischer emphasizes a social psychological approach that considers issues of social networks and identity as central. This shift of focus to networks from singular communities would lead to an analysis that demonstrates the interconnectedness of neighborhoods and communities presenting some other notions of urban. For Fischer, demonstrating the continuity in cities would approach some of the other nodes in the rural–urban continuum.

To accomplish this task, the ethnographer need rely not just upon the conventional implicit comparison, but on explicit study of and comparison between multiple sites in the city as well. While some might argue that implicit cross-community comparisons in ethnographic monographs remain consistent, work demonstrating the contentions across communities and networks has highlighted the complexity of urban space foreshadowed by Fischer's critiques. Here we might think of Elijah Anderson's *Streetwise*, which examines two communities, one that is being gentrified and one that is not (and the tensions that exist between the two communities), and Albert Hunter's analysis in *Symbolic Communities* of the ways networks create and shape the boundaries of communities, as exemplifying the sort of intervention Fischer is highlighting.[24]

Taking as his point of departure the cynical notions people share about the purpose of ethnography, Jack Katz offers a series of warrants that qualify the place and purpose of ethnographic methods.[25] According to Katz, "all ethnography is haunted by the paradox that its distinctive methodological respect for its subjects' meanings implies that its labors are gratuitous." This paradox raises particular questions that are asked of the ethnographer by both the sociological community and the audience at large. These questions Katz articulates as: "If all you have to offer is just a description of commonsense reality, then what is your contribution? If you claim to describe what everyone studied already knows, then who needs you?"[26] To address these questions, Katz calls for a naturalistic ethnographic approach. The naturalistic approach, as articulated by Katz, treats the field as a social phenomenon and is "sometimes more and sometimes less phenomenological in its execution, that evokes the distinctive social interactions and the unique cultures that create genuinely exceptional sensibilities."[27] Ultimately, for Katz, the naturalistic approach will treat the site as a phenomenological occurrence,[28] using thick description[29] to characterize the field as it is on its own and not as it should be, or how it is in relationship to mainstream or conventional sensibilities.

Examining issues of theory in ethnographic methodology, Michael Burawoy posits the notion of the "extended case method."[30] A departure from the convention of "grounded theory,"[31] which requires ethnographers to go into the field with as clean a slate as possible, Burawoy's conception of the ethnographic method is more explicitly tied to theory. In fact, theory seems more important than the field, at least in some instances.

As Burawoy asserts, this extended-case approach should begin by considering theories that "highlight some aspect of the situation under study as being anomalous."[32] In many ways this approach extends from Suttles's consideration of the normative approach to ethnography, as Burawoy's method advocates theory building at the point where observations in a site deviate from some assumed norm. We find this sort of approach evidenced in Mario Small's *Villa Victoria* and John Jackson's *Real Black*, wherein both build social theories from the anomalies of the sites they study.[33] Small highlights changes in neighborhood civic participation as a product of generationally distinctive cognitive frames and Jackson illustrates the tensions between authenticity and sincerity through an understanding of Harlem communities, but both seemingly begin with a theoretical question that is emergent from an anomalous aspect of a Latino or Black neighborhood.

Whereas Burawoy's extended-case method approach is concerned with reconstructing theory and making links between micro and macro as a somewhat singular endeavor, in the appendix of *Sidewalk* Duneier suggests an approach that uses microlevel observations to diagnose social issues and pinpoint structural problems. For Duneier, theory's place in ethnographic method is emergent from a thorough understanding of the relations between microrealities and the myriad macrosites that contribute to those realities. Explicitly connecting with the multisite ethnographic approach,[34] wherein singular sites are conceptualized through their relations to the dynamics of other influential sites (i.e., other neighborhoods, public spaces, other cities, legislation), Duneier argues for an ethnographic method, "diagnostic ethnography," that explicitly triangulates the observations of behaviors and beliefs of those in the field.

Using the example of men urinating in the street, in his study on sidewalk vendors in New York City, Duneier explains that by visiting and talking with people at varied sites (e.g., Washington Square Park, Madison Square Garden, and Greenwich Village) he was able to bring together a layered analysis that exposed the obstacles and social constraints that were manifest in the behavior of public urination. It is in this process of bringing together sites to understand one or more social situations that Duneier sees the place for theory in ethnographic method. Warning against the move away from a grounded theoretical approach, while also taking heed of Steinberg's ethnographic fallacy, Duneier's sees his conception of diagnostic ethnography as a fruitful alternative. According to Duneier, diagnostic ethnography looks to diagnose the primary causes of the behaviors and beliefs observed in the field. Dismissing much of the claims of Wacquant, Duneier not only envisions a place for urban ethnographic inquiry, but also sees issues of representation as being mitigated through the methods he outlines.[35]

Such debates and discourse on ethnographic method reveal that issues of access, ethnographic representation, and causality are epistemological linchpins. Moreover, this brief exposition also reveals that contemporary ethnographic research and researchers have shaped the discussion. Whereas existing examinations and debates center on contemporary ethnographic research and praxis, I seek to illuminate the critical takeaways historical ethnography offers along similar lines of debate and thought.

The Case for Historical Ethnography

How could I study a neighborhood and the community therein if they were no longer available? In my case, while much of the built environment once comprising the Black Seventh Ward was still present, the social clubs, organizations, and residents had migrated from the area to other parts of Philadelphia several decades after DuBois completed *The Philadelphia Negro*. I found that historical ethnography, like the previously discussed debates and ideas posited by urban ethnographers, also offered critical insights to key areas of the ethnographic process: (1) Access, (2) Representation, and (3) Causality.

Access

Getting access is perhaps the hallmark of participant observation. For the historical ethnographer this fact is equally resonant, though the dynamics regarding such access are different in some important ways.[36] When a site or people are no longer available to be observed or queried, the archives and libraries become critical proxies. The archives and libraries function as primary access points for the historical ethnographer to gauge the places, people, and documents betwixt and between past and present. Moreover, the archives are also a place "where the researcher as a person interacts with archive personnel, with other researchers and of course with the people who, to a greater or lesser extent, 'speak' through the historical documents." In this way, then, an archive "*is a field research site that holds its actors captive, that binds them, that does not release them.*"[37]

From the beginning, the historical ethnographer has to forge an ethnographic relationship with people (i.e., the archivists), places (i.e., the library or archive), and documents (i.e., ephemera, news media, institutional records, and letters) whose liminality must be examined so as to produce the tools to effectively conduct historical ethnographic research analysis. Much like contemporary respondents and "introductory agents"—those individuals or institutions that provide ethnographers with initial and/or primary access—archivists play a key role in the collection of data and can provide insights into the existing logics and organizing principles undergirding the archive. Though the task of forging a relationship with an archivist seems simple and straight-forward, in my time at a variety of archives in and around Philadelphia, I found this relationship complicated.

Like a contemporary field site, every archive has a language or code of its own, a way of thinking about and discussing data that determines what gets accessed, how its accessed, and who gets to access it.[38] Given this context, while building a relationship with an archivist is important for any researcher in the archives, for the historical eth-nographer it proves even more critical, as the archivists are not just guides but poten-tial ethnographic informants.[39] However, like many communities of professionals, there were several variations in the types of archivists I encountered and these differ-ences impacted my data outcomes; thus I was behooved to forge differing types of researcher–archivist relations based on the disposition of the archivist. Here, I will highlight two, as each illustrates the consequences of the archivist's disposition for the research and its specific influence on historical ethnographic research. As a gate-keeper, the archivist also serves to safeguard archival information and compel a certain deference for the data and the field. For my purposes, I use these characteriza-tions as hermeneutics or Weberian ideal types so as to illustrate the emergent ques-tions and outcomes.

First, is the *dubious archivist*. He or she is not easily impressed with the researcher, the research questions, and sometimes in the archival collection selected by the researcher for use. At some level, I found a version of the dubious archivist at each of my four primary archival sites. By dubious, I do not mean that they were without interest or belief in the research I was conducting. Rather, these sorts of archivists challenge the researcher to be clear about aspects of the inquiry into the archives: "What are your keywords, search terms?" "Tell me what your interested in, and I will see if we have something that fits?" "What will be the end result of this research?" Initially I found such questions challenging and often misread them as dismissive. Over time, however, I found that the dubious archivist was responding to the oversaturation of researchers in certain parts of the archives.

Why does this happen? In my view, the answer relates to how the researcher came to discover a particular archive. Secondary literature, conversations with experts in the area of research, and university librarians often provide a direct pathway to the archival holdings, highlighting what have been deemed as fruitful collections within the archive—those that have led to publications, those that have been used time and again, and those that have been mined so often that they can yield results with little energy expended and little time invested in the larger archive. As a result, some archivists antic-ipate a lack of interest in the total holdings due to many incidents of researchers "cherry picking" the archives.

Archives can be daunting places, with massive holdings that can take hours, days, or even years to fully examine. With limited time and (often) limited finances, the researcher may not be able to attend to the totality of the archive, and for some archivists such a disposition can produce skepticism. While initially an archivist's skepticism may look to be deterring, being queried up front provides the researcher an opportunity to converse with the archivist and clarify research terms in the language of the archive. In this way, then, the dubious archivist's challenges and disposition are more akin to the contemporary informant whose trust and confidence can dramatically impact access and research in important ways.

First, the dubious archivist can bring attention to the counterfactual at the onset of archival exploration: "Since X has happened and organizes this collection, your search for Y seems like a dead end." Second, conversations with a dubious archivist provide what can amount to very significant field notes regarding donors (families and individuals who have given personal ephemera and records for use at the archive), the origins of the documents, and the original purpose underlying its holdings. Last, once sold on the virtues of the research project, the dubious archivist can become an influential liaison with other collections and institutions, helping to develop an archival network of historical and ethnographic data vis-à-vis other archivists and data.

Next is the *eager archivist*. Unlike the dubious counterpart, eager archivists may meet the researcher with resounding (and sometimes distracting) assistance. To be clear, in order to understand this eagerness, it is important to note that archives themselves can be quiet, empty, and often underused, leaving many eager to interact with someone, especially a researcher interested in their archival treasures. Whereas the dubious archivist may greet the researcher with skepticism, the eager archivist welcomes the researcher with little questioning and/or vetting.

In the case of the eager archivist, the researcher may determine the filter used to pull from the archival holdings. Using the researcher's search terms to organize access, the eager archivist may make nearly all parts of the holdings relate to the researcher's indicated interests. In an effort to meet the researcher's needs, eager archivists translate the existing language and code of the archives into that of the researcher's.

This translation can be quite critical as it can reduce the time spent in examining holdings, streamline the connections across and within collections, and empower the researcher to access a variety of archives that he/she may not have originally planned to explore. Such streamlining and exploration, however, can create tremendous distractions. For example, in my research on the Black Seventh Ward, an eager archivist led me to a series of collections throughout the Northeast corridor related to W. E. B. DuBois. To be sure, some of these data, like DuBois's original neighborhood maps and survey cards, proved quite useful. However, there was a time when I spent three months following the sordid story of DuBois's daughter Yolande's short-lived marriage to Countee Cullen in the early twentieth century.

Here, then, there are several layers of temporality. First, is the fact that as the researcher I was entering the archives at a particular moment in time, a contemporary period relative to the documents examined. Second, the archivist is also an artifact of the present moment, although by virtue of her physical location in the archives, she is the voice of the collection and therefore herself betwixt and between. Then, there are the documents and so on themselves, which are squarely in the past; but as a researcher you enter that past and it becomes present, for you, in the moment (a fact evidenced by my following up of Yolande's marriage).

Distractions and distinctions notwithstanding, both types of archivists I have discussed animate the type of liminal spaces an historical ethnographer must contend with in an effort to collect data. In order to access the past and its relationship with conventional and assumed notions of the present, the historical ethnographer must see the archivists as both ethnographic informants and archival translators.

Given this context, the primary way to access historical counterfactuals and data from the past is to understand and respect the types of archivists one encounters and the subsequent versions of access they provide the researcher. Here, then, historical ethnography reveals that access is not just a problem for understanding present communities and places. Rather, historical ethnography, through its relations with and reliance on the archives, seeks to access both time (i.e., history) and place (i.e., the archives). Without this sort of dual access point, the historical ethnographer's efforts can be greatly impeded, as archivists, librarians, and historical documents provide the primary windows into figuring out "what was or is there."

After forging such bonds with archivists and producing field notes based upon such interactions, I was able to bring this knowledge and these relations to the examination of the archival documents which allowed access to the past; thus creating the "there" that most all researchers seek in the data collection and analysis process. In terms of access, then, historical ethnography reveals a complicated relationship with archives, access, and archivists than might be the case for discretely historical or sociological research endeavors. With an emphasis on field notes, the ethnographic sensibilities of a historical ethnographer require a nuanced relationship with the data and its keepers, the archivists. Key is the access provided by the archival informant like those I have highlighted, as well as the process of constructing field notes that take into account the daily happenings in the archives.

Representation

The successful ethnographer is able to use description and narrative to illuminate a given lifeworld vis-à-vis the sociopolitical lives of the peoples and places under study. In the case of contemporary ethnography, accomplishing this often entails living in the field site, interacting with those in the field, and keeping and analyzing copious field notes. Historical ethnography, however, requires a different approach though it usually relies on similar analytic tools, such as field notes, interviews, and content analysis.

Indeed, as one explores the archives one finds that what is there (in the archives) is often what is *left*, and not necessarily all that is or was "there." In the process of uncovering letters, documents, and institutional records, I discovered the liminality of histor-ical ethnography as pertains to minding history and time. Specifically, while in the archives one discovers the costs and benefits of accessing the "survivors," the lasting or remaining documentary evidence that will supply the historical ethnographic data necessary to (re)construct the stakes of a given time and community.

Much like its contemporary ethnographic counterpart, historical ethnographies must attempt to triangulate or validate their findings, and the documents upon which such suppositions are based, to fully represent the subject matter. The goal of historical ethnography, as with any other ethnography, is to gather and convey an internally valid description of a site and the peoples therein. In other words, the historical ethnographer must contend with the politics of representation: "How do I know what I know?" "What really happened in 1926?" "Did this event matter?" "Was this person I found in the archives of significance to the emergent story?"

Contemporary ethnographies facilitate the ability to examine field notes alongside qualitative interviews with those in the field, tagging along[40] with respondents and informants. Historical ethnography, then, presents a liminal dilemma regarding repre-sentation—how to bring the tools of history, anthropology, and sociology to represent a specific lifeworld betwixt and between the past and the present. Further, such repre-sentation requires both internal validity and some level of consistency with the ebb and flow of history that has led to the present moment or context.

In my research, I found that in order to gauge the veracity and comprehensive nature of my data I needed to combine *macro-level* historical documentation (such as US census records, national news media, government/institutional records, and secondary literature on urban United States history), *meso-level* records (i.e., local and state community surveys, local news media, local and state voting records, local and state election results, court records, and local community organizations and institutional records), and *micro-level* data (such as journals, letters, neighborhood-level news media, photographs, and oral history collections in the archives). Taken alongside the field notes provided through interactions in and with the archives and the archivists, these types of data helped to pinpoint moments of demographic change in the United States, urban America, Philadelphia, the Black Seventh Ward, and develop a general narrative about urban and neighborhood change. For example, in my research I discovered a tenement collapse in 1936 in the Black Seventh Ward that appeared to accelerate New Deal-era public-housing construction in Philadelphia. After discovering this event, I wanted to determine its significance both temporally and also in terms of its relative impact on patterns of change in Philadelphia over time. Enter the triangulation process.

Considering the convergence of the coverage of the event in local news media and similar events in other urban locales in the United States, examining the oral histories of leaders of the time, photographs of the neighborhood and the city before and after 1936, and combining the data from *The Philadelphia Negro*, allowed me to determine the key stakeholders and the "life-course" of this particular event. In other words, in order to follow this previously underanalyzed event and locate its relative historical significance I had to draw from the various levels of archival data available. In this way, in order to generate a sincere[41] and perhaps authentic ethnographic portrayal I was compelled to understand and employ the hierarchy or full range of historical data and their influence on the depiction of structure, communities, history and culture. Furthermore, in the process of developing a representation of a former neighborhood and community, considerations of the relations between data types and emergent ethnographic representations proved fruitful in the area of building sociological analysis and theory.

Causality

Building social theories through inferring notions of causality is often the heaviest burden of ethnographic research carried out by sociologists. In fact, much of the aforementioned debate among ethnographers has centered on the cost and benefits of theorizing before or after entering or leaving a given field site. While some proponents advocate a grounded approach,[42] and others suggest the power of operating with a toolkit of social theories,[43] the historical ethnographer discovers the liminality of their endeavor relative to these approaches to generating causal inferences. At the moment the historical ethnographer begins their research, "history" had already happened, and a master narrative always already exists in the organization of the archives and the conventional wisdom about historical events. In the case of my research on the Black Seventh Ward, I discovered a series of crises in the neighborhood that happened before and during the Great Depression, including the collapse of previously unexplored local black banks and a black-led boycott of white businesses in Philadelphia. Despite the compelling nature of such events, they initially appeared to be counterfactuals. This at first is not a problem, as ethnographic counterfactuals are useful tools to explore causality.[44]

Though in most historical accounts, causality regarding urban and neighborhood change heavily relied on the emergence and conclusion of the Great Depression, these seemingly counterfactual events provided an opportunity to *ethnographically revisit*[45] the Great Depression era through this predominantly black neighborhood in Philadelphia. Revisiting enabled me to ascertain the relative significance of a historical event through following the event to its historical end. Minding history in this longitudinal manner provides an opportunity to garner a clear sense of the stakeholders and players as the issue manifested itself over the course of the Great Depression. Along such lines, Diane Vaughan suggests that this type of causal inference, one which relies on an ethnographic longitudinal filter, is akin to analogic theorizing—a method that compares similar events or activities across different social settings.[46] Extending Vaughan's point, I found that the theorization process involved in historical ethnography requires a constant cycling between evaluating the ethnographic data discovered and the master narratives of extant history and accounts. In this way, then, historical ethnographers can produce theories that maintain the "bottom-up" theorizing under-girding a grounded approach while also bringing to bear the general theories that underpin the teleology inherent in conventional notions of the present.

What does this all mean as relates to causality and theorization? In my view, histor-ical ethnography helps to elucidate notions of causality emergent from the commu-nities, people, and organizations often made invisible in the general thrust of the historical record. In this way, the historical ethnographer can build causal inferences that lead to infrahistorical general social theories. In the case of my research, I found New Deal public housing in Philadelphia to be determined as much by political-eco-nomic dynamics of the time (i.e., the Great Depression, the Great Migration, and World War II) as by the multivocal lifeworld of the Black Seventh Ward. Here, then, I discovered the continued general importance of reception and framing of public pol-icies by residents, especially urban minorities.

Demonstrating the impact of the actions and attitudes of peoples and organiza-tions both across and within time, historical ethnographers can offer theories that bring together seemingly dissonant historical players and moments into a more com-prehensive narrative of change across micro, meso, and macro lines. If we are to have a more coherent and ethnographic notion of history, then we must seek to recover and examine the voices and impactful actions of players lost in the cracks of time. In this way, the types of causal inferences and theories that a historical ethnography can unlock are invaluable and necessary to deepen and clarify our larger sociological imagination.

Calling All Historical Ethnographers

In this appendix I have drawn out the major lessons of my endeavor to revisit W. E. B. DuBois's Black Seventh Ward. Indeed there are several takeaways. First, access to the archives is akin to accessing a contemporary field site like an impoverished neighbor-hood,[47] a nightclub,[48] or a gentrifying black neighborhood.[49] Such field notes derived from interaction in the archives play a similar role in helping to shape the ethnographic picture of the site and data. They also prove significant in minding the archives and determining subsequent causality. Second, ethnographic field notes remain key tools that enhance the internal validity of the research and the claims thereof. Third, history is itself a causal factor, both delimiting our imagination of the times that have long passed and providing a prevailing narrative to measure findings against.

Like their contemporary ethnographic counterparts, historical ethnographers seek to understand the specific as a means to bring together a cogent narrative of social action and events. A significant outcome of the liminality of historical ethnography as it pertains to gauging past and present is that it has the potential to produce a qualitative assessment of long-term big-picture causal effects. An important distinction, however, is that what is deemed general, namely the historical record, is in fact the instrument that is used to measure the significance of archival data, while also being the phenomena that are being implicitly disrupted and disentangled. While such virtues are seemingly most relevant for the study of those made invisible both by and through history, namely minorities, the ability to mind time and places with an ethnographic sensibility cannot be overstated.

My hope is that this exposition moves us towards a discussion of *all* potential forms of ethnographic inquiry, as each provides its own brand of costs and benefits. Fixing our methodological debates and discussion on contemporary ethnographies diminishes the possibilities of expanding the purpose and practice of participant observation. Furthermore, it prevents new ways of thinking ethnographically. Historical ethnography demonstrates that history is not purely a descriptive ethnographic tool but also a tool of theorization and determining causality.

As it stands, our anthropological peers have found historical ethnography to be quite useful both methodologically and epistemologically. Highlighting the liminality of historical ethnography as a practice and tool for theorization, I hope to ignite curiosity while also helping to legitimate the work of those sociologists conducting historical ethnographies in an effort to expand and challenge our sociological imagination. Besides generating fruitful dialogue on ethnographic methods and praxis, my greatest hope in this discussion is that it helps to move away from the question that haunted me—"What is an historical ethnography?"—toward questions that locate this type of participant observation within our broader conception of what constitutes ethnography today.

Notes

CHAPTER I

1. W. E. B. DuBois, *The Autobiography of W. E. B. DuBois: A Soliloquy on Viewing My Life for the Last Decade of Its First Century* (New York: International Publishers, [1967] 2007), 192.

2. DuBois, *Autobiography*, 195.

3. W. E. B. DuBois, *The Philadelphia Negro: A Social Study* (Philadelphia: University of Pennsylvania Press, 1899), 1.

4. DuBois, *Philadelphia Negro*; Roger Lane, *William Dorsey's Philadelphia & Ours* (New York: Oxford University Press, 1991); Roger Lane, *Roots of Violence in Black Philadelphia, 1860–1900* (Cambridge, MA: Harvard University Press, 1986); Robert Gregg, *Sparks From The Anvil of Oppression: Philadelphia's African Methodists and Southern Migrants, 1890–1940* (Philadelphia: Temple University Press, 1993); Gary B. Nash, *Forging Freedom: The Formation of Philadelphia's Black Community, 1720–1840* (Cambridge, MA: Harvard University Press, 1988); Theodore Hershberg, ed., *Philadelphia: Work, Space, Family and Group Experience in the 19th Century* (New York: Oxford University Press, 1981). Throughout this book I use the phrases "the Black Seventh Ward" and "South/Lombard street area" interchangeably.

5. St. Clair Drake and Horace Cayton, *Black Metropolis: A Study of Negro Life in a Northern City* (Chicago: University of Chicago Press, 1993). See also James Weldon Johnson, *Black Manhattan* (New York: Atheneum, 1968), and Blair Ruble, *Washington's U-Street* (Baltimore: Johns Hopkins University Press, 2010). In his analysis of black Harlem, Johnson also characterizes the area as a distinct area unto itself. Scholars of the urban South have also extended this characterization, arguing that in southern black communities, what emerges as a result of the racial geography and racial history of the South are black communities that constitute *separate cities*. For further discussion of this concept and southern black communities, see Christopher Silver and John V. Moeser, *The Separate City: Black Communities in the Urban South, 1940–1968* (Lexington: University of Kentucky Press, 1995).

6. The archival data I use are from a combination of holdings from the following locations: Philadelphia's City Archives, Temple University's Urban Archives, the Free Library of Philadelphia, the University of Pennsylvania's archives, the Historical Society of Pennsylvania, and the Library of Congress. These data include reports, memos, and studies conducted by local and neighborhood organizations, such as the Philadelphia City Planning Commission, the Redevelopment Authority, and the Housing Association of Delaware Valley, community organization participation records, records from local churches and schools in the area, and old leases and deeds. I also make use of nearly 250 previously collected oral histories. I also rely heavily on photographs and local newspapers, which include both mainstream and black press in Philadelphia, such as the *Philadelphia Inquirer*, the *Christian Recorder*, the *Evening Bulletin*, the *Public Ledger*, and the *Philadelphia Tribune* (a black newspaper founded in 1884) and the *Philadelphia Independent* (a black newspaper founded during the 1930s).

7. The approach I take to examine and analyze the social and political history of the Black Seventh Ward over time is perhaps best described as what scholars have referred to as a "path-dependent approach." Making clear the usefulness of critical junctures, James Mahoney offers critical junctures as an analytic and narrative tool that "demonstrate[s] the power of agency by revealing how long-term development patterns can hinge on distant decisions of the past." Mahoney adds that critical junctures enable "historical researchers to avoid the problem of infinite explanatory regress into the past," thus suggesting that critical junctures are a tool for pinpointing significant moments in history while also helping the researcher avoid seemingly endless discussions of the past. See James Mahoney, *Legacies of Liberalism: Path Dependence and Political Regimes in Central America* (Baltimore: Johns Hopkins University Press, 2001), 7. For further discussion on critical junctures and their analytic usefulness, see also Seymour Martin Lipset and Stein Rokkan, eds., *Party Systems and Voter Alignments: Cross-National Perspectives* (New York: Free Press, 1967), and Ruth Berins Collier and David Collier, *Shaping the Political Arena: Critical Junctures, the Labor Movement, and Regime Dynamics in Latin America* (Princeton: Princeton University Press, 1991).

8. See Eric Klinenberg, *Heat Wave: A Social Autopsy of Disaster in Chicago* (Chicago: University of Chicago Press, 2002).

9. Though there has been much debate about the notion of "agency" as perhaps having been overused, due to the lack of the concept and terms applicable to that of urban minorities in some social science literature the concept retains significant relevance. Further, the notions of power, involvement, and intentionality embedded within the broader concept of agency are particularly helpful for examining relations between urban and neighborhood change and the actions and attitudes of urbanites. The literature on agency is vast and quite rich. However, there have been two major strands in this area. That is, agency as a form of delegation and agency as a sense of free will. Perhaps influenced most heavily by sociologist Max Weber,

the work on agency has revealed that the actions and attitudes of "everyday" men and women have both an empirical and theoretical significance, especially to understanding structure and structural change. See for example: Margaret Archer, *Being Human: The Problem of Agency* (New York: Cambridge University Press, 2001); James S. Coleman, *Foundations of Social Theory* (Cambridge, MA: Harvard University Press, 1990); Max Weber, *The Theory of Social and Economic Organization* (New York: Free Press, 1964); Max Weber, *The Protestant Ethic and the Spirit of Capitalism* (New York: Routledge, 2002); Erving Goffman, *The Presentation of Self in Everyday Life* (New York: Doubleday, 1959); Arlie Hochschild, *The Managed Heart: The Commercialization of Human Feeling*, 2nd ed. (Berkeley: University of California Press, 2003); Hans Joas, *The Creativity of Action* (Chicago: University of Chicago Press, 1996); Talcott Parsons, *The Structure of Social Action: A Study in Social Theory with Special Reference to a Group of Recent European Writers*, Vol. 1 (New York: The Free Press, 1968); Charles Taylor, *Human Agency and Language: Philosophical Papers I* (New York: Cambridge University Press, 1985); Linda M. G. Zerilli, *Feminism and the Abyss of Freedom* (Chicago: University of Chicago Press, 2005); Jeffrey C. Alexander, *The Civil Sphere* (New York: Oxford University Press, 2006); Albert O. Hirschman, *Exit, Voice, and Loyalty: Responses to Decline in Firms, Organizations, and States* (Cambridge, MA: Harvard University Press, 1970); Mustafa Emirbayer and Ann Mische, "What is Agency?" *American Journal of Sociology* 103, no. 4 (1998): 962–1023; Susan P. Shapiro, "Agency Theory," *Annual Review of Sociology* 31 (2005): 263–84; Julia Adams, "Principals and Agents, Colonialists and Company Men: The Decay of Colonial Control in the Dutch East Indies," *American Sociological Review* 61, (1996): 12–28; Julia Adams, "1–800–How-Am-I-Driving?: Agency in Social Science History," *Social Science History* 35, no. 1 (2011): 1–17; Kevin Fox Gotham, "Toward an Understanding of the Spatiality of Urban Poverty: The Urban Poor as Spatial Actors," *International Journal of Urban and Regional Research* 27, no. 3 (2003): 723–37; and Marcus Anthony Hunter, "The Nightly Round: Space, Social Capital and Urban Black Nightlife," *City & Community* 9, no. 2 (2010): 165–86.

10. Frances Fox Piven and Richard A. Cloward, *Poor People's Movements: Why they Succeed, How they Fail* (New York: Pantheon Books, 1977), 2.

11. See Richard Iton, *In Search of the Black Fantastic* (New York: Oxford University Press, 2009); Robin D. G. Kelley, *Race Rebels: Culture, Politics, and the Black Working Class* (New York: Free Press, 1994); and Theda Skocpol, *States & Social Revolutions: A Comparative Analysis of France, Russia, & China* (New York: Cambridge University Press, 1979).

12. Hirschman, *Exit, Voice, and Loyalty*.

13. See Michael B. Preston, Lenneal J. Henderson, Jr., and Paul L. Puryear, eds., *The New Black Politics: The Search For Political Power*, 2nd ed. (New York: Longman, 1987); Katherine Tate, *From Protest to Politics: The New Black Voters in American Elections* (New York: Russell Sage Foundation, 1993); Albert K. Karnig and Susan

Welch, *Black Representation and Urban Policy* (Chicago: University of Chicago Press, 1980); Carol M. Swain, *Black Faces, Black Interests* (Cambridge, MA: Harvard University Press, 1995); Melissa Harris-Lacewell, *Barbershops, Bibles, and BET: Everyday Talk and Black Political Thought* (Princeton: Princeton University Press, 2006); and J. Phillip Thompson, III, *Double Trouble: Black Mayors, Black Communities, and the Call for a Deep Democracy* (New York: Oxford University Press, 2006).

14. See Adolph Reed, *Race, Politics, and Culture* (New York: Greenwood Press, 1986); Aldon Morris, *The Origins of the Civil Rights Movement: Black Communities Organizing for Change* (New York: Free Press, 1984); Preston, Henderson, and Puryear, eds., *New Black Politics*; Tate, *From Protest to Politics*; Karnig and Welch, *Black Representation and Urban Policy*; Thompson, *Double Trouble*.

15. See Michael C. Dawson, *Behind the Mule: Race and Class in African-American Politics* (Princeton: Princeton University Press, 1994); Charles P. Henry, *Culture and African American Politics* (Bloomington: Indiana University Press, 1990); and Cathy J. Cohen, *The Boundaries of Blackness* (Chicago: University of Chicago Press, 1999).

16. See Dawson, *Behind the Mule*; Cohen, *Boundaries of Blackness*; Adolph Reed, *Stirrings in the Jug: Black Politics in the Post-Segregation Era* (Minneapolis: University of Minnesota Press, 1999); and Mary Pattillo, *Black on the Block: The Politics of Race and Class in the City* (Chicago: University of Chicago Press, 2007).

17. Cohen, *The Boundaries of Blackness*.

18. See Reed, *Race, Politics, and Culture*; Aldon Morris, *Origins of the Civil Rights Movement*; Preston, Henderson, and Puryear, eds., *New Black Politics*; and Thompson, *Double Trouble*.

19. See Doug McAdam, *Political Process and the Development of Black Insurgency, 1930–1970* (Chicago: University of Chicago Press, 1982); Thomas Sugrue, *Origins of the Urban Crisis* (Princeton: Princeton University Press, 1996); Aldon Morris, *Origins of the Civil Rights Movement*; Charles Tilly, *From Mobilization to Revolution* (Reading, MA: Addison-Wesley, 1978); Francesca Polletta, *Freedom is an Endless Meeting* (Chicago: University of Chicago Press, 2002); Darnell Hunt, *Screening the Los Angeles Riots* (New York: Cambridge University Press, 1997); Martha Biondi, *To Stand and Fight* (Cambridge, MA: Harvard University Press, 2003); and Rhonda Y. Williams, *The Politics of Public Housing* (New York: Oxford University Press, 2004).

20. In my analysis I take cues from recent discussions around the concept of "black community," deploying the term sparingly to characterize the population I examine. See for example, Reed, *Stirrings in the Jug*, 15–16; and Pattillo, *Black on the Block*.

21. Hirschman, *Exit, Voice, and Loyalty*, 17; Isabel Wilkerson, *The Warmth of Other Suns* (New York: Vintage Books, 2011).

22. James C. Scott, *Seeing Like a State: How Certain Schemes to Improve the Human Condition Have Failed* (New Haven: Yale University Press, 1998), 6–8.

CHAPTER 2

1. "Brown & Stevens Bank Goes into Receivers Hands," *Philadelphia Tribune*, February 7, 1925; "Attorneys Clash at Hearing of Brown-Stevens," *Philadelphia Tribune*, May 30, 1925; "Bankers Form a Permanent Organization," *Philadelphia Tribune*, September 18, 1926; "Three Depositors Take Action in Case of Brown & Stevens," *Evening Bulletin*, February 18, 1925. All figures reported according to current standards are based upon the 2010 Consumer Price Index (CPI). The CPI is especially useful because I focus on black Americans as consumers. Using the CPI, I have produced estimates for all figures reported to facilitate an idea of how much money was involved in the banks discussed in the chapter. For more see: Samuel H. Williamson, "Seven Ways to Compute the Relative Values of a U.S. Dollar Amount, 1774 to Present," (Measuring Worth, 2011), http://measuringworth.com/uscompare/.

2. James Madison, Alexander Hamilton, and John Jay, *The Federalist Papers* (New York: SoHo, 2011); Adam Smith, *The Wealth of Nations* (New York: Penguin, 1986).

3. Michèle Lamont and Virág Molnár, "The Study of Boundaries in the Social Sciences," *Annual Review of Sociology* 28 (2002): 167–95, at 168.

4. Vivana Zelizer, "The Special Meaning of Money: 'Special Monies,'" *American Journal of Sociology* 95, no. 2 (1989): 342–77, at 343. Further explaining this concept Zelizer asserts: "For instance, a housewife's pin money or her allowance is treated differently from a wage or a salary, and each surely differs from a child's allowance. Or a lottery winning is marked as a different kind of money from an ordinary paycheck. The money we obtain as compensation for an accident is not quite the same as the royalties from a book" (343). Further discussion in this regard includes: Viviana Zelizer, "Human Values and the Market: The Case of Life Insurance and Death in 19th-Century America," *American Journal of Sociology* 84, no. 3 (1978): 591–610; Zelizer, *The Social Meaning of Money* (New York: Basic Books, 1994); Zelizer, *Morals and Markets: The Development of Life Insurance in the United States* (New York: Columbia University Press, 1979); Thomas Crump, *The Phenomenon of Money* (London: Routledge & Kegan Paul, 1981); Albert O. Hirschman, *Rival Views of Market Society* (New York: Viking, 1986); and Georg Simmel, *The Philosophy of Money*, trans. Tom Bottomore and David Frisby (London: Routledge & Kegan Paul, 1900). See also Bruce Carruthers and Wendy Espeland, "Money, Meaning, and Morality," *American Behavioral Science* 41 (1998): 1384–8; and Lisa A. Keister, "Financial Markets, Money, and Banking," *Annual Review of Sociology* 28 (2002): 39–61.

5. DuBois, *The Philadelphia Negro* (Philadelphia: University of Pennsylvania Press, 1899), 295.

6. Arnett G. Lindsay, "The Negro in Banking," *Journal of Negro History* 14, no. 2 (1929): 172; for further discussion on black banks, see also Lila Ammons, "The Evolution of Black-Owned Banks in the United States between the 1880s and 1990s," *Journal of Black Studies* 26, no. 4 (1996): 467–89; Abram L. Harris, *The Negro as Capitalist* (New York: Negro Universities Press, [1936] 1969); Edward D. Irons, "Black

Banking—Problems and Prospects," *Journal of Finance* 26, no. 2 (1971): 407–25; and Andrew F. Brimmer, "The Black Banks: An Assessment of Performance and Prospects," *Journal of Finance* 26, no. 2 (1971): 379–405; DuBois, *Philadelphia Negro*, 184.

7. US Senate, 46th Cong., 2nd sess., 1880, Rep. 440; US Senate, *The Freedman's Bank Bill*, 46th Cong., 3rd sess., 1881; U.S. Senate, 62nd Cong., 2nd Session, 1912, Rep. 759, 4; Lindsay, "Negro in Banking," 156–201.

8. Walter L. Fleming, The Freedmen's Savings Bank: A Chapter in the Economic History of the Negro Race (Westport: Negro Universities Press, 1970) 19; See also Ira Berlin et al., Free At Last: A Documentary History of Slavery, Freedom, and the Civil War (New York: New Press, 1992); Orlando Patterson, Rituals of Blood: Consequences of Slavery in Two America Centuries (New York: Basic Civitas, 1998).

9. Frederick Wherry, "The Social Characterizations of Price: The Fool, the Faithful, the Frivolous, and the Frugal," *Sociological Theory* 26, no. 4 (2008): 363–79, at 369.

10. Quoted from Lindsay, "Negro in Banking," 163; US Senate, 46th Cong., 2nd sess., 1880, Rep. 440.

11. As quoted in Fleming, *Freedmen's Savings Bank*, 26. See also *Congressional Globe*, 38th Cong., 2nd sess., 1865, pt. I and pt. II.

12. Fleming, Freedmen's Savings Bank, 35. See also Carl R. Osthaus, Freedmen, Philanthropy, and Fraud: A History of the Freedman's Savings Bank (Urbana: University of Illinois Press, 1976).

13. As quoted in Fleming, *Freedmen's Savings Bank*, 44.

14. Fleming, Freedmen's Savings Bank, 45.

15. As quoted in Osthaus, Freedmen, Philanthropy, and Fraud, 82.

16. Harris, *Negro as Capitalist*.

17. Fleming, *Freedmen's Savings Bank*, 42; see also US Senate, 46th Cong., 2nd sess., 1880, Rep. 440; *Congressional Globe*, 38th Cong., 2nd sess., 1865, pt. I and pt. II.

18. Harris, Negro as Capitalist.

19. Frederick Douglass, Life and Times of Frederick Douglass: His Early Life as a Slave, His Escape from Bondage, and His Complete History to the Present Time (Hartford: Park Publishing, 1881) 413.

20. Douglass, *Life and Times*, 414.

21. Douglass, *Life and Times*, 410–12.

22. Philip S. Foner, ed., *Frederick Douglass: Selected Speeches and Writings* (Chicago: Lawrence Hill, 1999), 680–81.

23. Douglass, Life and Times, 414.

24. Booker T. Washington, *The Story of the Negro*, Vol. 2 (New York: Doubleday, Page, 1909), 214–15.

25. W. E. B. DuBois, *The Souls of Black Folk* (New York: Penguin, 1982), 32.

26. DuBois, Souls of Black Folk.

27. Sam Bass Warner, *The Private City* (Philadelphia: University of Pennsylvania Press, 1968); Roger Lane, *Roots of Black Violence in Black Philadelphia* (Cambridge, MA: Harvard University Press, 1986); V. P. Franklin, *The Education of Black Philadelphia* (Philadelphia: University of Pennsylvania Press, 1979).

28. US Census Reports, 1890–1910; "Remarkable Progress Made by Colored People of this City," *Philadelphia Tribune*, March 21, 1914.

29. Warner, *Private City*; Lane, *Roots of Black Violence*; Franklin, *Education of Black Philadelphia*.

30. See Melvin L. Oliver and Thomas M. Shapiro, *Black Wealth/White Wealth* (New York: Routledge, 1997); see also Dalton Conley, *Being Black, Living in the Red* (Berkeley: University of California Press, 1999); for discussion of black wealth and racial differences in wealth accumulation, see Andrew F. Brimmer, "Income, Wealth, and Investment Behavior in the Black Community," *American Economic Review* 78, no. 2 (1988): 151–5; Robert L. Boyd, "Residential Segregation by Race and the Black Merchants of Northern Cities during the Early Twentieth Century," *Sociological Forum* 13, no. 4 (1998): 595–609; Frances K. Goldscheider and Calvin Goldscheider, "The Intergenerational Flow of Income: Family Structure and the Status of Black Americans," *Journal of Marriage and Family* 23, no. 2 (1991): 499–508; Ivan Light, "Gambling Among Blacks: A Financial Institution," *American Sociological Review* 42, no. 6 (1977): 892–904; A. Wade Smith and Joan V. Moore, "East-West Differences in Black Economic Development," *Journal of Black Studies* 16, no. 2 (1985): 131–54; Maury Gittleman and Edward N. Wolff, "Racial Differences in Patterns of Wealth Accumulation," *Journal of Human Resources* 39, no. 1 (2004): 193–227; Kyle Crowder et al., "Wealth, Race, and Inter-Neighborhood Migration," *American Sociological Review* 71, no. 1 (2006): 72–94; and Albert Karnig, "Black Economic, Political, and Cultural Development: Does City Size Make a Difference?" *Social Forces* 57, no. 4 (1979): 1194–211.

31. "Jews on South Street Request Removal of Colored Policemen," *Philadelphia Tribune*, June 24, 1916; "Plan on Foot to Boycott South Street Stores," *Philadelphia Tribune*, June 31, 1916.

32. *Philadelphia Tribune*, June 24, 1916; *Philadelphia Tribune*, June 31, 1916.

33. *Philadelphia Tribune*, June 31, 1916.

34. "Colored Citizens Boycott White South St. Stores," *Philadelphia Tribune*, July 8, 1916.

35. "Colored Citizens," *Philadelphia Tribune*.

36. "Colored Citizens," *Philadelphia Tribune*.

37. "Colored Citizens," *Philadelphia Tribune*.

38. *Philadelphia Tribune*, July 8, 1916; "Citizens Demand that Meetings Be Continued," *Philadelphia Tribune*, August 5, 1916.

39. Drake and Cayton, *Black Metropolis*, 430–31.

40. My thinking on and discussion of the "linked fate" perspective is informed by the work of scholars such as Michael C. Dawson, *Behind the Mule: Race and Class in*

African-American Politics (Princeton: Princeton University Press, 1994); Charles P. Henry, *Culture and African American Politics* (Bloomington: Indiana University Press, 1990); and Cathy J. Cohen, *The Boundaries of Blackness* (Chicago: University of Chicago Press, 1999). See Dawson, *Behind the Mule*; Cohen, *Boundaries of Blackness*; Adolph Reed, *Stirrings in the Jug: Black Politics in the Post-Segregation Era* (Minneapolis: University of Minnesota Press, 1999).

41. "Dr. W. E. B. DuBois Delivers Lecture Flays Politics," *Philadelphia Tribune*, March 9, 1918.

42. DuBois, *Philadelphia Negro*, 394–7.

43. Harris, *Negro as Capitalist*; "New Real Estate and Banking: For Philadelphia at 427 S. Broad Street," *Philadelphia Tribune*, January 18, 1913.

44. DuBois, *Philadelphia Negro*, 119 (emphasis in the original).

45. The larger North Carolina Bank, Metro Bank, later absorbed Crown, although that bank would later fail as well. For more information see Harris, *Negro as Capitalist*.

46. Harris, *Negro as Capitalist*; "Brown and Stevens to Erect Handsome Apartment Houses," *Philadelphia Tribune*, May 7, 1921.

47. "Brown and Stevens," *Philadelphia Tribune*, May 7, 1921.

48. *Philadelphia Tribune*, May 7, 1921. Such efforts to promote Brown and Stevens highlight the work indigenous institutions do to respond to consensus or common issues for urban blacks. Given the persistent negative impact an economic detour has on wealth accumulation and maintenance among blacks, indigenous institutions such as the black press, fraternal orders, and churches refrained from criticizing or interrogating the impact and intentions of those black entrepreneurs and leaders seemingly addressing such profound black needs.

49. Harris, *Negro as Capitalist*; *Philadelphia Tribune*, May 7, 1921; "The Mayor Hears Arguments on Play Ground Naming," *Philadelphia Tribune*, August 6, 1921; "Stockholders Vote to Sell Dunbar to John T. Gibson," *Philadelphia Tribune*, August 23, 1921.

50. *Philadelphia Tribune*, May 7, 1921.

51. Harris, *Negro as Capitalist*; *Philadelphia Tribune*, May 7, 1921; *Philadelphia Tribune*, August 6, 1921; *Philadelphia Tribune*, August 23, 1921.

52. Harris, *Negro as Capitalist*; *Philadelphia Tribune*, May 7, 1921; *Philadelphia Tribune*, August 6, 1921; *Philadelphia Tribune*, August 23, 1921.

53. Harris, *Negro as Capitalist*; *Philadelphia Tribune*, May 7, 1921; *Philadelphia Tribune*, August 6, 1921; *Philadelphia Tribune*, August 23, 1921; "The Doings of the Profession: On and Off the Board's Gibson Standard Theater," *Philadelphia Tribune*, September 17, 1921.

54. *Philadelphia Tribune*, February 7, 1925; "300 Draw Savings in Run on Bank," *Evening Bulletin*, February 9, 1925.

55. *Evening Bulletin*, February 9, 1925.

56. "Close Negro Bank after Depositors Storm its Office," *Evening Bulletin*, February 11, 1925.

57. Gary Alan Fine, "Redemption Rumors: Mercantile Legends and Corporate Beneficence," *Journal of American Folklore* 99, no. 392 (1986): 208–22.

58. *Philadelphia Tribune*, August 6, 1921; *Philadelphia Tribune*, August 23, 1921; *Philadelphia Tribune*, February 7, 1925; *Evening Bulletin*, February 9, 1925; "Receiver Named for Closed Bank," *Evening Bulletin*, February 10, 1925; *Evening Bulletin*, February 11, 1925; "900,000 is Lost in Brown and Stevens Smash," *Afro-American*, May 23, 1931.

59. *Philadelphia Tribune*, February 7, 1925; *Evening Bulletin*, February 9, 1925; *Evening Bulletin*, February 11, 1925. See also: Dawson, *Behind the Mule*; Henry, *Culture and African American Politics*; and Cohen, *Boundaries of Blackness*; Reed, *Stirrings in the Jug*.

60. "Uptown Negro Bank Suspends Business," *Evening Bulletin*, February 15, 1925; "Bank Patrons Face 'Substantial Loss' Conversion of Closed Institution's Assets into Cash Involve Substantial Financial Sacrifice," *Evening Bulletin*, February 16, 1925.

61. "Bank Patrons Face 'Substantial Loss'," *Evening Bulletin*...

62. In the matter of Edward C. Brown's and Andrew Stevens's bankruptcy proceedings and the larger banking investigation see: District Court of the United States, Eastern District Pennsylvania, Equity No. 9330, No. 14078; *Evening Bulletin*, February 11, 1925; "Aid for Depositors Hit by Closed Bank," *Evening Bulletin*, February 12, 1925; "Close Second Bank and Name Receiver," *Evening Bulletin*, February 14, 1925; *Evening Bulletin*, February 16, 1925; Brown was also reported to have written a bad check for $36,000 to Major Wright, who organized the Citizens & Southern Bank in 1925; see "Brown and Stevens Out in Bail for Bad Check," *Philadelphia Tribune*, July, 11, 1925 for further details.

63. District Court of the United States, Eastern District Pennsylvania, Equity No. 9330, No. 14078; *Evening Bulletin*, February 12, 1925.

64. "Banker E. C. Brown Transferred Valuable Real Estate to Wife," *Philadelphia Tribune*, May 23, 1925; *Philadelphia Tribune*, May 30, 1925; "19 Pieces of Property Transferred by Defunct Bank to Change Hands," *Philadelphia Tribune*, June 20, 1925; *Philadelphia Tribune*, July 11, 1925; "Depositors in Defunct Bank Must Wait Until Next Fall," *Philadelphia Tribune*, July 25, 1925; "Brown and Stevens Bank to Be Sold Monday," *Philadelphia Tribune*, August 1, 1925; "Brown Stevens Building Sold Monday for $94,000," *Philadelphia Tribune*, August 8, 1925; "If You Pay for Seven Pounds Get Full Weight," *Philadelphia Tribune*, August 22, 1925; "Fixtures of Brown–Stevens Bank Sold for $4,007," *Philadelphia Tribune*, August 22, 1925; "Cosmopolitan Bank has Deficit of Over Eighty-Six Thousand Banking Department Calls Upon Stockholders to pay $5,000 Into Busted Bank," *Philadelphia Tribune*, July 3, 1926; "Brown and Stevens Depositors Organize to Hasten Settlements," *Philadelphia Tribune*, July 31, 1926; "Brown–Stevens Depositors Tired of Promises," *Philadelphia Tribune*, October 16, 1926; "E. C. Brown Dies in New York City," *Philadelphia Tribune*, January 26, 1928; "Depositors to Get Four Percent Dividend,"

Philadelphia Tribune, November 29, 1928; "Trust Flop Hits Negroes Newsdealers Daughter Life's Savings Placed in Bank Whose Doors Close," *Philadelphia Tribune*, December 25, 1930; "Final Chapter Written In B. S. Bank Failure," *Philadelphia Tribune*, April 27, 1933; *Afro-American*, May 23, 1931; "Brown & Steven to Make First Payment Soon," *Afro-American*, February 13, 1926; "Only 45.93 Left of the Million Dollars E. C. Brown Amassed in Theatre Projects," *Afro-American*, May 6, 1933; "Death Closes Former Banker Brown's Accounts," *New York Amsterdam News*, February 1, 1928.

65. For a recent discussion of the persistence of the culture of distrust for banking and banks among the poor, see Christine Haughney, "City's Poor Still Distrust Banks," *New York Times*, August 18, 2009.

66. See Sandra Susan Smith, *Lone Pursuit: Distrust and Defensive Individualism among the Black Poor* (New York: Russell Sage Foundation, 2007); Jennifer Lee, *Civility in the City: Black, Jews, and Koreans in Urban America* (Cambridge, MA: Harvard University Press, 2002).

CHAPTER 3

1. "Horror Crash Killing 7, to Bring End to Slum Houses," "Oust Hundreds from Slum Homes as Result of Horror Crash that Claimed 7 Lives," "Gus Norris Writes on the Slum Conditions in 7th Ward," *Philadelphia Independent*, December 27, 1936; "Funeral for Crash Victims," *Philadelphia Independent*, January 3, 1937; "6 Killed, 20 Hurt as 2 Houses fall; Slum Probe Begun," *Philadelphia Inquirer*, December 21, 1936.

2. *Philadelphia Inquirer*, December 21, 1936; "Evicted Tenants Organize a Union for Better Housing," "Police Order Tenants Out of Bandboxes," *Philadelphia Inquirer*, December 26, 1936.

3. *Philadelphia Inquirer*, December 21, 1936; December 26, 1936; *Philadelphia Independent*, December 27, 1936.

4. ""$10,000 Bail is Set as 'Manslaughter' Trial Faces Lessee in Tragedy Probe," *Philadelphia Tribune*, December 24, 1936.

5. The Carl Mackley Houses were the first to be constructed. Originally known as Juniata Park Housing, the Mackley Homes are now a private apartment complex in the Juniata neighborhood of Philadelphia. They were built in 1933–1934 as single-family apartments and opened in 1935. Opening one year prior to the tenement collapse, the Mackley Houses were treated as a discrete project (especially from what later morphed into New Deal Era public housing construction). Sponsored by the American Federation of Full-Fashioned Hosiery Workers, with financing by the Housing Division of the Public Works Administration, the Mackley Houses were named for a striking hosiery worker killed by nonunion workers during the H. C. Aberle Company strike in 1930. For more on the Mackley Houses and the differing politics surrounding their construction, see John F. Bauman, *Public Housing, Race,*

and Renewal: Urban Planning in Philadelphia, 1920–1974 (Philadelphia: Temple University Press, 1987).

6. US Census Reports, 1900–1920.

7. "Court Refuses to Prosecute Man for Protecting his Home," *Philadelphia Tribune*, May 3, 1919.

8. "Court Refuses," *Philadelphia Tribune*.

9. Much of this discussion occurs in an analysis of the deterioration of urban black neighborhoods in the wake of deindustrialization. Scholars have emphasized the critical role that middle-class blacks played as social and political buffers between whites and poor blacks, as a result of the increasing social isolation of urban black poor and working-class residents. In these analyses, researchers often emphasize the out-migration and/or disappearance of the urban black middle class to explain the general dilapidation and decline of urban black neighborhoods in the post–civil rights context. For a more detailed discussion of this topic, see William Julius Wilson, *When Work Disappears* (Chicago: University of Chicago Press, 1996); and Elijah Anderson, *Streetwise: Race, Class, and Change in an Urban Community* (Chicago: University of Chicago Press, 1990). It should be noted, however, that there has been debate about the role and disappearance of the black middle class in research such as that noted above. Recent research has suggested that the black middle class continues to reside in urban black neighborhoods but it also points to a reciprocal relationship between poor and middle-class blacks. The most notable work in this regard includes Mary Pattillo-McCoy, *Black Picket Fences: Privilege and Peril Among the Black Middle Class* (Chicago: University of Chicago Press, 1999) and Mary Pattillo, *Black on the Block: The Politics of Race and Class in the City* (Chicago: University of Chicago Press, 2007).

10. My thinking on cross-cutting issues and its difference from consensus issues is guided by Cathy Cohen, *Boundaries of Blackness* (Chicago: University of Chicago Press, 1999).

11. "Mayor Moore would Clean-up Seventh Ward Section to Establish His Own Political Headquarters," *Philadelphia Tribune*, October 30, 1920.

12. "Amos M. Scott for Magistrate," *Philadelphia Tribune*, July 2, 1921; "Women Pick Scott Standard Bearer for Race Victory," *Philadelphia Tribune* August 27, 1921; "Voters of South Philadelphia Rally for Amos Scott," *Philadelphia Tribune*, September 3, 1921; "Vare Wards Carry Scott to Victory in Battle at Polls," *Philadelphia Tribune*, October 1, 1921; "Amos Scott wins by Over 60,000 Majority," *Philadelphia Tribune*, November 12, 1921.

13. "Mayor Moore Opens New playground, Phyllis Wheatley its Name," *Philadelphia Tribune*, July 16, 1921; "The Mayor Hears Argument on Play Ground Naming," *Philadelphia Tribune*, August 6, 1921.

14. See Miriam Ershkowitz and Joseph Zikmund II, eds., *Black Politics in Philadelphia* (New York: Basic Books, 1973); H. Viscount Nelson, *Black Leadership's Response to the Great Depression in Philadelphia* (Lewiston: Edwin Mellen, 2006); see also

Peter McCaffery *When Bosses Ruled Philadelphia* (University Park: Pennsylvania State University Press, 1993); and Charles T. Banner-Haley, *To Do Good and Do Well: Middle Class Blacks and the Depression Philadelphia, 1929–1941* (New York: Garland Press, 1993).

15. Once called the Philadelphia Housing Association, during the latter half of the twentieth century the organization renamed itself the Housing Association of Delaware Valley to account for the larger urban metropolitan area for which it was an advocate. In order to maintain consistency throughout the book I refer to the organization as the Housing Association of Delaware Valley, or HADV. Such terminology also helps avoid confusion between this housing advocacy organization and the Philadelphia Housing Authority, or PHA, the local authority formed to oversee housing programs and sites in Philadelphia.

16. W. E. B. DuBois, *The Philadelphia Negro* (Philadelphia: University of Pennsylvania Press, 1899), 292.

17. See Negro Migrant Study (1923–1924), Temple University Urban Archives; for similar discussions in cities such as Detroit, Chicago, and Milwaukee see Reynolds Farley et al., *Detroit Divided* (New York: Russell Sage Foundation, 2000); Allan H. Spear, *Black Chicago* (Chicago: University of Chicago Press, 1967); and Joe William Trotter, Jr., *Black Milwaukee* (Urbana: University of Illinois Press, 1985) respectively.

18. "Normal" at the time referred to schools that provided general education. The phrase "normal" was often used to distinguish such schools from vocational, or trade-oriented schools; see also Vincent P. Franklin, *The Education of Black Philadelphia* (Philadelphia: University of Pennsylvania Press, 1979); and Franklin, *Roger Lane's William Dorsey's Philadelphia & Ours* (New York: Oxford University Press, 1991).

19. "'Dying Like Flies' Undertakers Doing Big Business Because of Housing Situation," *Philadelphia Tribune*, March 21, 1925; "People 'Dying Like Flies' because of Unsanitary Conditions," *Philadelphia Tribune*, March 28, 1925.

20. "Yes, We Have a Democratic Club in Phila.; Officers and Executive Committee of the Colored Democratic Club of Phila.," *Philadelphia Tribune*, June 7, 1924.

21. Robin D. G. Kelley, *Race Rebels: Culture, Politics, and the Black Working Class* (New York: Free Press, 1994).

22. "Hagans Voted President of Citizens Club," *Philadelphia Tribune*, December 13, 1928.

23. *Negro Housing in Philadelphia* (1927), Housing Association of Delaware Valley Papers, Temple University Urban Archives; see also Sam Bass Warner, *The Private City: Philadelphia in Three Periods of Its Growth* (Philadelphia: University of Pennsylvania Press, 1968).

24. See Bauman, *Public Housing, Race, and Renewal.*

25. Bauman, *Public Housing, Race, and Renewal.*

26. Statement of J. Hampton Moore, July 4, 1933, J. Moore Hampton Collection, Historical Society of Pennsylvania; see also Newman to A. R. Clas, July 8, 1935,

Housing Association of Delaware Valley Papers, Temple University Urban Archives.

27. See Nelson, *Black Leadership's Response*, 74.

28. "Citizens Republican Club Shows Hesitance in Endorsing Hoover," *Philadelphia Tribune*, September 15, 1932; "Citizen's Club on Verge of Bankruptcy," *Philadelphia Tribune*, December 7, 1933.

29. "Citizens Republican Club Shows Hesitance," *Philadelphia Tribune*; "Citizen's Club on Verge of Bankruptcy," *Philadelphia Tribune*; see also Bauman, *Public Housing, Race, and Renewal*; and James Wolfinger, *Philadelphia Divided: Race and Politics in the City of Brotherly Love* (Chapel Hill: University of North Carolina Press, 2007).

30. "City Officials Indifferent to Crime Breeding Slum Section," *Philadelphia Tribune*, February 28, 1935; "Technique of Slums Profit Czars Aired," *Philadelphia Tribune*, March 7, 1935; see also Nelson, *Black Leadership's Response*; Bauman, *Public Housing, Race, and Renewal*; and Wolfinger, *Philadelphia Divided*.

31. See Kelley, *Race Rebels*.

32. Nelson, *Black Leadership's Response*; see also Banner-Haley, *To Do Good and Do Well*.

33. "Tribune Slum Area Campaign Prophetic," *Philadelphia Tribune*, June 27, 1935.

34. See Nelson, *Black Leadership's Response*; and Bauman, *Public Housing, Race, and Renewal*.

35. Nelson, *Black Leadership's Response*; and Bauman, *Public Housing, Race, and Renewal*.; see also Wolfinger, *Philadelphia Divided*.

36. Unnamed and undated newspaper, unnamed newspaper, December 22, 1936, Housing Association of Delaware Valley Papers, Temple University Urban Archives; unnamed newspaper, December 21, 1936, Housing Association of the Delaware Valley, Temple University Urban Archives; "The Housing Tragedy Challenge to Women," *Philadelphia Independent*, December 27, 1936; *Philadelphia Evening Bulletin*, December 28, 1936, Housing Association of the Delaware Valley Papers, Temple University Urban Archives.

37. For black female-led activism, see Lisa Levenstein, *A Movement Without Marches* (Chapel Hill: University of North Carolina Press, 2009); see also Rhonda Y. Williams, *The Politics of Public Housing* (New York: Oxford University Press, 2004).

38. "Outstanding Citizens Here Hit Neglect," *Philadelphia Tribune*, December 24, 1936.

39. "Outstanding Citizens Here Hit Neglect," *Philadelphia Tribune*.

40. Unnamed and undated newspaper, December 22, 1936, Housing Association of Delaware Valley Papers, Temple University Urban Archives; unnamed newspaper, December 21, 1936, Housing Association of Delaware Valley Papers, Temple University Urban Archives; *Philadelphia Independent*, December 27, 1936; *Philadelphia Evening Bulletin*, December 28, 1936, Housing Association of Delaware Valley Papers, Temple University Urban Archives.

41. *Philadelphia Inquirer*, December 28, 1936; "Outstanding Citizens Here Hit Neglect," *Philadelphia Tribune*; *Philadelphia Tribune*, December 24, 1936. *Philadelphia Record*, December 27, 1936; see also Nelson, *Black Leadership's Response*; Bauman, *Public Housing, Race, and Renewal*; Wolfinger, *Philadelphia Divided*.

42. *Philadelphia Tribune*, December 24, 1936.

43. "Plan Memorial for Victims of House Collapse," *Philadelphia Tribune*, December 9, 1937; "Tenants Urge Representation on housing Authority Here as housing Plans Progress," *Philadelphia Tribune*, December 23, 1937; "Local Groups Support Low Cost," *Philadelphia Tribune*, April 13, 1939; see also Nelson, *Black Leadership's Response*; Bauman, *Public Housing, Race, and Renewal*; and Wolfinger, *Philadelphia Divided*.

44. "Stood on the Brink of Grave—Live to Tell Graphic Stories!," *Philadelphia Tribune*, December 24, 1936.

45. *Philadelphia Tribune*, December 24, 1936; "Hold Landlord in Deaths of 7," *Philadelphia Tribune*, June 24, 1937.

46. "J. Austin Norris is Sworn in to $10,000 Post by Judge Bok," *Philadelphia Tribune*, July 22, 1937; see also Nelson, *Black Leadership's Response*; Bauman, *Public Housing, Race, and Renewal*; and Wolfinger, *Philadelphia Divided*.

47. See Nelson, *Black Leadership's Response*; Bauman, *Public Housing, Race, and Renewal*; Wolfinger, *Philadelphia Divided*; and Roger Biles, "Public Housing and the Postwar Urban Renaissance," in *From Tenements to the Taylor Homes: In Search of Urban Housing Policy in Twentieth Century America*, ed. John F. Bauman, Roger Biles, and Kristin M. Szylvian (University Park: Pennsylvania State University Press, 2000), 143–62.

48. Hirsch, *Making the Second Ghetto*.

49. *Philadelphia Tribune*, December 23, 1937.

50. *Philadelphia Tribune*, December 23, 1937.

51. *Philadelphia Tribune*, December 23, 1937; "Will Use Funds to End City's Slums," *Philadelphia Tribune*, January 13, 1938; "Slums Will Remain Slums Local Housing Plans Reveal," *Philadelphia Tribune*, February 10, 1938; Reports on Public Housing Plans, Housing Association of Delaware Valley, Temple University Urban Archives; "Philadelphia's Negro Population: Facts on Housing," October 1953, City of Philadelphia Commission on Human Relations Papers, City Archives; "A Study of Recent Negro Migrants Into Philadelphia: A Preliminary Report," August 3, 1957, Urban League Papers, Temple University Urban Archives; "The Negro Population and Sub-standard Housing Conditions," October 25, 1939, National Association for the Advancement of Colored People (NAACP), Housing Association of Delaware Valley Papers, Temple University Urban Archives.

52. *Philadelphia Tribune*, November 11, 1937; "Tribune Crusade 2 years ago, Cited Housing Dangers," *Philadelphia Tribune*, December 9, 1937; *Philadelphia Tribune*, December 23, 1937; "Democratic Ranks are Split as Two Groups Hold Election of

Officers for Committeemen," *Philadelphia Tribune*, December 30, 1937; *Philadelphia Tribune*, January 13, 1938; "Finances Seen Near Solution St. Thomas," *Philadelphia Tribune*, February 24, 1938; "Citizens Committee is Formed to Protest Demolition of Old Historic St. Thomas PE Church," *Philadelphia Tribune*, April 28, 1938; "St. Thomas P.E. Church to remain in possession of Parish, Say Officers," *Philadelphia Tribune*, May 5, 1938; "Effect Union of P.E. Church and Mission," *Philadelphia Tribune*, May 26, 1938; "Congregation Jams Doors at New St. Thomas Church," *Philadelphia Tribune*, June 2, 1938; "Norris Loses Leadership of Seventh Ward," *Philadelphia Tribune*, June 9, 1938; "Local Groups Support Low Cost Housing," *Philadelphia Tribune*, April 13, 1939; "Lombard Street Fifty Years Ago Home of City's Leading Figures," *Philadelphia Tribune*, November 30, 1939; "Lombard Street Seat of Negro Wealth Just 50 Years Ago," *Philadelphia Tribune*, December 14, 1939.

53. *Philadelphia Tribune*, June 9, 1939; "Mercy Hospital O.K.'s Merger," *Philadelphia Tribune*, February 6, 1941; "4 Who Favored Merger Quit Mercy Hospital's Board of Directors," *Philadelphia Tribune*, August 14, 1941.

54. *Philadelphia Tribune*, May 18, 1939; see also Nelson, *Black Leadership's Response*; Bauman, *Public Housing, Race, and Renewal*; and Wolfinger, *Philadelphia Divided*.

55. "Housing Authority Gets 'Conclusive Evidence' of Race Discrimination," *Philadelphia Tribune*, March 6, 1941; "Richard Allen Homes Soon Ready; Housing Authority Receiving Applications for Allen Homes," *Philadelphia Tribune*, April 10, 1941; "Racial Bias Admitted by Housing Authority," *Philadelphia Tribune*, May 29, 1941; "Housing Segregation held as legal as judge dismisses local suit," *Philadelphia Tribune*, July 17, 1941; "Allen Homes Shift Stirs City," *Philadelphia Tribune*, January 31, 1942; "Allen Homes Group Appeals Directly to President Roosevelt," *Philadelphia Tribune*, February 7, 1942; "Foes of Allen Homes Transfer Jubilant Fire Leaves Scores Homeless," *Philadelphia Tribune*, February 14, 1942; "Richard Allen Project was Dedicated last Sunday," *Philadelphia Tribune*, October 3, 1942.

56. Clippings from *Philadelphia Inquirer*, February 7, 1942; clippings from *Philadelphia Record*, February 4, 1942; clippings from *Philadelphia Record*, February 9, 1942; clippings from *Evening Bulletin*, February 4, 1942.

57. *Philadelphia Tribune*, March 6, 1941; April 10, 1941; May 29, 1941; July 17, 1941; January 31, 1942; February 7, 1942; October 3, 1942; "Foes of Allen Homes Transfer Jubilant Fire Leaves Scores Homeless," *Philadelphia Tribune*, February 14, 1942.

58. *Philadelphia Tribune*, April, 13, 1939; "First in Hew Houses," "5000 to live in New Richard Allen Homes," *Philadelphia Tribune*, October 3, 1940; *New York Times*, August 23, 1941; Mayor Lamberton's Statement, May 13, 1940, Housing Association of Delaware Valley Papers, Temple University Urban Archives.

59. See Martha Biondi, *To Stand and Fight* (Cambridge, MA: Harvard University Press, 2005), and Rhonda Y. Williams, *The Politics of Public Housing* (New York: Oxford University Press, 2004).

CHAPTER 4

1. "Royal Theatre Closed after 50 Yrs.: Now 'Gravestone' in a 'Dying Era,'" *Philadelphia Tribune*, December 7, 1968.

2. Ibid.

3. "6,000 Families Facing Loss of Home to Expressways," *Philadelphia Tribune*, April 15, 1967; *Philadelphia Tribune*, December 7, 1968.

4. Arnold R. Hirsch, *Making the Second Ghetto: Race and Housing in Chicago, 1940–1960*, 2nd ed. (Chicago: University of Chicago Press, [1983] 1998). For further elaboration of the concept of a "second ghetto," see Douglas S. Massey and Nancy Denton, *American Apartheid: Segregation and the Making of the Underclass* (Cambridge, MA: Harvard University Press, 1993); June Manning Thomas and Marsha Ritzdorf, eds., *Urban Planning and the African American Community* (Thousand Oaks, CA: Sage, 1996); Thomas Sugrue, *The Origins of Urban Crisis: Race and Inequality in Postwar Detroit* (Princeton: Princeton University Press, 1996); Raymond A. Mohl, "Making the Second Ghetto in Metropolitan Miami, 1940–1960," *Journal of Urban History* 21 (1995): 395–427; Michael B. Katz, ed., *The "Underclass" Debate: Views from History* (Princeton: Princeton University Press, 1993); Arnold Hirsch and Raymond Mohl, eds., *Urban Policy in Twentieth Century America* (New Brunswick: Rutgers University Press, 1993); Charles F. Casey-Leininger, "Making the Second Ghetto in Cincinnati: Avondale, 1925–1970," in *Race and the City: Work, Community, and Protest in Cincinnati, 1820–1970*, ed., Henry Louis Taylor Jr. (Urbana: University of Illinois Press, 1993), 232–57; William Julius Wilson, *The Truly Disadvantaged* (Chicago: University of Chicago Press, 1987); and *When Work Disappears* (New York: Random House, 1996). For some of the most notable discussions and studies of the "initial" ghetto, see Gilbert Osofky, *Harlem: The Making of a Ghetto, 1890–1930* (New York: Harper and Row, 1963); Allan Spear, *Black Chicago: The Making of a Negro Ghetto, 1890–1920* (Chicago: University of Chicago Press, 1967); and Kenneth L. Kusmer, *A Ghetto Takes Shape: Black Cleveland, 1870–1930* (Urbana: University of Illinois Press, 1976).

5. Robin D. G. Kelley, *Race Rebels: Culture, Politics, and the Black Working Class* (New York: Free Press, 1994), 6–7.

6. For more on Chicago's redevelopment of the Lakefront and Loop areas, see Hirsch, *Making the Second Ghetto*; for specific discussion of the "new" and old urban renewal measures in New York, see Derek Hyra, *The New Urban Renewal* (Chicago: University of Chicago Press, 2008), and Christopher Mele, *Selling the Lower Eastside: Culture, Real Estate, and Resistance in New York City* (Minneapolis: University of Minnesota Press, 2000).

7. US Census Report, 1950; *Philadelphia Tribune*, April 15, 1967; December 7, 1968.

8. The Philadelphia Housing Authority/City Planning Commission/Redevelopment Authority, *Southeast Central Area Report*, "The Philadelphia Housing Quality Survey," November 1949, City Archives.

9. Carolyn Adams et al., Philadelphia: Neighborhoods, Division, and Conflict in a Postindustrial City (Philadelphia: Temple University Press, 1991), 31; William A. Reynolds, Innovation in the United States Carpet Industry, 1947–1963 (Princeton: Van Nostrand, 1968); Steven S. Plice, "Manpower and Merger: The Impact of Merger on Personnel Policies in the Carpet and Furniture Industries," Manpower and Human Resources Studies, No. 5 (Philadelphia: Wharton School, Industrial Research Unit, 1976).

10. Adams et al., *Philadelphia*, 31; Reynolds, *Innovation in the United States Carpet Industry*; Plice, "Manpower and Merger."

11. Herbert Gans, *The Urban Villagers: Group and Class in the Life of Italian-Americans* (New York: Free Press, 1962), 285–86.

12. W. E. B. DuBois, *The Philadelphia Negro* (Philadelphia: University of Pennsylvania Press, 1899), 372.

13. My thinking on "growth coalitions" is informed by the following research: John R. Logan and Harvey L. Molotch, *Urban Fortunes: The Political Economy of Place* (Berkeley: University of California Press, 1987); John H. Mollenkopf, *The Contested City* (Princeton: Princeton University Press, 1983); Harvey Molotch, "The City as a Growth Machine: Toward a Political Economy of Place," *American Journal of Sociology* 83 (1982): 309–29; John F. Bauman, *Public Housing, Race, and Renewal: Urban Planning in Philadelphia, 1920–1974* (Philadelphia: Temple University Press, 1987).

14. Edmund Bacon, interview, January 1, 1975, Walter Phillips Oral History Collection, Temple University Urban Archives; Robert B. Mitchell, interview March 5, 1975, Walter Phillips Oral History Collection, Temple University Urban Archives; Norman Berson, interview, February 8, 1979, Walter Phillips Oral History Collection, Temple Urban Archives; Lenora Berson, interview, February 8, 1979, Walter Phillips Oral History Collection, Temple University Urban Archives; Citizens' Council on City Planning, "A Chronological History of the CCCP," in Citizens' Council on City Planning Papers, Temple University Urban Archives; see also Citizens' Council on City Planning, *Annual Reports* 1945–1965, Temple University Urban Archives; Bauman, *Public Housing, Race, and Renewal.*

15. Citizens' Council on City Planning, "A Chronological History of the CCCP"; Dorothy Schoell Montgomery to Mrs. William Wurster (Catherine Bauer), October 30, 1947, Housing Association of Delaware Valley Papers, Temple University Urban Archives; see also Citizens' Council on City Planning, *Annual Reports*; and Bauman, *Public Housing, Race, and Renewal.*

16. For more on Levittown, see Herbert Gans, *The Levittowners: Ways of Life and Politics in a New Suburban Community* (New York: Pantheon, 1967).

17. For Better Philadelphia Exhibit, see "Chronology of Significant Events in Relation to the Crosstown Expressway, 1947–1970," Housing Association of Delaware Valley Papers, Temple University Urban Archives; Dorothy Montgomery to Bryn J. Hovde, May 21, 1951, Housing Association of Delaware Valley Papers, Temple

University Urban Archives; Edmund Bacon, "A Case Study in Urban Design," *Journal of the American Institute of Planners* 26, no. 3 (1960): 224–35; For Lombard Street area redevelopment, "Lombard Street Re-development Project," Urban Traffic Committee, Housing Association of the Delaware Valley Papers, Temple University Urban Archives; Division of Land Planning, map "Redevelopment Areas," certified January 9, 1948, Philadelphia City Planning Commission Papers, City Archives; "Redevelopment Area No. 9 ('Southeast Central')," certified January 9, 1948, Philadelphia City Planning Commission Papers, City Archives; Henry S. Churchill, "City Redevelopment," *Architectural Forum* (1950): 72; and Bauman, *Public Housing, Race, and Renewal.*

18. Budgetary issues notwithstanding, the PHA was criticized by housing advocates who suggested it was a mere tool of the Republican regime, using political patronage to fill many of its jobs, often with people whom many deemed "unqualified." Those critical of the PHA's slow action were furthered angered by its failure to make use of the nearly $72,000 set aside for initial site selection studies in anticipation of federal housing legislation. By 1948, the CCCP and the HADV were not alone in their disapproval of the Republican administration's approach to housing and the PHA's inaction, as progressive downtown businessmen had also begun to loudly voice their discontent with the status quo. For PHA's postwar housing program, see Roland R. Randall, James McDevitt, Raymond Rosen, et al. to Edward Hopkinson, chairman of Planning Commission, July 23, 1945, Housing Association of Delaware Valley Papers, Temple University Urban Archives; for PHA's six-year plan see Housing Authority to Mayor Samuels, July 23, 1945, Philadelphia Housing Authority Records, City Archives; "Notes on Housing Authority Hearings of Saturday, May 12, 1945 at Bellevue Stratford," Housing Association of Delaware Valley Papers, Temple University Urban Archives; "Philadelphia Housing Authority Press Release," June 17, 1947, Housing Association of Delaware Valley Papers, Temple University Urban Archives; Dorothy Montgomery to Warren J. Vinton, July 5, 1949, Housing Association of Delaware Valley Papers, Temple University Urban Archives; Bauman, *Public Housing, Race, and Renewal*; and Kirk Petshek, *The Challenge of Urban Reform: Policies and Programs in Philadelphia* (Philadelphia: Temple University Press, 1973).

19. On investigation of Samuels and the Republican regime, see Joseph R. Fink, "Reform in Philadelphia, 1946–1951" (PhD diss., Rutgers University, 1971); "Richardson Dilworth, Press Release," August 10, 1949, Housing Association of Delaware Valley Papers, Temple University Urban Archives; Bauman, *Public Housing, Race, and Renewal*; and Jeanne Lowe, *Cities in a Race with Time: Progress and Poverty in America's Renewing Cities* (New York: Random House, 1967).

20. See "Report on Activities, 1949–1965," Greater Philadelphia Movement Papers, Temple University Urban Archives; Minutes, September 28, 1949, Greater Philadelphia Movement Papers, Temple University Urban Archives; Lowe, *Cities in a Race with Time*; Petshek, *Challenge of Urban Reform*; Miriam Ershkowitz and

Joseph Zikmund II, eds., *Black Politics in Philadelphia* (New York: Basic Books, 1973).

21. See "Report on Activities, 1949–1965," and Minutes, September 28, 1949, Greater Philadelphia Movement Papers; Lowe, *Cities in a Race with Time*; Petshek, *Challenge of Urban Reform*; Ershkowitz and Zikmund, eds., *Black Politics in Philadelphia.*

22. By 1951, the coalition of businessmen, civic leaders, and politicians successfully unseated the Republican mayor, and thus the stage was set for the growth coalition's redevelopment plans. Upon his election, Clark selected Dilworth to serve as district attorney, strengthened the Redevelopment Authority by appointing former US senator Francis J. Meyers as chairman, and selected as new members William F. Kurtz and Dorothy Montgomery. He also created in the mayor's office a new post of Housing Coordinator, selecting William Rafsky, his executive secretary, to the position. On the city charter see "Housing and the City Charter: Recommendations of the Philadelphia Housing Association and the City Charter Commission," April 1950, Philadelphia Housing Association and City Charter Commission, Housing Association of Delaware Valley Papers, Temple University Urban Archives; Lowe, *Cities in a Race with Time*; Petshek, *Challenge of Urban Reform*; and John Hadley Strange, "The Negro in Philadelphia Politics, 1963–1965," (PhD diss., Princeton University, 1966). Strange also notes that reapportionment did not impact the racial composition of the areas, despite administrative changes.

23. Martha Biondi, *To Stand and Fight* (Cambridge, MA: Harvard University Press, 2005); John Bauman, Roger Biles, and Kristin M. Szylvian, *From Tenements to the Taylor Homes: In Search of Urban Housing Policy in Twentieth-Century America* (University Park: Pennsylvania State University Press).

24. See "Lombard Street Re-development Project," HADV Papers; David Clow, "House Divided: Philadelphia's Controversial Expressway," *Society for American Regional Planning*, 1989; Division of Land Planning, map "Redevelopment Areas," certified January 9, 1948, Philadelphia City Planning Commission Papers, City Archives; "Redevelopment Area No. 9 ('Southeast Central')," certified January 9, 1948, Philadelphia City Planning Commission Papers, City Archives; "Chronology of Significant Events," HADV Papers; Bauman, *Public Housing, Race, and Renewal.*

25. See "Lombard Street Re-development Project," HADV Papers; Division of Land Planning, map "Redevelopment Areas"; "Redevelopment Area No. 9 ('Southeast Central')"; "Chronology of Significant Events," HADV Papers; Bauman, *Public Housing, Race, and Renewal.*

26. Letter from Ned Hosier, March 25, 1952, Philadelphia City Planning Commission Papers, City Archives; Letter from Elisabeth Nesbitt, August 2, 1952, Philadelphia City Planning Commission, City Archives; "Redevelopment Area No. 9 ('Southeast Central')," certified January 9, 1948, Philadelphia City Planning Commission, City Archives.

27. See "Relocation in Philadelphia," November 1958, Housing Association of Delaware Valley Papers, Temple University Urban Archives; "To the Present Owner, Tenant, or Occupant of the Above Premises," March 21, 1955, Redevelopment Authority of Philadelphia, Francis J. Lammer, Executive Director, Philadelphia Housing Authority Records, City Archives; and Bauman, *Public Housing, Race, and Renewal*, 170–73; see also Thomas and Ritzdorf, eds., *Urban Planning and the African American Community*.

28. Matthew Countryman, *Up South: Civil Rights and Black Power in Philadelphia* (Philadelphia: University of Pennsylvania Press, 2006), 45.

29. Countryman, *Up South*, 43.

30. Countryman, *Up South*, 45.

31. "Where you Live: A South Philadelphia Oasis Stands the Test of Time," *Philadelphia Tribune*, October, 23, 1991; "Alice Lipscomb, 87, Phila. Activist," *Philadelphia Inquirer*, October, 10, 2003.

32. "Where you Live," *Philadelphia Tribune*; "Alice Lipscomb, 87, Phila. Activist," *Philadelphia Inquirer*.

33. Kelley, *Race Rebels*.

34. Kelley, *Race Rebels*; "Redevelopment Authority: Housing Concerns Did Not Go Unnoticed in 1960s Movement," *Philadelphia Tribune*, November 3, 1978; "15th Annual Report of the Redevelopment Authority of Philadelphia," 1961, Housing Association of Delaware Valley Papers, Temple University Urban Archives.

35. "Chronology of Significant Events," HADV Papers; "Planning Assistance: Crosstown Expressway, Summer 1967," Citizens' Committee to Preserve and Develop the Crosstown Community, Philadelphia City Planning Commission Papers, City Archives; *Philadelphia Tribune*, April 15, 1967; "Crosstown Expressway Described As 'Carbon Monoxide' Curtain," *Philadelphia Tribune*, April 29, 1967; "Crosstown Rally Set for Saturday," *Philadelphia Tribune*, November 4, 1967; "Housing Association Urges Phila. to Abandon New Expressway Plan," *Philadelphia Tribune*, April 16, 1968.

36. Bauman, *Public Housing, Race, and Renewal*, 170.

37. For discussions of a similar sentiment among urban blacks in other cities see: (on Chicago) Hirsch, *Making the Second Ghetto*; (on New York City) Biondi, *To Stand and Fight*; (on Baltimore) Williams, *The Politics of Public Housing*.

38. Countryman, *Up South*, 93.

39. NAACP newsletter, January 31, 1958, NAACP papers, III C 221, Library of Congress; "Blue-printing the Future for the Negro Citizen," March 29, 1958, Floyd Logan Collection, Temple University Urban Archives; "Design for the Future," n.d., NAACP papers, III C 135, Library of Congress; Countryman, *Up South*.

40. DuBois, *Philadelphia Negro*, 388.

41. Minutes, Pennsylvania Equal Rights Council, October 3, 1958, Housing Association of Delaware Valley collection, Temple University Urban Archives; "Minutes," Pennsylvania Equal Rights Council, November 14, 1958, Urban League collection,

Temple University Urban Archives; "Special Memorandum on Housing," Philadelphia Fellowship Commission, Fellowship Commission papers, Temple University Urban Archives; Countryman, *Up South*.

42. Writing of the distinction between consensus and cross-cutting issues, Cohen argues that consensus issues are "framed as somehow important to every member of 'the black community,' either directly or symbolically," while cross-cutting issues "are presented as affecting only specific segments of" the "black community." Cathy Cohen, *Boundaries of Blackness* (Chicago: University of Chicago Press, 1999), 11–13.

43. "Chronology of Significant Events," HADV Papers; Hirsch, *Making the Second Ghetto*, 170; Peter H. Rossi and Robert A. Dentler, *The Politics of Urban Renewal: The Chicago Findings* (New York: Free Press, 1962); Harold Kaplan, *Urban Renewal Politics: Slum Clearance in Newark* (New York; Columbia University Press, 1963). "Planning Assistance: Crosstown Expressway Summer 1967," Citizens' Committee to Preserve and Develop the Crosstown Community, Philadelphia City Planning Commission Papers, City Archives; *Philadelphia Tribune*, April 15, 1967; "Crosstown Expressway Described As 'Carbon Monoxide' Curtain," *Philadelphia Tribune*; "Crosstown Rally Set For Saturday," *Philadelphia Tribune*; "Housing Association Urges Phila. to Abandon New Expressway Plan," *Philadelphia Tribune*, April 16, 1968.

44. "Chronology of Significant Events," HADV Papers; for the history of Delaware and Schuylkill Expressways, see http://www.phillyroads.com/roads/delaware/ and http://www.phillyroads.com/roads/schuylkill/, accessed September 12, 2012; for background on the roots of the interracial coalition efforts, see "The Crosstown Community Development Corporation—Its Background Program and Financial Needs," Crosstown Community Development Corporation, Philadelphia City Planning Commission Papers, City Archives; and "Planning Assistance: Crosstown Expressway, Summer 1967," Citizens' Committee to Preserve and Develop the Crosstown Community, Philadelphia City Planning Commission Papers, City Archives; "3 Expressways Will be Built Here by State," *Philadelphia Inquirer*, January 18, 1966.

45. John H. Staples, "Urban Renewal: A Comparative Study of Twenty-Two Cities, 1950–1960," *Western Political Quarterly*, 23, no. 2 (1970): 294–304, at 297.

46. Staples, "Urban Renewal"; Gans, *Urban Villagers*, 281.

47. *Philadelphia Tribune*, October 23, 1992.

48. Ibid.

49. "Redevelopment Authority: Housing Concerns Did Not Go Unnoticed in 1960s Movement," *Philadelphia Tribune*, November 3, 1978; Bauman, *Public Housing, Race, and Renewal*.

50. "Redevelopment Authority," *Philadelphia Tribune*: Bauman, *Public Housing, Race, and Renewal*.

51. "Redevelopment Authority," *Philadelphia Tribune*; Bauman, *Public Housing, Race, and Renewal*.

52. Lenora Berson, *Case Study of a Riot: The Philadelphia Story* (New York: Institute of Human Relations Press, 1966), 15–16; "Commission on Human Relations Memorandum to Community Leaders and Intergroup Health & Welfare Agencies from Larry Groth," Fellowship Commission Papers, Temple University Urban Archives, September 3, 1964; Countryman, *Up South*, 156–57.

53. Sugrue, *Origins of the Urban Crisis*, 260–61; see also John C. Leggett, *Class, Race, and Labor: Working-Class Consciousness in Detroit* (New York: Oxford Press, 1968); Countryman, *Up South*; Thomas J. Sugrue, *Sweet Land of Liberty: The Forgotten Struggle for Civil Rights in the North* (New York: Random House, 2008); Biondi, *To Stand and Fight*; Janet L. Abu-Lughod, *Race, Space, and Riots: In Chicago, New York, and Los Angeles* (New York: Oxford University Press, 2007).

54. Sugrue, *Origins of the Urban Crisis*, 260–61, and *Sweet Land of Liberty*; Leggett, *Class, Race, and Labor*; Countryman, *Up South*; Biondi, *To Stand and Fight*; Abu-Lughod, *Race, Space, and Riots*.

55. Sugrue, *Origins of the Urban Crisis*, 260–61, and *Sweet Land of Liberty*; Leggett, *Class, Race, and Labor*; Countryman, *Up South*; Biondi, *To Stand and Fight*; Abu-Lughod, *Race, Space, and Riots*.

56. Petshek, *Challenge of Urban Reform*; and Strange, "Negro in Philadelphia Politics."

57. Countryman, *Up South*.

58. "Interview with Charyn Sutton," as quoted in Countryman, *Up South*, 213.

59. "The Crosstown Community Development Corporation," Philadelphia City Planning Commission Papers; and "Planning Assistance: Crosstown Expressway Summer 1967," Citizens' Committee to Preserve and Develop the Crosstown Community, Philadelphia City Planning Commission Papers, City Archives; *Philadelphia Tribune*, April 15, 1967; "Crosstown Expressway Described As 'Carbon Monoxide' Curtain," *Philadelphia Tribune*, April 29, 1967; "Crosstown Rally Set For Saturday," *Philadelphia Tribune*.

60. See "Chronology of Significant Events," HADV Papers; "Crosstown Highway Facing Stiff Protest from Grays Ferry," *Philadelphia Inquirer*, May 15, 1966; "Crosstown Complex Envisioned," *Philadelphia Inquirer*, June 15, 1967; "Crosstown Opportunity," *Philadelphia Inquirer*, June 16, 1967; "Homes Doomed: No Place to Go," *Philadelphia Inquirer*, June 20, 1967; "Planners Assailed over Relocation for Expressway," *Evening Bulletin*, May 4, 1967; *Philadelphia Tribune*, April 15, 1967.

61. "Chronology of Significant Events," HADV Papers; "Crosstown Highway Facing Stiff Protest," *Philadelphia Inquirer*; "Crosstown Complex Envisioned," *Philadelphia Inquirer*; "Crosstown Opportunity," *Philadelphia Inquirer*; "Homes Doomed," *Philadelphia Inquirer*; "Planners Assailed," *Evening Bulletin*; *Philadelphia Tribune*, April 15, 1967.

62. See "Chronology of Significant Events," HADV Papers; *Philadelphia Tribune* April 15, 1967.

63. "Chronology of Significant Events," ," HADV Papers; *Philadelphia Tribune*, April 15, 1967; "The Crosstown Expressway," speech delivered by Hon. Norman S. Berson, April 11, 1967, 3–6, HADV Papers, Temple University Urban Archives.

64. See "Chronology of Significant Events," HADV Papers; "Crosstown Highway Facing Stiff," *Philadelphia Inquirer*; "Crosstown Complex Envisioned," *Philadelphia Inquirer*; "Crosstown Opportunity," *Philadelphia Inquirer*; "Homes Doomed," *Philadelphia Inquirer*; "Planners Assailed," *Evening Bulletin*; *Philadelphia Tribune* April 15, 1967; Jane Jacobs, *The Death and Life of Great American Cities* (New York: Vintage, 1961), 349; see also, Herbert Gans, *Urban Villagers*.

65. "25 Groups Blast Crosstown Xway," *Philadelphia Tribune*, April 26, 1969; See "Chronology of Significant Events," HADV Papers; "Crosstown Highway Facing Stiff Protest," *Philadelphia Inquirer*; "Crosstown Complex Envisioned," *Philadelphia Inquirer*; "Crosstown Opportunity," *Philadelphia Inquirer*; "Homes Doomed," *Philadelphia Inquirer*; "Planners Assailed over Relocation," *Evening Bulletin*; *Philadelphia Tribune* April 15, 1967; Jane Jacobs, *The Death and Life of Great American Cities* (New York: Vintage Books, 1961), 349; See also, Herbert Gans, *Urban Villagers*.

66. "Chronology of Significant Events," HADV Papers; "Letter to Mayor James H. Tate," April 13, 1967, Philadelphia Anti-Poverty Action Committee, Philadelphia City Panning Commission Records, City Archives; Letter to Albert Greenfield, July 23, 1956, Armstrong Association of Philadelphia, Housing Association of Delaware Valley Papers, Temple University Urban Archives; "Memo to the Crosstown Business Committee," June 29, 1967, 1, Citizens' Committee to Preserve and Develop the Crosstown Community, Philadelphia City Planning Commission Records, City Archives; Benedict Anderson, *Imagined Communities* (New York: Verso, [1983] 1991); *Philadelphia Tribune*, April 15, 1967; "Black Leaders Rap New Expressway as Negro Removal Fear 'Burma Road' for South Philadelphia Residents; Easy Street for Whites," *Philadelphia Tribune*, March 18, 1969.

67. See "Chronology of Significant Events," HADV Papers; "Crosstown Expressway Rally Set for Saturday," *Philadelphia Tribune*; Letter to George Dukes from Mayor James H. J. Tate, November 6, 1967, Philadelphia City Planning Commission Records, City Archives; Statement of George Dukes, November 9, 1967, Philadelphia City Planning Commission Papers, City Archives.

68. See "Chronology of Significant Events," HADV Papers; "Crosstown Expressway Rally Set for Saturday," *Philadelphia Tribune*; Letter to George Dukes from Mayor James H. J. Tate, November 6, 1967, Philadelphia City Planning Commission Records, City Archives; Statement of George Dukes, November 9, 1967, Philadelphia City Planning Commission Papers, City Archives.

69. Letter from Robert B. Mitchell to Mayor James H. J. Tate, December 5, 1967, Philadelphia City Planning Commission Papers, City Archives.

70. See "Chronology of Significant Events," HADV Papers; "Relocation, Planning Challenged: Crosstown Paralysis," *Evening Bulletin*, April 22, 1968; "Memo to Members," January 16, 1970, City Wide Coalition to Oppose the Crosstown Expressway, Philadelphia City Planning Commission Papers, City Archives; Letter from Alice Lipscomb to William B. Walker, Chairman of the City Planning

Commission, May 27, 1968, City Planning Commission Papers, City Archives; Letter from Robert B. Mitchell to Mayor James H. J. Tate, December 5, 1967, Philadelphia City Planning Commission Papers, City Archives; Robert B. Mitchell, interview, March 5, 1975, Walter Phillips Oral History Collection, Temple University Urban Archives.

71. "Chronology of Significant Events," HADV Papers; "The Crosstown Community Development Corporation," Philadelphia City Planning Commission Records; "Tate Rapped for Dropping Road Plans," *Evening Bulletin*, March 31, 1968; "Crosstown Link is Dead, Smallwood Tells Planners," *Evening Bulletin*, June 27, 1968; "Tate Proposes Crosstown Housing Plan," *Evening Bulletin*, July 2, 1968; "The Crosstown Expressway," *Evening Bulletin*, August 25, 1968; "Expressway Planner Calls for New Approach," *Evening Bulletin*, August 28, 1969; "Directional Sign Indicates Crosstown Route May Be Alive," *Evening Bulletin*, December 30, 1969; "Crosstown Expressway Revived as Tate Reverses Stand," *Philadelphia Inquirer*, June 2, 1968; "The Crosstown Impasse," *Philadelphia Inquirer*, November 9, 1969.

72. "Crosstown Committee Selects Consultants For 14-Month Study," *Philadelphia Inquirer*, November 26, 1969; "Analysis of the Centralized Relocation Bureau's Crosstown Expressway Survey," April 1968, Housing Association of Delaware Valley Papers, Temple University Urban Archives; "Vorhees Report," Philadelphia City Planning Commission Papers, City Archives; "Position on the Crosstown Expressway," May 5, 1970, Greater Philadelphia Chamber of Commerce, Philadelphia City Planning Commission Papers, City Archives; Memo to Members, August 19, 1969, City Wide Coalition to Oppose the Crosstown Expressway, Philadelphia City Planning Commission Papers, City Archives; Memo from Linda Meyers, Chairwoman, August 22, 1969, Center City Stop the Crosstown Committee, Philadelphia City Planning Commission Papers, City Archives; Statement on the Crosstown Expressway, September 29, 1969, American Institute of Planners, Philadelphia Region Chapter, Philadelphia City Planning Commission Papers, City Archives; Letter to Robert J. Sugarman, Esq. (Legal Counsel to the Citizens Committee to Develop the Crosstown Community), October 31, 1969, American Institute of Planners, Philadelphia Region Chapter, Philadelphia City Planning Commission Papers, City Archives; News Release, December 3, 1970, Office of the Mayor, Philadelphia City Planning Commission Papers, City Archives.

73. "Southbridge: An Urban Development Proposal," Philadelphia City Planning Commission Records, City Archives; http://venturiscottbrown.org/pdfs/PhiladelphiaCrosstownCommunity01.pdf, accessed June 5, 2011; "Citizens Ask Rizzo 'to Bury' the Crosstown Expressway," *Philadelphia Tribune*, May 27, 1972; "Interview with Frank Rizzo," *Philadelphia Inquirer*, October 19, 1971; "City Unveils $750 Million Crosstown Corridor; Includes Expressway, Housing, Businesses," *Philadelphia Inquirer*, April 23, 1972; "City to Proceed With Renewal of Crosstown Link Section," *Philadelphia Inquirer*, May 31, 1972; "Businessmen

Oppose Plan for Crosstown," *Evening Bulletin*, April 18, 1972; "Planners Set Public Hearing on Crosstown," *Evening Bulletin*, April 20, 1972; "Community Groups Plan Rally Against Crosstown," *Evening Bulletin*, April 21, 1972; "Residents Hit City's New Plan for Crosstown," *Evening Bulletin*, April 23, 1972; Petshek, *Challenge of Urban Reform*.

74. *Philadelphia Tribune*, May 27, 1972; *Philadelphia Inquirer*, October 19, 1971; April 25, 1972; May 31, 1972; *Evening Bulletin*, April 18, 1972; April 20, 1972; April 21, 1972; April 23, 1972; Petshek, Challenge of Urban Reform.

75. "Wilson Goode Lecture," Yale University Urban Ethnography Workshop, October 17, 2011; W. Wilson Goode, *In Goode Faith* (Valley Forge: Judson Press, 1992), ix–xiii.

76. "Testimony Given before the Delaware Valley Regional Planning Commission on the Southbridge Proposal," April 26, 1972, by Shirley Dennis, Managing Director of the Housing Association of Delaware Valley, Housing Association of Delaware Valley Papers, Temple University Urban Archives; "Southbridge: An Urban Development Proposal," Philadelphia City Planning Commission Papers, City Archives.

77. "Testimony Given before the Delaware Valley Regional Planning Commission on the Southbridge Proposal," April 26, 1972, by Shirley Dennis, HADV Papers, Temple University Urban Archives; "Southbridge," Philadelphia City Planning Commission Papers.

78. Countryman, *Up South*.

79. Cohen, *Boundaries of Blackness*.

80. Jeffrey Alexander, *The Civil Sphere* (New York: Oxford University Press, 2006), 265.

81. For more on Washington, DC, see Howard Gillette, *Between Justice and Beauty: Race, Planning, and the Failure of Urban Policy in Washington, D.C.* (Washington, DC: Howard University Press, 1995); Steven Gregory, *Black Corona* (Chicago: University of Chicago Press, 1999).

CHAPTER 5

1. "City Honors Housing Activist," *Philadelphia Tribune*, January 20, 1989.

2. DuBois, The *Philadelphia Negro*, 372–73.

3. Joe R. Feagin, *The New Urban Paradigm: Critical Perspectives on the City* (New York: Rowman & Littlefield, 1998). See also M. Gottdiener and Chris G. Pickvance, *Urban Life in Transition* (Newbury: Sage, 1991), John R. Logan and Harvey L. Molotch, *Urban Fortunes: The Political Economy of Place* (Berkeley: University of California Press, 1987); John H. Mollenkopf, *The Contested City* (Princeton: Princeton University Press, 1983); Mollenkopf, *Power, Culture, and Place: Essays on New York City* (New York: Russell Sage Foundation, 1988); John Walton, "Urban Sociology: Contributions and Limits of Political Economy," *Annual Review of*

Sociology 19 (1993): 301–20. Floyd Hunter, *Community Power Structure: A Study of Decisions Makers* (Chapel Hill: University of North Carolina Press, 1953); Robert Dahl, *Who Governs?* (New Haven: Yale University Press, 1961); Charles M. Bonjean, Terry N. Clark, and Robert L. Lineberry, eds., *Community Politics: A Behavioral Approach* (New York: Free Press, 1971); Rufus P. Browning, Dale Rogers Marshall, and David H. Tabb, *Protest is Not Enough* (Berkeley: University of California Press, 1984); Floyd Hunter, Ruth Connor Schaffer, and Cecil G. Sheps, *Community Organization: Action and Inaction* (Chapel Hill: University of North Carolina Press, 1956). Robert Park, Ernest Burgess, and Roderick D. McKenzie, eds., *The City*, 2nd ed. (Chicago: University of Chicago Press, 1924).

4. Any discussion of neighborhood change and the social realities of urban blacks would be incomplete without a discussion of the local sociopolitical landscape. People live locally. People's lives are shaped by events and processes of change at the local level, such as gentrification, urban renewal, and the rise and decline of public and affordable housing. One basic question has been central to research in this area: How and why do cities grow? Usually invoking the concept of "community," to distinguish such discussions of local politics and urban development from that occurring at the national level, scholars have emphasized multiple lines of argument, often highlighting the importance of local economies and power-brokers. While for some a conception of urban development is tied to the principles of a free-market economy, others have been informed by a Marxist conception critiquing the inequality inherent in local capitalist enterprises. Notwithstanding such differing dispositions, research thus far has emphasized the importance of competition, particularly over urban land. Some of the most notable research demarcating the difference between local and national-level politics and growth include: Hunter, *Community Power Structure*; Dahl, *Who Governs?*; Bonjean, Clark, and Lineberry, *Community Politics*; Browning, Marshall, and Tabb, *Protest is Not Enough*; Hunter, Schaffer, and Sheps, *Community Organization*. For arguments asserting a free-enterprise perspective of urban development, in which local political advances and shifts in representation reflect a continual process of change within cities, see Robert Park, Ernest Burgess, and Roderick D. McKenzie, eds., *The City*, 2nd ed. (Chicago: University of Chicago Press, 1924). Others have contended, however, that free-market conceptions elide the inequality emergent in urban capitalistic regimes; see for example: Manuel Castells, *The City and the Grassroots* (Berkeley: University of California Press, 1983); Robert Bailey Jr., *Radicals in Urban Politics: The Alinsky Approach* (Chicago: University of Chicago Press, 1974); see also Manuel Castells, *The Urban Question: A Marxist Approach* (Cambridge, MA: MIT Press, 1977); David Harvey, "Government Policies, Financial Institutions and Neighborhood Change in United States Cities" in *Captive cities*, ed. Michael Harloe (London: John Wiley, 1977); Kevin Cox, ed., *Urbanization and Conflict in Market Societies* (Chicago: Methuen, 1978); William K. Tabb and Larry Sanders, eds., *Marxism and the Metropolis: New Perspectives in Urban Political Economy* (New York: Oxford University Press, 1984). Arguments

about the importance of networks for understanding urban development are furthered in other works, particularly Barry Wellman's discussion of the "community liberated" perspective. Accounting for the shifts in local social urban relationships Wellman suggests that advances in mass transit, technology, and communication have shifted social networks so that they are no longer rooted in singular neighborhoods, but are ramified across a series of neighborhoods and cities; Barry Wellman, "The Community Question: Intimate Networks of East New Yorkers," *American Journal of Sociology* 84, no. 5 (1979): 1201–21; see also Barry Wellman, ed., *Networks in the Global Village: Life in Contemporary Communities* (Boulder: Westview Press, 1999); Barry Wellman and Barry Leighton, "Networks, Neighborhoods, and Communities: Approaches to the Study of the Community Question," *Urban Affairs Quarterly* 14, no. 3 (1979): 363–90; Claude Fischer, *The Urban Experience* (New York: Harcourt, Brace, Jovanovich, 1976); Louis Wirth, "Urbanism as a Way of Life," *American Journal of Sociology* 44, no. 1 (1938): 1–24.

5. Adolph Reed, *Stirrings in the Jug: Black Politics in the Post-Segregation Era* (Minneapolis: University of Minnesota Press, 1999), 79. Importantly Reed's analysis outlines the black urban regime as potentially constitutive of the move from protest to politics, whilst also noting that there are several important consequences. "First, the dynamics that make possible the empowerment of black regimes are the same as those that produce the deepening marginalization and dispossession of a substantial segment of the urban black population. Second, the logic of progrowth politics, in which black officialdom is incorporated, denies broad progressive redistribution as a policy option and thereby prohibits direct confrontation of the problem of dispossession among the black constituency. Third, the nature of the politics that black regimes govern is such that the relation between the main components of their electoral and governing coalitions is often zero-sum." In my view, while such consequences relate to the Philadelphia case, they are perhaps more emblematic of a "regime"-style politics, such as those in Detroit and Atlanta that Reed also examines (ibid., 88–89).

6. Matthew J. Countryman, *Up South: Civil Rights and Black Power in Philadelphia* (Philadelphia: University of Pennsylvania Press, 2006).

7. Mary Pattillo, *Black on the Block: The Politics of Race and Class in the City* (Chicago: University of Chicago Press, 2007), 3; Katherine Tate, *From Protest to Politics: The New Black Voters in American Elections* (New York: Russell Sage Foundation, 1993); Michael B. Preston, Lenneal J. Henderson Jr., and Paul L. Puryear, *The New Black Politics: The Search for Political Power*, 2nd ed. (New York: Longman, 1982 [1987]); Carol M. Swain, Black Faces, *Black Interests: The Representation of African Americans in Congress* (Cambridge, MA: Harvard University Press, 1995); Rufus R. Browning, Dale Rogers Marshall, and David H. Tabb, *Protest is Not Enough: The Struggle of Blacks and Hispanics for Equality in Urban Politics* (Berkeley: University of California Press, 1984). For a discussion of the larger rise of black mayors in the post–civil rights era see: J. Phillip Thompson III, *Double Trouble: Black Mayors, Black Communities, and the Call for a Deep Democracy* (New York: Oxford University Press, 2006).

8. Tate, *From Protest to Politics*; Thompson, *Double Trouble*.

9. St. Clair Drake and Horace Cayton, *Black Metropolis: A Study of Negro Life in a Northern City* (Chicago: University of Chicago Press, 1993); see also James Weldon Johnson, *Black Manhattan* (New York: Atheneum, 1968).

10. For a more comprehensive discussion of post–civil rights black politics, see Swain, *Black Faces, Black Interests*; Tate, *From Protest to Politics*; Preston, Henderson, and Puryear, eds., *New Black Politics*, and Thompson, *Double Trouble*; Michael C. Dawson, *Behind the Mule: Race and Class in African-American Politics* (Princeton: Princeton University Press, 1994), Cathy J. Cohen, *The Boundaries of Blackness* (Chicago: University of Chicago Press, 1999), Reed, *Stirrings in the Jug*. For larger discussion of black politics in Philadelphia during the post–civil rights era, see Countryman, *Up South*; Kirk R. Petshek, *The Challenge of Urban Reform* (Philadelphia: Temple University Press, 1973); Carolyn Adams et al., *Philadelphia: Neighborhoods, Division, and Conflict in a Postindustrial City* (Philadelphia: Temple University Press, 1991); W. Wilson Goode, *In Goode Faith* (Valley Forge, PA: Judson Press, 1992); John F. Bauman, *Public Housing, Race, and Renewal: Urban Planning in Philadelphia 1920–1974* (Philadelphia: Temple University Press, 1987); and Miriam Ershkowitz and Joseph Zikmund II, eds., *Black Politics in Philadelphia* (New York: Basic Books, 1973).

11. William H. Chafe, *The Unfinished Journey: America Since World War II* (New York: Oxford University Press, 2003), 240; Countryman, *Up South*; For more on the "culture of poverty" thesis see: Oscar Lewis, "The Culture of Poverty," in *Urban Life*, eds., G. Gmelch and W. Zenner (Long Grove, IL: Waveland Press, 1966); Daniel Patrick Moynihan, *The Negro Family: The Case for National Action* (Washington DC: Office of Policy Planning and Research, US Department of Labor, 1965); William Julius Wilson, *The Truly Disadvantage: The Inner City, the Underclass, and Public Policy* (Chicago: University of Chicago Press, 1987); William Julius Wilson, "The Moynihan Report and Research on the Black Community," *Annals of the American Academy of Political and Social Science* 621 (2009): 34–46; and David Harding, "Cultural Context, Sexual Behavior, and Romantic Relationships in Disadvantaged Neighborhoods," *American Sociological Review* 72, no. 3 (2007): 341–64. For more on the war on poverty, the following offer some of the best historical discussions: Michael B. Katz, *The Undeserving Poor: From the War on Poverty to the War on Welfare* (New York: Pantheon, 1989); Thomas Jackson, "The State, the Movement, and the Urban Poor: The War on Poverty and Political Mobilization in the 1960s," in *The "Underclass" Debate: Views from History*, ed., Michael B. Katz (Princeton: Princeton University Press, 1993), 403–39; and Allen J. Matusow, *The Unraveling of America: A History of Liberalism in the 1960s* (New York: Harper and Row, 1984).

12. "Indigent Win Role in City's Antipoverty Bid," *Philadelphia Inquirer*, February 6, 1965; "Another try for Antipoverty Funds," *Evening Bulletin*, December 30, 1964; "Labor Attacks Tate Plan for Antipoverty Funds," *Evening Bulletin*, January 29, 1965;

"Mayor Defends Antipoverty Program," *Evening Bulletin*, February 8, 1965; "Tate Shakes Up City's Antipoverty Forces," *Evening Bulletin*, February 10, 1965; "City Defines 12 Pockets of Poverty," *Evening Bulletin*, March 26, 1965; "Antipoverty-War Troops Complain about Cramped 'Command Post,'" *Evening Bulletin*, November 28, 1965. These articles also indicate that in two previous attempts the administration's version of the local antipoverty effort was rejected by the Office of Economic Opportunity as they did not give adequate representation of the poor; Matusow, *Unraveling of America*; Matthew Countryman also makes the point that previous attempts by the administration to create the antipoverty organization were unsuccessful, as Mayor Tate hoped to "exclude local civil rights activists—in particular Cecil Moore and the leadership of Philadelphia CORE—from the program." Given both the NAACP's and CORE's prominence in dealing with black poverty, the final version of the antipoverty committee indicates that the Mayor Tate had accepted that these organizations would be represented on the PAAC. Countryman, *Up South*, 392; City of Philadelphia, "Executive Order 1–65," February 22, 1965, Greater Philadelphia Federation of Settlements Collection, Temple University Urban Archives. The twelve poverty districts were determined using data from the 1960 census. All residents in each of these districts were eligible to vote in the election, and those who fell below a certain income limit were eligible to run in those elections. In addition to having a representative on the citywide PAAC, each CAC also received a budget of $25,000; "Philadelphia Antipoverty Action Committee Statistical Survey of Candidates of the May 26, 1965 Election," n.d., Greater Philadelphia Federation of Settlements Collection, Temple University Urban Archives.

13. "Bowser Seen as 7th Anti-Poverty Head Possibility," *Philadelphia Tribune*, January 23, 1965; "Profile of New Administrator; Bowser was Born, Bred, Schooled in North Phila.," *Philadelphia Tribune*, April 17, 1965; "City Antipoverty Group OKs Tate's Picking Director," *Evening Bulletin*, March 6, 1965; "Poverty Unit Proposes Bowser as Executive," *Evening Bulletin*, April 2, 1965; "Dispute Perils Poverty War, Aides Contend," *Evening Bulletin*, April 4, 1965; "Moore Sees Selfish Motives Behind Selection of Bowser," *Evening Bulletin*, April 5, 1965; "Cecil Moore Says Poverty Fight Is 'Not for Power, But For People,'" *Evening Bulletin*, April 9, 1965; "Both Bowser, Crippins Gets Poverty Jobs," *Evening Bulletin*, April 13, 1965; "Crippins Takes Poverty Job Despite Moore's Disclaimer," *Evening Bulletin*, April 14, 1965; "Moore Insists Poverty Post Go to Crippins," *Philadelphia Inquirer*, April 3, 1965; Countryman, *Up South*.

14. PAAC held a series of town-hall meetings to publicize CAC elections and to explain the purposes of the antipoverty program. Countryman, *Up South*; David Fineman, "Community Action Councils—A Philadelphia First: A Freedom Report of the Philadelphia Chapter, Congress of Racial Equality," n.d., Greater Philadelphia Federation of Settlements Collection, Temple University Urban Archives; "300,000 Urged to Attend Meetings Wednesday on Poverty Program," *Evening Bulletin*,

April 25, 1965; "Local Leaders Plan to Keep Control of Poverty War," *Evening Bulletin*, April 27, 1965; "War-on-Poverty Vote Hailed Here as Success," *Evening Bulletin*, May 27, 1965; "Meeting is Told Politicians May Grab Poverty Funds," *Evening Bulletin*, January 19, 1965; "W. Phila. Unit Rejects City Poverty Plan," *Evening Bulletin*, February 4, 1965; "U.S. Gives City $5.9. Million to Fight Poverty," *Evening Bulletin*, June 23, 1965; Philadelphia Antipoverty Action Committee, Community Action Council Representatives, June 8, 1965, Housing Association of Delaware Valley Papers, Temple University Urban Archives.

15. Quoted in Countryman, *Up South*, 300; Fineman, "Community Action Councils"; "PAAC Urged to Put Salaried Workers Under Civil Service or Merit System," *Evening Bulletin*, January 25, 1966; "PAAC Plans 2nd Harrisburg Bus Trip to Push for Higher Relief Payments," *Evening Bulletin*, May 17, 1966; "PAAC Official's Dual Role Threatens Funds, U.S. says," *Evening Bulletin*, January 19, 1967; "Most Elected Aides on PAAC Panel Turn up on Payroll," *Philadelphia Inquirer*, July 20, 1966; "Philadelphia's Plan to Give Poor a Voice in Poverty Drive Called a Failure," *New York Times*, July 17, 1966; William Meek, interview, June 27, 1979, Walter Phillips Oral History Collection, Temple University Urban Archives; "Memorandum to Council Chairmen, PAAC Representatives, CAC Office Staff from Miss Barbara L. Weems," October 28, 1966, Greater Philadelphia Federation of Settlements Collection, Temple University Urban Archives.

16. "Moore, Coleman Tangle At Anti-Poverty Meet; Sam Evans' Role Hit," *Philadelphia Tribune*, January 29, 1966; "Poor Lacked Power in Philadelphia," *Evening Bulletin*, January 6, 1966; "Fired Aide Again Blasts Poverty Setup," *Evening Bulletin*, January 20, 1966; *Evening Bulletin*, January 25, 1966; "City Hall for Lack of Support to Poverty Units," *Evening Bulletin*, March 28, 1966; *Evening Bulletin*, May 17, 1966; "Rejected Aide to Direct War on Poverty Here," *Evening Bulletin*, January 19, 1967; Philadelphia Antipoverty Action Committee, Community Action Council Representatives, June 8, 1965, Housing Association of Delaware Valley Papers, Temple University Urban Archives; Countryman, *Up South*; Fineman, "Community Action Councils"; "Mrs. Anderson Page to Dr. John O. Reinemann," December 16, 1966, Greater Philadelphia Federation of Settlements Collection, Temple University Urban Archives.

17. Following Bowser's resignation, Barbara Weems assumed the role of executive director. Countryman, *Up South*; "26,000 Poor Vote in PAAC Election Here," *Evening Bulletin*, July 23, 1966; "Bigger Vote Turnout of Poor Shows their Faith in Democracy," *Evening Bulletin*, July 24, 1966; "Rival Faction and PAAC Chart Collision Course," *Evening Bulletin*, August 5, 1966; "PAAC Oks Federal Guidelines; Moore Quits with Blast at U.S.," *Evening Bulletin*, December 28, 1966; *Evening Bulletin*, January 19, 1967; *Evening Bulletin*, January 30, 1967; "Tate Names 31 to New Antipoverty Commission," *Evening Bulletin*, February 20, 1968.

18. Cohen, *Boundaries of Blackness*.

19. In their recent book *The Separate City*, Christopher Silver and John V. Moeser use this idea to underscore the ways in which racial segregation facilitated the rise of a distinct black social, economic and political community. Such a notion builds on the assertions of scholars such as James Weldon Johnson and St. Clair Drake and Horace Cayton's characterizations of postwar urban black communities as collectively comprising a "city within a city." See: Silver and Moeser, *The Separate City: Black Communities in the Urban South, 1940–1968* (Lexington: University Press of Kentucky, 1995); Johnson, *Black Manhattan*; Drake and Cayton, *Black Metropolis*; Allen Spear, *Black Chicago: The Making of a Negro Ghetto, 1890–1920* (Chicago: University of Chicago Press, 1967).

20. "Black Political Forum to Honor 10 Community Leaders at Dinner," *Philadelphia Tribune*, April 15, 1970; Richard Hatcher quoted in *Evening Bulletin*, April 27, 1970; "In for the 'Long Haul': John White, Raised in Politics, Civil Rights," *Philadelphia Inquirer*, February 23, 1999. On John White, see "J. White Sr., Dies," *Philadelphia Inquirer*, September 16, 1999; "Farewell Brother: John White Sr. Dies; He Helped Bring End to 'Plantation Politics,'" *Philadelphia Daily News*, September 16, 1999; "A Legend Eulogized at His Funeral: John White Sr. Remembered as Great Leader," *Philadelphia Inquirer*, September 21, 1999; Countryman, *Up South*; Goode, *In Goode Faith*.

21. "Black Political Forum to Honor Community Leaders," *Philadelphia Tribune*; Hatcher, *Evening Bulletin*, April 27, 1970; "In for the 'Long Haul,'" *Philadelphia Inquirer*; "J. White Sr., Dies," *Philadelphia Inquirer*; "Farewell Brother," *Philadelphia Daily News*; "Legend Eulogized at His Funeral," *Philadelphia Inquirer*, September 21, 1999; Countryman, *Up South*; Goode, *In Goode Faith*; Dianne Pinderhughes, *Race and Ethnicity in Chicago Politics* (Chicago: University of Illinois Press, 1987); Carol M. Swain, *Black Faces, Black Interests* (Cambridge, MA: Harvard University Press, 1995); Mack H. Jones, "Black Office-Holding and Political Development in the Rural South," *Politics* 2, (1971): 64–72.

22. "Black Political Forum to Honor Community Leaders," *Philadelphia Tribune*; Hatcher, *Evening Bulletin*, April 27, 1970; "In for the 'Long Haul,'" *Philadelphia Inquirer*; "J. White Sr., Dies," *Philadelphia Inquirer*; "Farewell Brother," *Philadelphia Daily News*; "Legend Eulogized at His Funeral," *Philadelphia Inquirer*.

23. *Philadelphia Tribune*, April 15, 1970; "Black Political Forum Dinner Speakers Accuse Politicians of Ignoring the Constituents," *Philadelphia Tribune*, April 28, 1970; *Evening Bulletin*, April 27, 1970; *Philadelphia Inquirer*, February 23, 1999; September 16, 1999; September 21, 1999; Countryman, *Up South*; Goode, *In Goode Faith*.

24. Goode, *In Goode Faith*; Bernard C. Watson, *Colored, Negro, Black: Chasing the American Dream* (Philadelphia: JDC Books, 1997); Adams et al., *Philadelphia*; Countryman, *Up South*; Lisa Levenstein, *A Movement without Marches: African American Women and the Politics of Poverty in Postwar Philadelphia* (Chapel Hill: University of North Carolina Press, 2009).

25. "Decent Housing Uppermost to Council Campbell," *Philadelphia Tribune*, February 7, 1970; Williams received a total of 3,408 compared to the 2,333 votes for Lawson. "Jack Saunders Says," *Philadelphia Tribune*, March 7, 1970; March 14, 1970; and June 5, 1970; Goode, *In Goode Faith*; S. A. Paolantonio, *Frank Rizzo: The Last Big Man in Big City America* (Philadelphia: Camino, 1993); Countryman, *Up South*.

26. *Philadelphia Tribune*, February 7, 1970; March 7, 1970; March 14, 1970; June 5, 1970; "John and Milton Street: What are They Planning From their North Philadelphia Power Bases," *Philadelphia Tribune*, November 9, 1979; "Brothers Picket and Protest Way to Power," *New York Times*, January 1, 1980; Goode, *In Goode Faith*; Paolantonio, *Frank Rizzo*; Countryman, *Up South*; Lenora Berson, interview, November 16, 1978, Walter Phillips Oral History Collection, Temple University Urban Archives; Norman Berson, interview, February 8, 1979, Walter Phillips Oral History Collection, Temple University Urban Archives; *Evening Bulletin*, June 25, 1968; September 9, 1969; August 1978; *New York Times*, January 1, 1980.

27. Paolantonio, *Frank Rizzo*; Goode, *In Goode Faith*; "Black Political Convention Planners See Rizzo's Candidacy as Good Omen," *Philadelphia Tribune*, February 6, 1971; "Hardy Williams' Real intention Subject of Crystal Ball Gazing," *Philadelphia Tribune*, February 9, 1971; "Black Political convention: No Place for Personal Advancement," *Philadelphia Tribune*, February 13, 1971; "Black Convention Ignores Machine Politicians," *Philadelphia Tribune*, February 16, 1971; "Thacher Longstreth Banking on Black Vote to Beat Rizzo," *Philadelphia Tribune*, May 22, 1971; "Jack Saunders Says," *Philadelphia Tribune*, May 25, 1971; Countryman, *Up South*.

28. Paolantonio, *Frank Rizzo*; Goode, *In Goode Faith*; William Meek, interviews, May 22, 1979, June 27, 1979, Walter Phillips Oral History Collection, Temple University Urban Archives; "Black Political Power in Phila. Has Come Far in a Generation," *Philadelphia Inquirer*, November 16, 1998; *Philadelphia Inquirer*, February 23, 1999; "The Philadelphia Party," *Philadelphia Tribune*, April 17, 1976; "Bowser Rips GOP For Crowding his Phila. Party," *Philadelphia Tribune*, May 3, 1977; "Bowser Says Mayor Would Change Charter for Personal Political Gain," *Philadelphia Tribune*, September 15, 1978; "Black Elected Officials to Candidates: Make Commitment in Exchange for Support," *Philadelphia Tribune*, December 5, 1978; "Williams Backs Bowser; Black Ward Leaders are Expected to Follow," *Philadelphia Tribune*, March 20, 1979; "GOP Courts Bowser, Black Leaders," *Philadelphia Tribune*, December 19, 1980; "The Key in 1983," *Philadelphia Tribune*, October 12, 1982; Countryman, *Up South*.

29. Paolantonio, *Frank Rizzo*; Goode, *In Goode Faith*; Meek, interviews; "Black Political Power in Phila.," *Philadelphia Inquirer*; *Philadelphia Inquirer*, February 23, 1999; "Philadelphia Party," *Philadelphia Tribune*; "Bowser Rips GOP," *Philadelphia Tribune*; "Bowser Says Mayor Would Change Charter," *Philadelphia Tribune*; "Black Elected Officials to Candidates," *Philadelphia Tribune*; "Williams Backs

Bowser," *Philadelphia Tribune;* "GOP Courts Bowser," *Philadelphia Tribune;* "Key in 1983," *Philadelphia Tribune;* Countryman, *Up South.*

30. "More Minorities Get City Contracts," *Philadelphia Tribune,* March 8, 1985; Adams et al., *Philadelphia.*

31. Rufus P. Browning, Dale Rogers Marshall, and David H. Tabb, *Protest in Not Enough: The Struggle of Blacks and Hispanics for Equality in Urban Politics* (Berkeley: University of California Press, 1984); Kenneth Mladneka, "Blacks and Hispanics in Urban Politics," *American Political Science Review* 83 (1989): 165–69.

32. "Budget Foes: Neighborhoods Ignored," *Philadelphia Inquirer,* April 11, 1983.

33. Adams et al, *Philadelphia,* 84; Mathew Creighton and Michael Katz, "Immigrants and Suburbs: Growth and Distribution in Greater Philadelphia, 1970–2000: A Tract-Level Analysis," Working Paper series, Immigrant Suburbanization Project (August 2007), University of Pennsylvania. Creighton and Katz also find that populations in suburbs they characterize as "bedroom developing" also increased during the same period, relative to population decreases in the urban core, from 5.8 to 10.4 percent; thus representing a near double in size of the white population of such suburbs. Thompson, *Double Trouble.* For more on Burlington, New Jersey, see Gans, *The Levittowners: Ways of Life and Politics in a New Suburban Community* (New York: Pantheon Books, 1967). For more on white flight see Kevin M. Kruse, *White Flight: Atlanta and the Making of Modern Conservatism* (Princeton: Princeton University Press, 2005); Amanda Seligman, *Block by Block: Neighborhoods and Public Policy on Chicago's West Side* (Chicago: University of Chicago Press, 2005).

34. Thompson, *Double Trouble,* 5.

35. Goode, *In Goode Faith,* 186; Paolantonio, *Frank Rizzo;* "Goode's historic victory did not come easy," *Philadelphia Tribune,* May 20, 1983; "Election of Black Mayor in Philadelphia Reflects a Decade of Change," *New York Times,* November 10, 1983; Countryman, *Up South.*

36. "Reflections and Predictions: Dr. Grant Views South St., Home of Business for 40 Years," *Philadelphia Tribune,* March 30, 1979.

37. "Black Merchants Seeking Financial Aid; West Side of South Street Suffers while East Side Suffers," *Philadelphia Tribune,* July 21, 1995.

38. "S. Phila. Community Leader to Join Redevelopment Board," *Philadelphia Inquirer,* January 10, 1984; "Alice Lipscomb, 87, Phila. Activist," *Philadelphia Inquirer,* October 10, 2003; "Redevelopment Authority Member to Seek End to Dispute with Fumo," *Philadelphia Inquirer,* November 24, 1987.

39. "S. Phila. Community Leader to Join Redevelopment Board," *Philadelphia Inquirer;* "Alice Lipscomb," *Philadelphia Inquirer;* "Redevelopment Authority Member to Seek End to Dispute," *Philadelphia Inquirer;* and "Threatened by Displacement, Area Has Built a Base for Itself," *Philadelphia Inquirer,* July 26, 1984.

40. "S. Phila. Community Leader to Join Redevelopment Board," *Philadelphia Inquirer;* "Alice Lipscomb," *Philadelphia Inquirer;* "Redevelopment Authority Member to

Seek End to Dispute," *Philadelphia Inquirer*, November 24, 1987; and "Threatened by displacement," *Philadelphia Inquirer*.

41. *Philadelphia Inquirer*, January 10, 1984; October 10, 2003; July 26, 1984.

42. "Housing Will Return Life to Empty S. Phila School," *Philadelphia Inquirer*, February 2, 1985; "New Home Evokes School Memories," *Philadelphia Inquirer*, June 3, 1987; *Philadelphia Tribune*, October 23, 1992.

43. "Housing Will Return Life," *Philadelphia Inquirer*; "New Home Evokes Memories," *Philadelphia Inquirer*; *Philadelphia Tribune*, October 23, 1992.

44. Lois Fernandez, "Oral History of Odunde," December 8–10, 1999, Temple University Urban Archives; "Philadelphia Has 'Odunde,'" *Philadelphia Tribune*, July 13, 1979; "A Riverside Offering Starts New Year's Fest," *Philadelphia Inquirer*, July 12, 1982; "The History of Odunde by One of Its Founders," *Philadelphia Tribune*, June 7, 1991; "Odunde Festival Begins this Sunday," *Philadelphia Tribune*, June 6, 1997. Much like their business, the Uhuru Hut, black residences and business along the west side of South Street were in a persistent struggle to survive, with many forced to leave. For more on this, see: "Black Merchants Seeking Financial Aid," *Philadelphia Tribune*, July 21, 1995.

45. Fernandez, "Oral History of Odunde"; "Philadelphia Has 'Odunde,'" *Philadelphia Tribune*; "Riverside Offering," *Philadelphia Inquirer*; "History of Odunde," *Philadelphia Tribune*; "Odunde Festival Begins this Sunday," *Philadelphia Tribune*; "Black Merchants Seeking Financial Aid," *Philadelphia Tribune*.; "Odunde May Move From South Street," *Philadelphia Tribune*, March 2, 1993; Maurice Halbwachs, *On Collective Memory*, ed. and trans. Lewis A. Coser, (Chicago: University of Chicago Press, 1992) 84.

46. Fernandez, "Oral History of Odunde"; *Philadelphia Tribune*; "Odunde Festival Celebrates Unity," *Philadelphia Inquirer*, June 13, 1979; "The Sun Shines on Tribute to African River Goddess," *Philadelphia Inquirer*, June 11, 1984.

47. "A Happy African New Year Festival," *Philadelphia Inquirer*, June 10, 1985; "Odunde: Bigger, Better," *Philadelphia Tribune*, June 11, 1985; "City Grants $8.1 Million to Community Organizations," *Philadelphia Inquirer*, July 5, 1985; "Yuppies and Trendy Shops Are Taking over Once a Hub of Black Life, South Street West is Being Transformed," *Philadelphia Inquirer*, January 27, 1986; "Odunde Festival to Go on as Planned," *Philadelphia Tribune*, June 7, 1988; "A Celebration of African New Year," *Philadelphia Inquirer*, June 9, 1986; "S. Phila. Enjoys Day of African Ambiance," *Philadelphia Inquirer*, June 15, 1987; "African Festival has a spicy, rich texture," Philadelphia Inquirer, June 13, 1988; "Thousands Jam Odunde Festival," *Philadelphia Tribune*, June 14, 1988; "Odunde Fete Enlivens South St.," *Philadelphia Inquirer*, June 12, 1989; "South St. Odunde Festival Will Celebrate African New Year," *Philadelphia Inquirer*, June 1, 1990; "An African New-Year Fete Music, Culture and Food at 15th Odunde," *Philadelphia Inquirer*, June 8, 1990; "Odunde Festival to Liven South Street," Philadelphia Tribune, June 7, 1991; "The Spirited Offerings of Odunde," *Philadelphia Inquirer*, June 10, 1991.

48. Fernandez, "Oral History of Odunde"; "Sights, Sounds and Tastes of Africa on Tap as Odunde Festival," *Philadelphia Inquirer*, June 5, 1992; *Philadelphia Tribune*, March 5, 1993; "2 Women Are Shot at Street Festival Odunde," *Philadelphia Inquirer*, June 14, 1993; "The Odunde Festival Will Feature Boukman Eksperyans—for Starters," *Philadelphia Inquirer*, June 4, 1993; "Should Odunde be Moved?" *Philadelphia Tribune*, June 22, 1993; E. A. Kennedy, *Life, Liberty, and the Mummers* (Philadelphia: Temple University Press, 2007); Patricia Anne Masters, *The Philadelphia Mummers: Building Community Through Play* (Philadelphia: Temple University Press, 2007).

49. Fernandez, "Oral History of Odunde"; "Sights, Sounds and Tastes of," *Philadelphia Inquirer*; *Philadelphia Tribune*, March 5, 1993; "2 Women Are Shot at Street Festival Odunde," *Philadelphia Inquirer*; "Odunde Festival Will Feature Boukman Eksperyans," *Philadelphia Inquirer*; "Should Odunde be Moved?" *Philadelphia Tribune*; Kennedy, *Life, Liberty, and the Mummers*; Masters, *Philadelphia Mummers*; "Odunde Fete Has Organizers, Officials and Residents at Odds," *Philadelphia Tribune*, June 7, 1994; "Lamenting a Center of Black Life in the City," *Philadelphia Inquirer*, March 21, 1994; Japonica Brown-Saracino, *A Neighborhood that Never Changes: Gentrification, Social Preservation, and the Search For Authenticity* (Chicago: University of Chicago Press, 2009); Brown-Saracino, "Social Preservation and the Quest for Authentic Community," *City and Community* 3, no. 2 (2004): 125–56.

50. "Odunde Fete Has Organizers, Officials and Residents at Odds," *Philadelphia Tribune*; "Lamenting a Center," *Philadelphia Inquirer*; Brown-Saracino, *Neighborhood that Never Changes*; Brown-Saracino, "Social Preservation"; "Spiritual Strength on a Weekend; Community Support Gives Odunde Life," *Philadelphia Tribune*, June 10, 1994; "Showcasing African Culture with Odunde," *Philadelphia Tribune*, June 13, 1994; "Odunde Festival: A Vision Realized," *Philadelphia Inquirer*, June 11, 1995; *Philadelphia Tribune*, June 6, 1997; "Odunde Still Full of Spirit," *Philadelphia Inquirer*, June 12, 2000.

CHAPTER 6

1. "Flash Mob Disrupts South Street," *Philadelphia Inquirer*, March 21, 2010; "Police Struggle with 'Flash Mob' on South Street," *Philadelphia Inquirer*, March 21, 2010; "Calm Returns to South Street," *Philadelphia Inquirer*, March 22, 2010; "Editorial: Terror in a Flash," *Philadelphia Inquirer*, March 23, 2010; "10 Teens Found Guilty of Rioting in February 16 'Flash Mob,'" *Philadelphia Inquirer*, March 23, 2010; "Flash Mob Teens Face the Music at Family Court," *Philadelphia Daily News*, March 23, 2010; "18 Teens Sentenced for Felony Rioting in Flash Mob," *Philadelphia Inquirer*, March 24, 2010; "Nutter Shows up; Flash Mobs Stay Home," *Philadelphia Inquirer*, March 28, 2010; "What's behind 'Flash Mobs'?," *Philadelphia Inquirer*, March 28, 2010; "Boy, 11, among 4 Charged in Flash-Mob Attacks," *Philadelphia Daily News*,

August 1, 2011; "Did Mob Youths 'Damage their Race'," *Philadelphia Tribune*, August 9, 2011; "Flash Mobs Have Deep Rooted Causes, Advocates Say," *Philadelphia Tribune*, August 11, 2011; "Flash-Mob Violence Raises Weighty Questions," *Philadelphia Inquirer*, August 14, 2011.

2. Cathy J. Cohen, *Democracy Remixed* (New York: Oxford University Press, 2010).

3. "Nutter Shows up; Flash Mobs Stay Home," *Philadelphia Inquirer*, March 28, 2010.

4. William H. Sewell Jr., "A Theory of Structure: Duality, Agency, and Transformation," *American Journal of Sociology* 98, no. 1 (1992): 1–29, at 2.

5. See Mustafa Emirbayer and Ann Mische, "What is Agency?" *American Journal of Sociology* 103, no. 4 (1998): 962–1023; Jeffrey C. Alexander, *Action and Its Environments* (New York: Columbia University Press, 1988); William H. Sewell Jr., "A Theory of Structure"; and David A. Snow and Robert D. Benford, "Ideology, Frame Resonance, and Participant Mobilization" *International Social Movement Research* 1, (1988):197–217.

6. See Aldon Morris, *The Origins of the Civil Rights Movement: Black Communities Organizing for Change* (New York: Free Press, 1984); Doug McAdam, *Political Process and the Development of Black Insurgency: 1930–1970* (Chicago: University of Chicago Press, 1982); Thomas Sugrue, *The Origins of the Urban Crisis* (Princeton: Princeton University Press, 1996); Chris Rhomberg, *No There There* (Berkeley: University of California Press, 2004); Francesca Polletta, *Freedom is an Endless Meeting* (Chicago: University of Chicago Press, 2002); and Frances Fox Piven and Richard A. Cloward, *Poor People's Movements: Why They Succeed, How They Fail* (New York: Vintage Books, 1979).

7. Mario Small, *Unanticipated Gains: Origins of Network Inequality in Everyday Life* (New York: Oxford University Press, 2009); see also Martín Sánchez Jankowski, *Cracks in the Pavement: Social Change and Resilience in Poor Neighborhoods* (Berkeley: University of California Press, 2008).

8. James C. Scott, *Seeing Like A State* (New Haven: Yale University Press, 1999).

9. W. E. B. DuBois, *The Philadelphia Negro* (Philadelphia: University of Pennsylvania Press, 1899), 310.

10. See Elijah Anderson, *Streetwise: Race, Class, and Change in an Urban Community* (Chicago: University of Chicago Press, 1990).

11. William Julius Wilson, *When Work Disappears* (Chicago: University of Chicago Press, 1996).

12. Robert Sampson, et al., "Neighborhoods and violent crime: a multilevel study of collective efficacy," *American Journal of Public Health* 95, (1997): 225–32. See also Lee Rainwater, *Behind Ghetto Walls: Black Families in a Federal Slum.* (Chicago: Aldine, 1970); Carol B. Stack, *All or Kin: Strategies for Survival in a Black Community* (New York: Harper & Row, 1974); Ulf Hannerz, *Soulside: Inquiries into Ghetto Culture and Community* (New York: Columbia University Press, 1969).

13. Sudhir Venkatesh, *Off the Books* (Cambridge, MA: Harvard University Press, 2006).

14. Some notable exceptions include: Robin D. G. Kelley, *Yo Mama's Disfunktional: Fighting the Culture Wars in Urban America* (Boston: Beacon Press, 1997); Cathy J. Cohen, *Democracy Remixed* (New York: Oxford University Press, 2010); and Marcus Anthony Hunter, "The Nightly Round: Space, Social Capital and Urban Black Nightlife," *City & Community* 9, no. 2 (2010): 165–86.

15. According to the US Census report from 2000, Majority–minority cities whose population is predominantly black included Detroit (83 percent), Baltimore (65 percent), Memphis (62 percent), Washington DC (61 percent), and New Orleans (67 percent). In that same year, Philadelphia's black population accounted for 44 percent of its total population. For further details, see Michael A. Stoll, *The American People Census 2000: African Americans and the Color Line* (New York: Russell Sage Foundation, 2004).

16. See Mary Waters, *Black Identities* (New York: Russell Sage Foundation, 1999).

17. Sudhir Venkatesh, *American Project* (Cambridge, MA: Harvard University Press, 1999); Anderson, *Streetwise*; Mary Pattillo, *Black on the Block: The Politics of Race and Class in the City* (Chicago: University of Chicago Press, 2007); Omar McRoberts, *Streets of Glory* (Chicago: University of Chicago Press, 2003); Steven Gregory, *Black Corona* (Princeton: Princeton University Press, 1998); William Julius Wilson and Richard P. Taub, *There Goes the Neighborhood* (New York: Vintage, 2006); and Karyn Lacy, *Blue-Chip Black* (Berkeley: University of California Press, 2007).

18. See William Julius Wilson, *Truly Disadvantaged* (Chicago: University of Chicago Press, 1987); *When Work Disappears*; Amanda Seligman, *Block By Block: Neighborhoods and Public Policy on Chicago's West Side* (Chicago: University of Chicago Press, 2005); and Kevin M. Kruse, *White Flight: Atlanta and the Making of Modern Conservatism* (Princeton: Princeton University Press, 2005).

19. See Wilson, *Truly Disadvantaged*; Wilson, *When Work Disappears*; see also Anderson, *Streetwise*.

20. Mary Pattillo, *Black on the Block*, 301. Wilson, *Truly Disadvantaged*; Wilson, *When Work Disappears*; See also Mary Pattillo-McCoy, *Black Picket Fences: Privilege and Peril among the Black Middle Class* (Chicago: University of Chicago Press, 1999), and Gregory, *Black Corona*.

21. See Wilson, *Truly Disadvantaged*; Wilson, *When Work Disappears*; Venkatesh, *American Project*; Pattillo, *Black on the Block*; McRoberts, *Streets of Glory*; Gregory, *Black Corona*.

22. "Did Mob Youths 'Damage their Race'?" *Philadelphia Tribune*, August 9, 2011.

23. Christopher Silver and John V. Moeser, *The Separate City: Black Communities in the Urban South, 1940–1968* (Lexington: University Press of Kentucky, 1995) x.

24. Pattillo, *Black on the Block*, 3.

25. See for example: Sampson et al., "Neighborhoods and violent crime.".

26. See for example: Stack, *All or Kin.*

27. See for example: Douglas Massey and Nancy Denton, *American Apartheid* (Cambridge, MA: Harvard University Press, 1993); Camille Zubrinsky Charles, "The Dynamics of Racial Residential Segregation," *Annual Review of Sociology* 29, (2003): 167–207.

28. David Harding, "Cultural Context, Sexual Behavior, and Romantic Relationships in Disadvantaged Neighborhoods," *American Sociological Review* 72, no. 3 (2007): 341–64.

29. Michelle Boyd *Jim Crow Nostalgia: Reconstructing Race in Bronzeville* (Minneapolis: University of Minnesota Press, 2008); Derek Hyra, *The New Urban Renewal* (Chicago: University of Chicago Press, 2008); Kesha Moore, "What's Class Got to Do With it?" *Journal of Urban Affairs* 27, no. 4 (2005): 437–51.

30. Some notable examples of this work include: Anderson, *Streetwise*; Venkatesh, *Off the Books*; Venkatesh, *American Project*; Mitchell Duneier, *Sidewalk* (New York: Farrar, Strauss, and Giroux, 1999); Pattillo, *Black on the Block*; Pattillo-McCoy, *Black Picket Fences*; Gregory, *Black Corona*; Hannerz, *Soulside*; William G. Hawkeswood, *One of the Children: Gay Black Men in Harlem* (Berkeley: University of California Press, 1992); John L. Jackson, *Harlemworld: Doing Race and Class in Contemporary Black America* (Chicago: University of Chicago Press, 2001); Jane Jacobs, *The Death and Life of Great American Cities* (New York. Random House, 1981); Elliot Liebow, *Tally's Corner* (Boston: Little Brown, 1967); Herbert Gans, *The Urban Villagers: Group and Class in the Life of Italian-Americans* (New York: Free Press, 1962); and Jay MacLeod, *Ain't No Makin' It: Aspirations and Attainment in a Low-Income Neighborhood* (Boulder: Westview Press, 1987).

31. Rhomberg extends the concept of reiterated problem-solving from the work of Jeffrey Haydu to demonstrate that "structural conditions generate recurrent problems that are solved by alternative sets of arrangements in successive periods, and solutions worked out at earlier conjunctures become part of the context for changes at later points." Chris Rhomberg, *No There There: Race, Class, and Political Community in Oakland* (Berkeley: University of California Press, 2004) 205; see also Jeffrey Haydu, "Making Use of the Past: Time Periods as Cases to Compare and as Sequences to Problem Solving," *American Journal of Sociology* 102, no. 2 (1998): 339–71.

32. DuBois, *Philadelphia Negro*, 385.

33. See Matthew J. Countryman, *Up South: Civil Rights and Black Power in Philadelphia* (Philadelphia: University of Pennsylvania Press, 2006), and Kelley, *Yo' Mama's Disfunktional*; Sugrue, *Origins of the Urban Crisis*; and John F. Bauman, *Public Housing, Race, and Renewal* (Philadelphia: Temple University Press, 1987).

METHODOLOGICAL APPENDIX

1. Claude Levi-Strauss, *Structural Anthropology* (New York: Basic Books, 1963), 16–17; emphasis in the original.

2. Diane Vaughan, "Theorizing Disaster: Analogy, historical ethnography, and the Challenger accident," *Ethnography* 5, no. 3 (2004): 315–47, p. 321; emphasis added.

3. Jürgen Habermas, *The Theory of Communicative Action*, Volume 2: *Lifeworld and System: A Critique of Functionalist Reason*, trans. Thomas McCarthy (New York: Beacon Press, 1985).

4. Diane Vaughan, *The Challenger Launch Decision: Risky Technology, Culture, and Deviance at NASA* (Chicago: University of Chicago Press, 1996), and "Theorizing Disaster: Analogy, historical ethnography, and the Challenger accident," *Ethnography* 5, no. 3 (2004): 315–47.

5. Though this is true of historical ethnography in the research product and process, in the interpretation of data and live respondents' sentiments, "contemporary" ethnographers are doing a similar activity, particularly if they are doing the unstructured sort of oral/life history collection.

6. Victor Witter Turner, *The Forest of Symbols* (Ithaca: Cornell University Press, 1967); Turner, *The Ritual Process: Structure and Anti-structure* (Chicago: Aldine, 1969); Turner, *Dramas, Fields, and Metaphors: Symbolic Action in Human Society* (Ithaca: Cornell University Press, 1974).

7. While Turner's work popularized the concept of "liminality," the origins of this concept can be traced back to Arnold Van Gennep's *Les Rites de passage* (New York: Psychology Press, 1909). Further, since Turner's seminal work in this area, notions of "middleness" have recently been proffered as an extension of his ideas of liminality, perhaps most notable in this regard is Pattillo's discussion of the positionality of middle-class black Americans: Mary Pattillo, *Black on the Block: The Politics of Race and Class in the City* (Chicago: University of Chicago Press, 2007).

8. While there is significant research that quantitatively explores issues of urbanism and the organization of the city, ethnography has been key as a method of inquiry in the field of urban sociology; see Andrew Abbott, *Department and Discipline: Chicago Sociology at One Hundred* (Chicago: University of Chicago Press, 1999).

9. For more see Abbott, *Department and Discipline*.

10. Gerald Suttles, "Urban Ethnography: Situational and Normative Accounts," *Annual Review of Sociology* 2 (1976): 1–18.

11. Suttles, "Urban Ethnography," 1.

12. Suttles, "Urban Ethnography," 1.

13. Harvey W Zorbaugh, *The Gold Coast and the Slum* (Chicago: University of Chicago Press, 1929); Sudhir Alladi Venkatesh, *Off the Books* (Cambridge, MA.: Harvard University Press, 2006).

14. Suttles, "Urban Ethnography," 2.

15. Ulf Hannerz, *Soulside: Inquiries into Ghetto Culture and Community* (New York: Columbia University Press, 1969); Gerald D Suttles, *The Social Order of the Slum: Ethnicity and Territory in the Inner City* (Chicago: University of Chicago Press, 1968).

16. Suttles, "Urban Ethnography," 16.

17. Loïc Wacquant, "Scrutinizing the Street: Poverty, Morality, and the Pitfalls of Urban Ethnography," *American Journal of Sociology* 107, no.6 (2002): 1468–532.

18. See Elijah Anderson, *Code of the Street: Decency, Violence, and the Moral life of the Inner City* (New York: Norton, 1999), and Anderson, "The Ideologically Driven Critique," *American Journal of Sociology* 107 no. 6 (2002): 1533–50; Katherine Newman, *No Shame in My Game: The Working Poor In the Inner City* (New York: Vintage, 1999), and Newman, "No Shame: The View from the Left Bank," *American Journal of Sociology* 107, no. 6 (2002): 1577–99; Mitchell Duneier, "What Kind of Combat Sport is Sociology?" *American Journal of Sociology* 107, no. 6 (2002): 1551–76, and Mitchell Duneier, *Sidewalk* (New York: Farrar, Strauss and Giroux, 1999).

19. Wacquant, "Scrutinizing the Street," 1469, emphasis in the original.

20. Stephen Steinberg, "The Urban Villagers," *Radical History Review* 69 (1997): 243–60. Although both Newman, "No Shame," and Anderson, "The Ideologically Driven Critique," levied a response, it is within Duneier's response, "What Kind of Combat Sport is Sociology?" and his larger text, *Sidewalk*, that we find a specific discussion of urban ethnographic methodology. Incorporating the ideas of Burawoy's extended-case method and George Marcus's multisited ethnography, Duneier links ethnographic method and theory with his notion of "extended place method," while also troubling Wacquant's concerns around representations in urban ethnography. See Michael Burawoy, *Ethnography Unbound: Power and Resistance in the Modern Metropolis* (Berkeley: University of California Press, 1991), and Burawoy, "The Extended Case Method," *Sociological Theory* 16, no. 1 (1998): 4–33; George Marcus, *Ethnography through Thick and Thin* (Princeton: Princeton University Press, 1995).

21. Claude Fischer, "The Study of Urban Community and Personality," *Annual Review of Sociology* 1 (1975): 67–89.

22. Fischer, "Study of Urban Community and Personality," 81.

23. Fischer, "Study of Urban Community and Personality," 81.

24. Elijah Anderson, *Streetwise: Race, Class and Change in an Urban Community* (Chicago: University of Chicago Press, 1990); Albert Hunter, *Symbolic Communities: The Persistence and Change of Chicago's Local Communities* (Chicago: University of Chicago Press, 1974).

25. Jack Katz, "Ethnography's Warrants," *Sociological Methods and Research* 25, no. 4 (1997): 391–423.

26. Katz, "Ethnography's Warrants," 392.

27. Katz, "Ethnography's Warrants," 408.

28. For more see for example, Maurice Merleau-Ponty, *The Visible and the Invisible* (Evanston: Northwestern University Press, 1968), and Merleau-Ponty, "Science and the Experience of Expression," in *The Prose of the World*, ed. Claude Lefort, 9–46 (Evanston: Northwestern University Press, 1973); Michael Polanyi, *Personal Knowledge: Towards a Post-critical Philosophy* (Chicago: University of Chicago Press, 1962); Jean Paul Sartre, *Being and Nothingness: An Essay on Phenomenological Ontology* (New York: Washington Square Press, 1956).

29. Clifford Geertz, *Local Knowledge* (New York: Basic Books, 1985).

30. Burawoy, *Ethnography Unbound*; Burawoy, "Extended Case Method."

31. Lyn Lofland and John Lofland, *Analyzing Social Settings* (Belmont, CA: Wadsworth, 1984).

32. Burawoy, *Ethnography Unbound*, 21.

33. John L. Jackson, *Real Black: Adventures in Racial Sincerity* (Chicago: University of Chicago Press, 2005); Mario Small, *Villa Victoria: The Transformation of Social Capital in a Boston Barrio* (Chicago: University of Chicago Press, 2004).

34. See Marcus, *Ethnography Through Thick and Thin*.

35. Duneier, "What Kind of Combat Sport is Sociology?"; Duneier, *Sidewalk*.

36. My discussion of historical ethnography is informed by works such as John Comaroff and Jean Comaroff, *Ethnography and the Historical Imagination* (Boulder: Westview, 1992); Vaughan, "Theorizing Disaster"; and Gail Kligman and Katherine Verdery, *Peasants Under Siege* (Princeton: Princeton University Press, 2011).

37. Michaela Fenske, "Micro, Macro, Agency: Historical Ethnography as Cultural Anthropology Practice," trans. John Bendix, *Journal of Folklore Research* 44, no.1 (2007): 67–99, at 76, emphasis added.

38. Comaroff and Comaroff, *Ethnography and the Historical Imagination*; Michael Burawoy, "Revisits: An Outline of a Theory of Reflexive Ethnography," *American Sociological Review* 68, no.5 (2003): 645–79; William Kornblum, "Discovering Ink: A Mentor for an Historical Ethnography," *Annals of the Academy of Political and Social Science* 595 (2004): 176–89.

39. See for example, Fenske, "Micro, Macro, Agency"; William M. Reddy, "Postmodernism and the Public Sphere: Implications for Historical Ethnography," *Cultural Anthropology* 7, no. 2 (1992): 135–68.

40. Margaret Kusenbach, "Street Phenomenology: The Go-Along as Ethnographic Research Tool," *Ethnography* 4 (2003): 455–85.

41. For more on the distinction between sincerity and authenticity see Jackson, *Real Black*.

42. Lofland and Lofland, *Analyzing Social Settings*.

43. Burawoy, *Ethnography Unbound*; Burawoy, "The Extended Case Method."

44. Robert Emerson et al., *Writing Ethnographic Fieldnotes* (Chicago: University of Chicago Press, 1995).

45. Burawoy, "Revisits."

46. Vaughan, "Theorizing Disaster," 315.

47. See Small, *Villa Victoria*.

48. See Marcus Anthony Hunter, "The Nightly Round: Space, Social Capital and Urban Black Nightlife," *City & Community* 9, no. 2 (2010): 165–86.

49. See Anderson, *Streetwise*; Pattillo, *Black on the Block*.

Index

CPSIA information can be obtained
at www.ICGtesting.com
Printed in the USA
BVOW08s0958160217
476342BV00003B/8/P